The
FATHERS
of the Church 3rd Edition

An Introduction to the First Christian Teachers

The
FATHERS
of the Church 3rd Edition

An Introduction to the First Christian Teachers

Mike Aquilina

Our Sunday Visitor Publishing Division
Our Sunday Visitor, Inc.
Huntington, Indiana 46750

ISBN: 978-1-61278-561-5 (Inventory No. T1259)
RELIGION / Christianity /Catholic
RELIGION / History Religion / Monasticism

eISBN: 978-61278-318-5
LCCN: 2013933398

Cover design by Amanda Falk
Interior design by Lindsey Riesen

Cover background and interior graphic by Shutterstock

Cover art: Art Resource, NY,
The Evangelists of Cappadocia St. Gregory Nazianzus, St. John Chrysostom, and St. Basil the Great, Byzantine, seventeenth century

PRINTED IN THE UNITED STATES OF AMERICA

For Terri

"An intelligent, discreet, and pious young woman
is worth more than all the money in the world.
Tell her that you love her more than your own life,
because this present life is nothing,
and that your only hope is that the two of you pass
through this life in such a way that,
in the world to come,
you will be united in perfect love."
— St. John Chrysostom

TABLE OF CONTENTS

ABBREVIATIONS

Abbr.	Series or Book Title	Recent Publisher
ACC	Ancient Christian Commentaries	InterVarsity Press
ACW	Ancient Christian Writers	Paulist Press
ANF	Ante-Nicene Fathers	Hendrickson
APL	Alba Patristic Library	Alba House
CCC	Catechism of the Catholic Church	United States Conference of Catholic Bishops
CWS	Classics of Western Spirituality	Paulist Press
ECF	The Early Church Fathers	Routledge
FC	Fathers of the Church	Catholic University of America Press
LF	Library of Fathers of the Holy Catholic Church	John Henry Parker
MFC	Message of the Fathers of the Church	Michael Glazer
NPNF1	Nicene and Post-Nicene Fathers, Series 1	Hendrickson
NPNF2	Nicene and Post-Nicene Fathers, Series 2	Hendrickson
OCT	Outstanding Christian Thinkers	Geoffrey Chapman
Patr.	Patrology (ed. Johannes Quasten)	Christian Classics
PP	Popular Patristics	St. Vladimir's Seminary Press
SECT	Sources of Early Christian Thought	Fortress Press
SPCK	Society for Promoting Christian Knowledge	SPCK
WSA3	The Works of Saint Augustine, Series III	New City Press

ACKNOWLEDGMENTS

Greg Erlandson, it seems, has been involved in this project since its earliest prehistory. When he was a reporter, many years ago, he wrote about the discovery of a cache of long-lost homilies of St. Augustine. I was a faraway reader, one of many thousands, but something about the story made me want to read more about the early Christians. Years down the road, Greg rose to editor-in-chief of the publisher that brought out the first edition of this book. Now, Greg is president and publisher of the same company and must bear some responsibility for the third edition. I thank him for that.

If Greg Erlandson whetted my appetite for the Fathers, Father Ron Lengwin fed the hunger with books from his library. I'm grateful to him.

Bob Lockwood conceived the idea for this book back in 1994 or so, and he cast about for a writer who could produce the book he wanted. I was way too young, clueless, and inexperienced, but he believed in me, and so he gave me the job — and, in doing so, he changed my life. Since then I've written around twenty books, given hundreds of talks, and taped more than a hundred television shows, all touching on the Fathers.

Several friends volunteered to be critical readers of the manuscript of that first edition. Their advice made the book far better than it would have been. Three of those readers have since gone to their reward: Fr. Ronald Lawler, O.F.M. Cap., Brad Fallon, and John Murdock. Two others — Mark Sullivan and Cary Valyo — are still here with me, and I'm grateful for their continued encouragement.

My editors, down the editions, have been an inspiration. I salute them: Jim Manney, Jackie Lindsey, Cindy Cavnar.

Two great webmasters and titans of online patristics, Kevin Knight and Roger Pearse, have been unfailingly generous in allowing me to use and adapt their e-texts for my books. May God bless them abundantly.

It's been a joy to get to know readers, especially those who have tracked me down to suggest improvements. I thank the following men whose comments were very helpful as I prepared this edition: Dr. William Varner, Dr. Jamie Blosser, Dr. Matthew Bunson, Fr. Malcolm Kennedy, Archimandrite Joseph (Lee), Fr. Joseph Linck (may he rest in peace), Fr. Peter Stravinskas, and Mr. Robert Guinan.

And then I must thank the friends who regularly lead me to good books, old and new: Terry Fenwick, David Scott, Chris Bailey, Paul Crawford, Rob Corzine, Scott Hahn, and Fr. Fred Cain.

I reverence my wife, who pays for all the books I buy — and who bought me my own set of the Fathers, many years ago. That's true love.

Above all: I must thank the God who put such good people in my life, not least these friends, not least the Fathers.

PREFACE

I t was a brilliant summer day. My father, then pushing eighty, took me with him on a long drive down a country road. Our local reservoir had been contaminated, and we were going to draw water by the gallon jug from a remote stream.

Usually a silent man, Pop was talkative that day, and as he drove along and as we hiked to the spring, he told me many stories — about his childhood, his father's early death from tuberculosis, my Uncle Leo's paternal care for the family after Grandfather died. These were stories I had never heard in our three decades of casual conversation at home.

I drank in every word — more eagerly, I must admit, than I would later sip the spring water — and when we got back to the house, I wrote down all I could recall, as near to Pop's own words as my memory would allow.

The words of our natural fathers are precious to us. Our fathers are key to a mystery we spend a lifetime trying to solve: ourselves. Their past is our own, given to us in so many silent ways as they guide our childhood steps. The paths we walk are paths to which they led us, or drove us. Their words and deeds are critical details in the story of our own lives and our salvation.

If all that is true of our natural fathers, how much more true of our fathers in Christian faith — the Fathers of the Church that gave us new life in Baptism?

Because of this desire to know my ancestors in faith, and because I believe you share this desire, I wrote this book. I am not a scholar, and this is not a scholarly exploration of the lives or works of the Fathers. For simplicity's sake, I have tried to avoid most of the academic controversies and just tell the story. Readers who want to dig deeper should look up each and all of the works included in my bibliography in the appendix at the back of this book.

I have taken most of my selections and quotations (though not all) from the nineteenth-century Edinburgh edition of the Fathers, published in thirty-eight volumes as *The Ante-Nicene Fathers* and *The Nicene and Post-Nicene Fathers*. When doing so, I have indicated the edition, series, volume number, and page number. Thus, NPNF1 2:129 would represent page 129 of volume 2 of the *Nicene and Post-Nicene Fathers*, Series 1.

The Edinburgh edition is praiseworthy for its clarity, but language does change over the course of a century. So, in most cases, I have adapted the translations to make them intelligible to today's reader. I have, whenever possible, compared the end product to other translations (and even, occasionally, to the Latin or Greek originals) to ensure accuracy. Some of the Fathers' poems I have chosen from alternative sources: St. Gregory of Nazianzus's *Soul and Body*, for example, appears in Elizabeth Barrett Browning's translation; and I have used Venerable John Henry Newman's renderings of St. Ambrose's hymns. In formal poetry, I have left the archaic language untouched; to do otherwise might be a mortal sin.

For dates, place names, and other basic information, I am dependent upon Dr. Matthew Bunson's very useful *Encyclopedia of Catholic History*. When there is a question of whether an individual should be called "Saint," I have considered Dr. Bunson's *Encyclopedia of Saints* to be my final authority — except in one instance when, to settle the matter, I phoned the great Dr. Bunson himself.

Most, but not all, Scripture quotations come from the *Revised Standard Version, Catholic Edition*, of the Holy Bible.

THE WORLD OF THE FATHERS

Introduction

─────────WHAT IS A FATHER?─────────

At the dawn of the age of the Fathers, Luke the Evangelist wrote of the first Christians: "Now the company of those who believed were of one heart and soul" (Acts 4:32). That single line illumines the history of the first six Christian centuries. As heirs to the Apostles, the leaders and teachers of the early Church — the Fathers of the Church — were intensely concerned with preserving the unity and integrity of the "company of those who believed," even as that company grew from a small band of several hundred to encompass millions of people speaking dozens of languages and dispersed throughout the Roman Empire. The unity of believers — unity in the Person of Jesus Christ — was the precious inheritance of the Church Fathers.

Many books tell the story of the first Christian centuries as a succession of creeds, councils, persecutions, and heresies. But it was far more than that, and far more interesting. It was the story of a family, and of how the Fathers of that family strove to keep their household together, to preserve the family's patrimony, to teach and discipline their children, and to protect the family from danger. Only when we understand them *as fathers* can we truly understand the Church Fathers. That, after all, is the way they understood themselves. "I myself," said St. Basil the Great when he was ordained a bishop, "have been appointed to the position of a father by reason of the station the Lord has appointed for me."[1]

The Fathers of the Church are a select group of early Christian teachers, around a hundred in number, depending on the list you consult. The Catholic Church has long revered them and given them a privileged place of doctrinal authority. Many of them are also revered by the Orthodox Churches and the other churches of the East. The Fathers, generally speaking, meet four criteria, which were established by St. Vincent of Lérins[2] in the fifth century:

1. Sound doctrine
2. Holiness of life
3. Church approval
4. Antiquity

The age of the Fathers, sometimes called the Patristic Era, stretched from the middle of the first century to the middle of the eighth, at the death of St. John of Damascus. Some of the earliest Fathers were disciples of the Apostles themselves, and the teaching of these men — called the Apostolic Fathers — has always received special veneration within the Church. Their witness is invaluable, because these Fathers were nearest to the Apostles, who were, in turn, nearest to Jesus Christ. Thus, the Apostolic Fathers are sometimes called the "first echo" of the Apostles. But, even beyond the first echo, the Church considers the Patristic Era in general to be a time of extraordinary graces for the expression and development of Christian doctrine.

In the New Testament, the Apostles clearly see themselves as fathers to the newborn Church. St. Paul reminded the Christians of Corinth that he was their "father in Christ Jesus" (1 Cor 4:15), and he addressed both Timothy and Titus as his true children (1 Tim 1:2; Ti 1:4). St. John also greeted his flock as "my children" (3 Jn 4) and "my little children" (1 Jn 2:1). St. Peter explicitly referred to Christians of his own generation as "the fathers" (2 Pt 3:4).

The custom of calling bishops "Father" continued with the passing of the Apostles' generation. The word "pope" comes from Latin and Greek words meaning "father," and in the early centuries it was applied to diocesan bishops as well as the bishop of Rome. Eventually, common usage extended the application of the title "Father" to priests, too, as is today the custom in English-speaking countries.

There was yet another usage for the term. At the very beginning of the Christian Church, bishops and teachers used "the Fathers" and "our

Fathers" as terms encompassing all their ancestors in the faith. When St. Irenaeus of Lyons, at the end of the second century, speaks of "the Fathers," he is referring not only to the Apostles and Apostolic Fathers, but also to the patriarchs and prophets of ancient Israel. Gradually, however, "Fathers of the Church" came precisely to mean only those Christian teachers who were designated as Fathers by long tradition.

Like the rabbis of early Judaism, these teachers took care to demonstrate that their teaching was not their own, but rather stretched back to the beginning. We see this already in the generation after the Apostles. St. Clement of Rome (writing well before A.D. 100) showed that his pedigree came from not one, but two Apostles, Sts. Peter and Paul. Papias of Hierapolis, writing a few decades later, also staked his authority on the fact that he was a "hearer" of the Apostle John. As the generations passed, it became increasingly important for a teacher to demonstrate his continuity with the apostolic teaching. St. Irenaeus explained that he had learned the faith from St. Polycarp of Smyrna, who in turn had learned from St. John the Apostle.

It was St. Irenaeus who first (as far as we know) showed how apostolic succession had been *institutionalized* in the line of bishops in every Church. His list of the popes, compiled around A.D. 170, is the earliest witness we have to the immediate successors of St. Peter.

In the third century, more teachers began to justify their doctrine by showing a *catena* (Latin for "chain") of unbroken teaching stretching, from Father to Father, back to the Apostles. By the fifth century, this practice had become almost a requirement for theologians and teachers.

As disputes multiplied, however, it became necessary to designate which ancient teachers were authoritative and which were not. Thus, in the fifth century, we find, in a decree attributed to Pope Gelasius I, history's first list of Church Fathers designated as such. In the same century, St. Vincent of Lérins sketched out the ground rules for the field known today as "patristics" or "patrology," the study of the Church Fathers. St. Vincent, who would himself eventually win recognition as a Father, ventured a definition. The Fathers, he wrote, are "those alone who, though in diverse times and places, yet persevering in the communion and faith of the one Catholic Church, have been approved teachers."[3]

Again, in the first centuries, use of the term "Father" was reserved for bishops, and especially for those bishops who were revered as seminal teachers (the "Fathers of the Council of Nicaea"). Yet we see a similar fatherly sense in deacons, priests, and laymen of the early Church. In the second century, the African lawyer Tertullian vigorously confronted heretics as poachers on his family's estate, trespassers who threatened his patrimony: "Who are you ... Marcion, by what right do you chop my wood? By whose permission, Valentinus, are you diverting my streams? By what power, Apelles, are you removing my landmarks? This is my property.... I hold sure title-deeds from the original owners themselves, to whom the estate belonged. I am the heir of the Apostles."[4]

Thus, in the fourth century, ecclesiastical writers began to apply the term "Father" to other men who were exceptional teachers: priests such as St. Jerome and laymen such as Tertullian, St. Justin (a philosopher), and Hermas (a farmer and family man).

WHO ARE THE FATHERS?

Knowing that the Fathers were expected to meet St. Vincent's four criteria — orthodoxy, holiness of life, Church approval, and antiquity — we might expect them to be a fairly uniform group. They appear on icons as long lines of nearly identical men with bald heads and long gray beards; in art, the Fathers seem interchangeable except for the obscure symbols that artists traditionally place in their hands.

But perception, here as elsewhere, is not necessarily reality. We should stop to consider that the Fathers lived in an era that stretched from the middle of the first century to the middle of the eighth. If we want to gain perspective, we should ponder that that span is roughly equivalent to the centuries passed between the time of Marco Polo and the development of the microchip, from Dante's *Inferno* to the landing on the moon. The Fathers lived in cultures as varied as the high Roman Empire and the first Muslim caliphates, in cosmopolitan cities and in barbarian backwaters, in times of war and in times of peace, through periods of persecution and, finally, through centuries of triumph.

They were a varied lot, ethnically, stylistically, and temperamentally. Tertullian, from North Africa, was a hothead. Origen of Alexandria, in Egypt, was cool and cerebral. St. Jerome, from what is today Croatia, was irascible, almost perpetually annoyed. St. Benedict of Nursia, Italy, was contemplative; St. Basil of Caesarea was an ace administrator who organized prodigious social outreach; St. Augustine, another North African, managed to be both extraordinarily active and extraordinarily contemplative.

Some Fathers wrote and spoke Syriac, others Latin or Greek, still others Coptic or Armenian. Some adhered to one or another theological method, and these were as different as are modern Catholic currents of thought. Vastly differing schools flourished, for example, in Cappadocia (in what is now Turkey) and Lérins (in what is today France). For centuries, Fathers of the Alexandrian school of biblical scholarship sparred with Fathers of the Antiochene school as, in more recent times, Thomists have uneasily coexisted with Christian phenomenologists and existentialists.

The Fathers could be further distinguished according to their work. Some were preachers. Some were popes. Some were teachers and lawyers. Some were monks and hermits. Some wrote "apologies," explaining and defending the Christian faith before hostile or skeptical pagans and Jews. Others were "exegetes," analyzing and expounding the Scriptures.

Often, the Fathers are divided according to the period in which they lived: the Apostolic Fathers inhabiting the generation of the Apostles and its immediate aftermath; the Ante-Nicene Fathers leading Christians till the fourth century; the Nicene Fathers guiding the Church through the early fourth century, which, with the great Council of Nicaea, was something of a golden age of doctrinal expression; and the Post-Nicene Fathers guiding the development of the Church's fundamental doctrines of the Trinity and Christology.

In every era, the Fathers had their disagreements and debates, and sometimes they called each other names. The fourth-century historian Eusebius of Caesarea, in Palestine, opined that Papias — an Apostolic Father — was a dimwit, "a man of very little intelligence."[5] St. Jerome suspected St. Augustine of being proud, conniving, and insincere — and he told him so.

From generation to generation, they were an odd mix. The Fathers represent a Church united because it is something divine, yet united only with difficulty because it is something human, suffering the effects of original sin. The Fathers show forth the richness of Christian faith in the Incarnation of God.

Still, when an English-speaker in the twenty-first century sees the Fathers' names in long lists, they *do* seem uniform in their strangeness and remoteness. The names are exotic, unusual, and many of the Fathers' cities and nations of origin no longer exist.

Often, the Fathers are divided into two lists — Greek and Latin, or Eastern and Western. The binary categories are problematic, since some Fathers used languages other than Greek and Latin (Syriac, for instance, or Coptic, or Armenian). Some Fathers, too, were Eastern in origin, but did their most important work in the West (Justin and Irenaeus, to cite just two examples). And some Fathers wrote originally in Greek, but their works survive mostly in Latin translation.

The lists themselves highlight further differences among the Fathers; most striking is that some are designated "Saint" while others are not. Yet we know that holiness is one of the four criteria the Church uses to designate a Father. Apparently, all the criteria do not apply evenly to each of the Fathers.

Consider orthodoxy, too. The Church reveres Tertullian for his early fervor and his teaching. He was, however, impetuous to a fault and a rigorous, demanding moralist. Tertullian's passions and perfectionism led him, eventually, right out of the Church and into the "purist," separatist sect of Montanus. Eusebius, for his part, is often called "the Father of Church history," yet not called "Saint." As a bishop, he opposed the excommunication of Christians who followed the Arian heresy; instead, he sought common ground with them in statements vague enough to satisfy both parties. Church councils rejected Eusebius's approach. Thus, Church history has regarded its own Father with some measure of suspicion. And Origen, who was one of the first "speculative theologians" as we understand the term today, occasionally took his speculation too far. Some of his propositions were condemned by Church councils in later centuries, though the Church stopped short of declaring Origen himself a heretic. Others, too, strayed dangerously close to questionable doctrine or practice. Yet the Church considered their good teachings too good to lose, and tradition has named them Fathers, almost in spite of themselves.[6]

The Fathers who were odd or somewhat errant make a history more colorful, and they rather vividly show the diversity of the Church. But the cranks are the exceptions. Among the Fathers, holiness and orthodoxy are the rule.

St. Gregory of Pontus's sanctity showed forth in great miracles, thus earning him the title of "Wonderworker." St. Augustine and St. Paulinus of Nola matched great learning with greater holiness, and in many ways they exemplify the virtue of Christian friendship. St. John Chrysostom preached with such clarity and vigor that his homilies continue to change lives, more than a millennium and a half later. Still other Fathers are known today only for their holiness and a reputation for teaching, as almost none of their writings have survived. After earning his place as a Father, St. Melito of Sardis fell silent for most of Christian history, until one of his texts was discovered in the mid-twentieth century.

THE FATHERS

There is no canonical list of the Fathers, and the Church has no process for naming them, as it has for naming saints and blesseds. There is a general (if not universal) consensus about which ancient authors may be cited as authorities in doctrinal matters. About some (for example, Tertulllian, Origen, Eusebius, Theodore), even the experts disagree. This list is compiled from data in Dr. Matthew Bunson's Encyclopedia of Catholic History *and other sources.*

St. Ambrose of Milan (d. 397) *
St. Anastasius Sinaita (d. 700)
St. Andrew of Crete (d. 740)

St. Aphrahat (fourth century)
St. Archelaus (d. 282)
Arnobius (d. 330)
St. Asterius of Amasea (fourth century)
St. Athanasius (d. 373) *
St. Augustine of Hippo (d. 430) *
St. Athenagoras (second century)
St. Basil the Great (d. 379) *
St. Benedict of Nursia (d.c. 550)
St. Caesarius of Arles (d. 542)
St. Caesarius of Nazianzus (d. 369)
St. Celestine I, Pope (reigned 422–432)
St. Clement of Alexandria (d. 215)
St. Clement I of Rome, Pope (reigned 88–97)
St. Cornelius, Pope (reigned 251–253)
St. Cyprian of Carthage (d. 258)
St. Cyril of Alexandria (d. 444)
St. Cyril of Jerusalem (d. 386)
St. Damasus I, Pope (reigned 366–384)
Didymus the Blind (d.c. 398)
Diodore of Tarsus (d. 392)
St. Dionysius, Pope (reigned 259–268)
St. Dionysius the Great (d.c. 264)
St. Ennodius (d. 521)
St. Ephrem of Syria (d. 373)
St. Epiphanius (d. 403)
St. Eucherius of Lyons (d.c. 450)
Eusebius of Caesarea (d. 340)
St. Eustathius of Antioch (fourth century)
St. Firmillian (d. 268)
St. Fulgentius (d. 533)
Gennadius I of Constantinople (fifth century)
St. Germanus (d. 732)
St. Gregory I the Great, Pope (reigned 590–604) *
St. Gregory of Elvira (d.c. 392)

St. Gregory of Nazianzus (d. 390) *
St. Gregory of Nyssa (d. 395)
St. Gregory of Pontus (d. 268)
Hermas (second century)
St. Hilary of Poitiers (d. 367)
St. Hippolytus (d. 236)
St. Ignatius of Antioch (d.c. 107)
St. Innocent I, Pope (reigned 401–417)
St. Irenaeus of Lyons (d.c. 202)
St. Isidore of Pelusium (d.c. 450)
St. Isidore of Seville (d. 636)
St. Jacob of Serugh (d. 521)
St. Jerome (d. 420) *
St. John Cassian (d. 435)
St. John Chrysostom (d. 407) *
St. John Climacus (d. 649)
St. John of Damascus (d. 749)
St. Julius I, Pope (reigned 337–352)
St. Justin Martyr (d. 165)
Lactantius (d. 323)
St. Leo I the Great, Pope (reigned 440–461)
St. Leontius of Byzantium (sixth century)
St. Macarius (d.c. 390)
Marius Mercator (d. 451)
Marius Victorinus (fourth century)
St. Maximus the Confessor (d. 662)
St. Melito of Sardis (d.c. 180)
St. Methodius of Olympus (d.c. 311)
Minucius Felix (second century)
St. Nilus the Elder (d.c. 430)
Novatian (d.c. 257)
St. Optatus (fourth century)
Origen (d. 254)
St. Prudentius (fourth and fifth centuries)
St. Pacian (d.c. 390)

St. Pamphilus (d. 309)
St. Paulinus of Nola (d. 431)
St. Peter Chrysologus (d. 450)
St. Phoebadius of Agen (fourth century)
St. Polycarp (d.c. 155)
St. Proclus (d.c. 446)
Pseudo-Dionysius the Areopagite (sixth century)
St. Romanus the Melodist (sixth century)
Rufinus of Aquileia (d. 410)
Salvian (fifth century)
St. Serapion (d.c. 370)
St. Siricius, Pope (reigned 384-399)
St. Sophronius (d. 638)
Tatian (second century)
Tertullian (d.c. 222)
Theodore of Mopsuestia (d. 428)
Theodoret of Cyrrhus (d.c. 458)
St. Theophilus of Antioch (second century)
St. Venantius Fortunatus (sixth century)
St. Vincent of Lérins (d.c. 450)

* Listed among the eight "Great Fathers" by the Catholic Church.

THE FATHERS AND THE GOSPEL

What did Tertullian mean when he thundered that he was "heir of the Apostles"? Like all the Fathers, he saw himself as the inheritor and protector of a certain patrimony: a revelation from God regarding His singular work of redemption in Jesus Christ. "Christianity came into history as a fact," wrote the twentieth-century theologian Yves Congar. "It was and is the fact of a new life given by God through Christ and in the name of Christ."[7]

And, in the beginning, the fact of the "Good News," or "Gospel," was the entirety of the message. The biblical Acts of the Apostles can give the impression that it was enough for the first Christians simply to preach Jesus Christ crucified and risen, and mass conversions followed. Yet the New Testament's later books show also that the Church, from the beginning, struggled against aberrant doctrine. Arising in the Apostles' lifetime was the "Docetic" heresy, which claimed that Jesus only *seemed* to be human, to suffer and die; according to the Docetists, the Savior was really a pure spirit, a ghost in the machine of a human body. It was probably against the Docetists that St. John wrote: "By this you know the Spirit of God: every spirit which confesses that Jesus Christ has come in the flesh is of God, and every spirit which does not confess Jesus is not of God" (1 Jn 4:2-3). St. Paul and St. Jude seem also to struggle against emerging Christian Gnosticism, an elitist, hyperspiritual heresy emphasizing secret revelations (see, for example, 1 Tim 6:20-21).

Such misunderstandings, willful and otherwise, became more pronounced as the Church expanded outward. As the Gospel traveled along the trade routes, Christian preachers more often encountered pagans unfamiliar with the Jewish roots of Christian faith. Also, as time wore on, Jesus' culture, language, and native customs grew increasingly remote. Would this additional distance make the Gospel ever less intelligible to ever more people?

For the Church, this was a matter of some urgency, because doctrine was not incidental to Christian faith. It was essential. To believe in the Jesus of the Docetists or the Gnostics was to believe in a false messiah. Jesus Christ was true God and true man. False doctrine obscured and distorted these all-important facts and so offered a vastly different person in the place of Jesus. To counter this, the Fathers, in their preaching, writing, and liturgy, strove to shine forth the Person of Jesus Christ, in His words and miracles, His suffering and rising. If any element marks the early Fathers' spirituality in a special way, it is their sense of nearness to their Lord. They firmly believed that fidelity and devotion to Jesus Christ would ensure the accuracy of their teaching. St. Clement of Rome, the fourth pope and a disciple of St. Peter, described the first-century Christians of Corinth in this way: "Content with the provision which God had made for you, and carefully attending to His words, you were inwardly filled with His teaching, and His sufferings were before your eyes."[8]

The Fathers' primary source of Jesus' acts, teachings, and suffering was "the Gospel." Today, we take this word to represent the books of the New Testament, especially the four books of the life of Christ. But in the time of the Apostolic Fathers, and even into the succeeding centuries, "the Gospel" meant the received Tradition, whether in written or oral form (see 2 Thess 2:14). The first generations of Christians did not so much read the Gospel as absorb it, through the liturgy and other prayers of the Church, through the catechetical homilies of their local bishop, and through everyday life in the Church community. Relatively rare was the believer who could read, and rarer still was the literate Christian who could afford to own pages of the Gospels copied out for study. Moreover, through most of the era of the Fathers, the Church had no universal canon of Scriptures, and there was considerable disagreement over which books belonged to "the Gospel" and which did not.

"Faith comes by hearing," St. Paul said (Rom 10:17), and the early Christians heard the Word from the men they revered as their Fathers. And the Fathers, for their part, especially the Apostolic Fathers, saw themselves as chosen vessels of the Gospel, having received it intact from the Apostles. St. Clement's words to the Corinthians ring with conviction: "The Apostles have preached the Gospel to us from the Lord Jesus Christ.... Christ therefore was sent forth by God, and the Apostles by Christ. Both these appointments, then, were made in an orderly way, according to the will of God." He went on to explain that the Apostles, in turn, "appointed the first-fruits [of their labors] ... to be bishops and deacons of those who should afterwards believe."[9]

St. Clement's credentials were his connections with Jesus Christ through St. Peter, the prince of the Apostles, and St. Paul. Later Fathers would prove the validity of their teaching by showing its continuity with the oral and written traditions of the Apostles, or by tracing the authority of their episcopal office back to the Apostles, and thus to Jesus.

──────────THE GOSPEL AND THE GOSPELS──────────

While the oral Tradition was paramount to the Apostolic Fathers, the Fathers did show a singular devotion to the sacred Scriptures, both the Old Testament and the New. St. Augustine said that reading Scripture is like reading letters from the other world, letters from our Father and from our fatherland.[10] Origen likened the Gospels read aloud to the Real Presence of Jesus in the Eucharist.[11] For St. Ambrose, the Bible was "the feast of wisdom, and the individual books are the various dishes."[12] St. Jerome wrote, "To be ignorant of Scripture is to be ignorant of Christ."[13]

The Fathers' own writings testify that they would have no Christian ignorant of Scripture. In homilies, letters, theological tracts, and catechetical books, practically every page is laden with quotations from the New and Old Testaments. Pope Leo XIII wrote in 1893: "If we consider the immediate disciples of the Apostles, St. Clement of Rome, St. Ignatius of Antioch, St. Polycarp — or the apologists, such as St. Justin and St. Irenaeus — we find that in their letters and their books, whether in defense of the Catholic faith or in its commendation, they drew faith, strength, and unction from the Word of God."[14] As that was true of the earliest Fathers, so it was true of the very last, St. John of Damascus, who moved to Palestine so that he could be nearer the scenes of the Gospels.

Yet for as much as half of the Patristic Era, the list of the sacred writings was not precisely, universally, officially defined. The writings credibly attributed to the Apostles — what we today know as the New Testament — were widely circulated. But so were many other works that claimed authorship by the disciples of Jesus. Epistles, gospels, acts, and apocalypses abounded, purporting to convey the teaching of Peter, John, James, Philip, the Virgin Mary, Mary Magdalene, Nicodemus, Barnabas, and even Pontius Pilate. These works varied widely in orthodoxy, literary quality, and historical accuracy. The *Gospel of Nicodemus*, for example, checked out on style and doctrine, but utterly failed in its accounts of Roman law and Jewish custom. "Infancy gospels" make up a genre by themselves, purporting to tell the spectacular miracles performed by the boy Jesus; the results are sometimes quite silly, as when the little Savior turns his cruel playmates into goats or withers the hand of an uppity schoolteacher. Other gospels, like those attributed to Philip and Thomas, went beyond the tawdry to the downright heretical, placing denials of the Incarnation in the mouth of Jesus Himself.

The question of authenticity, then, was a crucial one, and the Fathers approached the issue with an impressive degree of scientific rigor. In the century after Jesus' ascension into heaven, Christians were already discussing and debating which books should be read in the Church's public worship. Lists were drawn up, and these would eventually be known as "canons" — from the Greek word for "measuring stick."

By the beginning of the second century, there was general agreement on the canonicity of the four Gospels — Matthew, Mark, Luke, and John — and most of St. Paul's letters. But just about everything else was under debate. Hebrews and Revelation were contested by some Fathers even up to the moment the universal canon was defined.

Until the early fifth century, canons were mostly an affair of the local church, and these lists varied from region to region. Some churches counted St. Clement of Rome's *Letter to the Corinthians* as canonical. The so-called *Letter of Barnabas* was also considered canonical by many, including Origen, until well into the fourth century. Some churches in Egypt included a fifth gospel, often called the *Gospel of the Egyptians*.

The oldest surviving list of Christian books is the Muratorian Canon, from about 150. The fragment includes all the books of the New Testament except Hebrews, James, 1 Peter, and 2 Peter, and counts as canonical the *Apocalypse of Peter* and *The Shepherd by Hermas*, both of which were eventually excluded from the Church's definitive canon.

St. Athanasius, the bishop of Alexandria, provides the earliest list that matches exactly the twenty-seven books of the New Testament as we know it today. He promulgated it in 367, and he said it was binding on the whole Church. Still, there remained disputes, and the New Testament canon was not conclusively settled until the North African synods of Hippo Regius (393) and Carthage (397, 419), whose conclusions were approved by the pope.

The settling of the canon was just part of the greater drama of God's self-revelation to man. The Scriptures were texts that must be opened to the laity, not just in the sense of reading them to a congregation, but also interpreting them. In a 1993 document on "The Interpretation of the Bible in the Church," the Pontifical Biblical Commission summed up the Fathers' belief that "there is nothing in [Scripture] which is to be set aside as out of date or completely lacking meaning. God is constantly speaking to His Christian people a message that is ever relevant for their time."[15]

For the Fathers, that message shone through in many ways. Most of the Fathers discerned in the Scriptures at least two levels of meaning: the *literal* sense and the *spiritual* sense. Some Fathers further divided the spiritual sense into *allegorical, moral,* and *anagogical* senses. Thus, they acknowledged that each text told a literal truth, describing a historical event, person, or precept; but, at the same time, the passage might also tell a moral truth about how Christians should live, an allegorical truth about Jesus Christ, and a revelation (anagogical) about the Christian's heavenly destiny.

The *Catechism of the Catholic Church* explains that all the Fathers' teaching depends on their harmonizing of the two testaments of the Bible. "This catechesis unveils what lay hidden under the letter of the Old Testament: the mystery of Christ. It is called 'typological' because it reveals the newness of Christ on the basis of the 'figures' (types) which announce him in the deeds, words, and symbols of the first covenant" (n. 1094).

The *Catechism's* definition ends with an example: "By this re-reading in the Spirit of Truth, starting from Christ, the figures are unveiled.[16] Thus the flood and Noah's ark prefigured salvation by Baptism,[17] as did the cloud and the crossing of the Red Sea. Water from the rock was the figure of the spiritual gifts of Christ, and manna in the desert prefigured the Eucharist, 'the true bread from heaven'[18]" (n. 1094).

There were two major schools of biblical studies in the ancient Church. The school of Alexandria favored an allegorical reading of Scripture, and its most famous proponent was Origen, who is said to have written several thousand books. The school of Antioch, on the other hand, promoted a deep study of the literal sense of Scripture, emphasizing historical and linguistic scholarship. Perhaps the greatest exegete of the Antiochene school was Theodore of Mopsuestia.

Both methods of Scripture study had strengths and weaknesses. At their best, practitioners of the allegorical method could vividly demonstrate God's omniscience and providence as, from the first moment of creation, He prepared the way for redemption. At their worst, the Alexandrians could weave allegories so fanciful, complex, and improbable as to leave readers utterly bewildered. The literal method, used rightly, could render the Scriptures so vivid that believers seem transported into the scenes. Used to excess, a literalist reading could degenerate into rationalism or a sort of fundamentalism. Wayward students of the Alexandrian school sometimes strayed into Gnosticism. But it was an alumnus of Antioch who founded Arianism, the most far-reaching and rationalist of all the ancient heresies.

The greatest of the later Fathers, Jerome and Augustine, managed to integrate both methods, literal and allegorical, and to employ each according to the moment's need, in their commentaries and their homilies.

In reading the Scriptures, the Fathers held themselves accountable to a community of interpretation — the Church, the communion of saints. To consider the Gospel apart from the Tradition was unthinkable to the Fathers. St. Polycarp wrote that "whoever interprets according to his own perverse inclinations is the firstborn of Satan."[19] The heretics Arius and Eutyches both aroused horror in their judges when they sought to interpret Scripture in ways contrary to all the Fathers who had gone before.

Interpreting the Gospels, the Fathers sought to communicate the Gospel to the faithful, whose faith came by hearing. St. Jerome was representative of all the Fathers when he wrote, "A man who is well grounded in the testimonies of Scripture is the bulwark of the Church."[20]

THE FATHERS AT THE ALTARS

The Church's normal place for the reading of Scripture was in the context of the liturgy, which was itself a deeply biblical prayer. The oldest text that has survived from the Patristic Era is a liturgical manual called the *Didache* (meaning "Teaching"), probably composed between A.D. 48 and 90. Its guidelines suggest a spare, dignified ritual, borrowing heavily from the Jewish liturgies of the home and synagogue. Yet there is also clear continuity with the overwhelming New Testament witness of the Eucharist (see Mt 26:26-28; Mk 14:22-24; Lk 22:19-20; Lk 24:30, 35; Jn 6:25-65; Acts 2:42, 46; and 1 Cor 11).

It is apparent, even in this most ancient document, that the Church viewed the Mass as a sacrifice, a word the *Didache* uses many times. Moreover, the liturgy was seen as the believer's participation in the one sacrifice of Jesus Christ: His suffering, death, and resurrection. Said the *Didache* of the Mass: "It is this sacrifice that was spoken of by the Lord."[21]

"On the Lord's own day, gather yourselves together and break bread and give thanks," runs the instruction. The Greek word for "give thanks" is *eucharistesate*, which can also be rendered "make Eucharist." The *Didache* then goes on to provide eucharistic prayers for the presider to offer over the bread and wine. And the document recommends confession before Communion: "First confess your sins, so that your sacrifice may be pure."[22]

The *Didache* was probably composed in Antioch, Syria, even before some of the New Testament documents were written. So the Fathers' witness of the Eucharist is unbroken, from the four Gospels onward.

At the beginning of the second century, St. Ignatius of Antioch spoke of the Mass as a sacrifice, and of the Church as "the place of sacrifice."[23] His letters contain the most graphic, outside the Bible, of the early witnesses to Jesus' Real Presence in the Eucharist. He refers to the sacrament as "the blood of God,"[24] and for the sacramental "flesh" he consistently uses the Greek word *sarx*, which could be used for meat hanging in the marketplace. "Take care, then, to have but one Eucharist. For there is one flesh of our Lord Jesus Christ, and one cup to show forth the unity of His blood; one altar; as there is one bishop, along with the priests and deacons, my fellow servants."[25]

To the Smyrnaeans, Ignatius outlined the requirements for a valid liturgy: "Let that be deemed a proper Eucharist, which is administered either by the bishop, or by one to whom he has entrusted it."[26] He noted that already there were heretics who denied the Real Presence:

"From the Eucharist and prayer they hold aloof, because they do not confess that the Eucharist is the flesh of our Savior Jesus Christ."[27]

St. Ignatius precedes St. Justin who, in 155, wrote to the pagan emperor Antoninus Pius, describing the Christian liturgy as it was celebrated in Rome. Justin's account will be familiar to anyone who attends a Mass today, almost two thousand years later. In fact, the *Catechism of the Catholic Church* uses an extensive quotation from St. Justin in its section on the Holy Eucharist (n. 1345):

> On the day we call the day of the sun, all who dwell in the city or country gather in the same place.
>
> The memoirs of the apostles and the writings of the prophets are read, as much as time permits.
>
> When the reader has finished, he who presides over those gathered admonishes and challenges them to imitate these beautiful things.
>
> Then we all rise together and offer prayers* for ourselves ... and for all others, wherever they may be, so that we may be found righteous by our life and actions, and faithful to the commandments, so as to obtain eternal salvation.
>
> When the prayers are concluded we exchange the kiss.
>
> Then someone brings bread and a cup of water and wine mixed together to him who presides over the brethren.
>
> He takes them and offers praise and glory to the Father of the universe, through the name of the Son and of the Holy Spirit and for a considerable time he gives thanks (in Greek: *eucharistian*) that we have been judged worthy of these gifts.
>
> When he has concluded the prayers and thanksgivings, all present give voice to an acclamation by saying: "Amen."
>
> When he who presides has given thanks and the people have responded, those whom we call deacons give to those present the "eucharisted" bread, wine and water and take them to those who are absent.[28]

St. Justin affirmed: "The food that has been made the Eucharist by the prayer of His word, and which nourishes our flesh and blood by assimilation, is both the flesh and blood of that Jesus who was made flesh."[29]

The ritual of the Eucharist continued to evolve through the Patristic Era. Local churches developed their own traditions. Liturgies survive from the ancient churches in a great variety of languages. Yet they all retain the same elements: the confession of sins, the reading of Scripture (with preaching), the offering of the gifts, the blessing of the elements, and the reception of Holy Communion.

And the understanding of the Eucharist deepened with each successive generation, with loving consideration of ever-finer points of doctrine. The last of the Fathers, St. John of Damascus, marveled in the eighth century at the Presence St. Ignatius had so well described in the second, but now proceeding from the *what* of it to the *how*: "You ask how the bread becomes the Body of Christ, and the wine … the Blood of Christ. I shall tell you: the Holy Spirit comes upon them and accomplishes what surpasses every word and thought.… Let it be enough for you to understand that it is by the Holy Spirit, just as it was of the Holy Virgin and by the Holy Spirit that the Lord, through and in Himself, took flesh."[30]

FAMILY UNITY

We began this study by remarking on the Fathers' fatherhood: how they acted in a paternal way, concerned with preserving the unity of the Christian family. Taking their cue from St. Paul, the early Christians saw the unity of the Church as an enduring sign of the unity of Christ's divine and human natures, and of the unity of the Persons of the Blessed Trinity. The idea is central to the earliest documents, such as the *Didache* and St. Clement's *Letter to the Corinthians*, and finds perhaps its most famous and moving patristic expression in St. Cyprian's tract *On the Unity of the Church*.

St. Ignatius of Antioch saw the unity of the Church as a reflection of the unity of the Godhead:

As the Lord was united to the Father and
did nothing without Him ... so neither
should you do anything without the bishop
and priests.... Let there be one prayer, one
supplication, one mind, one hope, in love
and in joy undefiled. There is one Jesus
Christ, and nothing is more excellent than
He. Come together, then, as into one temple
of God, to one altar, to one Jesus Christ,
who came forth from one Father, and is with
one, and has gone to one.[31]

For all the Church Fathers, the Eucharist was the sacrament of
Christian unity. It signified the unity of the Church and, by the power
of God's grace, it effected that unity. This idea appears in that most
ancient liturgy of the *Didache*: "As this broken bread was scattered
upon the mountains, and gathered together became one, so may Your
Church be gathered together from the ends of the earth into Your
kingdom; for Yours is the glory and the power through Jesus Christ for
ever and ever."[32]

The Eucharist was a gathering of God's family, presided over
by the bishop, and later by his priests, whom the faithful reverently
addressed as their "Fathers." The office of bishop, established in the
New Testament, recurs in all the Apostolic Fathers, and they speak of
it as a type of fatherhood. "Let a man respect his bishop," wrote St.
Ignatius, and he continued: "For whoever is sent by the Master to run
His house, we ought to receive him as we would receive the Master
Himself."[33] In another letter, St. Ignatius wrote: "Be obedient to your
bishop and to one another, as Jesus Christ in His human nature was
subject to the Father and as the Apostles were to Christ and the Father.
In this way there will be union of body and spirit."[34] Thus the bishop,
as father, became a force for unity in the Church. Said St. Jerome: "Be
obedient to your bishop and welcome him as the parent of your soul."[35]

The Church's great Father on earth was the bishop of Rome, who
from the early days was called Papa — "Pope." Many Fathers attest
that the bishop of Rome was the successor to St. Peter, who was prince

of the Apostles. All the ancient traditions tell of Peter's martyrdom in Rome, and not a single source places it elsewhere. Very few events of the Apostolic Church are so well attested. The event was said to have consecrated the city.

In this, as in all things, the earliest Fathers trace a clear continuity with the New Testament (see Mt 16:18-19; Jn 21:15-17). One of the oldest surviving Christian texts, aside from the Bible, is St. Clement of Rome's *Letter to the Corinthians*. There we see the Church of Rome intervening in a controversy in a faraway church in Greece. St. Clement speaks from a position of authority and does not hesitate to demand obedience: "But should any disobey what has been said by [God] through us, let them understand that they will entangle themselves in transgression and no small danger."[36] A century later, St. Clement's letter was still read aloud on feast days in the Corinthian church. In the fourth century, the historian Eusebius attested that St. Clement's letter was read in churches throughout the Christian world.[37]

St. Ignatius of Antioch, in the early 100s, wrote letters of guidance to churches of the Near East, all along the path he traveled to martyrdom in Rome. In each he spoke as if imminent martyrdom has conferred a certain authority upon him — except when he addressed his letter to the Christians of Rome. It is only to the Roman Church that St. Ignatius showed deference.

At the end of the second century, St. Irenaeus confirmed the primacy of Rome and the papacy. The bishop of Lyons cited

that tradition derived from the Apostles,
of the very great, the very ancient, and
universally known Church founded and
organized at Rome by the two most
glorious Apostles, Peter and Paul ... which
comes down to our time by means of the
successions of the bishops. For it is a matter
of necessity that every Church should
agree with this Church, on account of its
preeminent authority — that is, the faithful
everywhere inasmuch as the apostolic

tradition has been preserved continuously by
faithful men everywhere.

St. Irenaeus went on, then, to give a history of the papacy up until
his own time:

> The blessed Apostles, then, having founded
> and built up the Church, committed into the
> hands of Linus the office of the episcopate.
> Of this Linus Paul makes mention in the
> Epistles to Timothy. To him succeeded
> Anacletus; and after him, in the third place
> from the Apostles, Clement....
> This man, as he had seen the blessed
> Apostles, and had been conversant with
> them, might be said to have the preaching
> of the Apostles still echoing in his ears,
> and their traditions before his eyes.... To
> this Clement there succeeded Evaristus.
> Alexander followed Evaristus; then, sixth
> from the Apostles, Sixtus was appointed;
> after him, Telephorus, who was gloriously
> martyred; then Hyginus; after him, Pius;
> then after him, Anicetus. Sorer having
> succeeded Anicetus, Eleutherius now, in the
> twelfth place from the Apostles, holds the
> inheritance of the episcopate.

He concludes: "In this order, and by this succession, the ecclesiastical
Tradition from the Apostles, and the preaching of the truth, have come
down to us. And this is most abundant proof that there is one and the
same vivifying faith, which has been preserved in the Church from the
Apostles until now, and handed down in truth."[38]
It is only in later centuries that history shows distant bishops
struggling for power against the popes. It is only later, too, that history
shows some popes willing to usurp the legitimate authority of local

bishops. Though the first successors of St. Peter were surely confident in their authority, they were just as surely aware that they were servants, after the model of their master. Indeed, most of the first popes followed their master in death as well as life. Good shepherds, they gave their lives as martyrs, for the sake of their sheep.

THE WITNESS OF BLOOD

The title "Father" signified a bishop's authority. But there was yet another great authority in the ancient Church, an honorary office we might call it. The early Christians revered the words, the witness, and the acts of the martyrs, those who died for the faith.

Also honored were the confessors, those who had been arrested or tortured for their Christian faith. Martyr means "witness" in Greek, and the willingness of many people to die for the Christian faith was indeed the most powerful testimony for the value of that faith. St. Justin, who would himself die a martyr's death, said as much in the mid-second century: "Though beheaded, and crucified, and thrown to wild beasts, in chains and fire, and all other tortures; we do not give up our confession; but the more such things happen, the more others, in larger numbers, become believers."[39] Tertullian put it most memorably and succinctly: "The more often you mow us down, the more in number we grow; the blood of Christians is seed."[40] Indeed, during the centuries when Christians were most severely persecuted, the Church grew by a steady 40 percent per decade.

This was an essential difference in Christianity. Most of the popular strains of paganism made no exclusive claims on their adherents. A pagan was free to mix and match his devotions from the various temples of his city. And new religions were flourishing at the time of the Church's emergence; merchants traveled the trade routes and brought their deities with them. In the third century, St. Hippolytus set out to write a refutation of all the major varieties of religious experience; by the end of his study, he had sprayed fire on hundreds of sects, movements, philosophies, and systems of astrology.

Most of the Eastern cults found their way to Rome. But because paganism was a buyer's market, and a saturated market at that, religious consumers were skeptical. The cults demanded little of their devotees, and so they received little in the way of long-term loyalty. The pagan cults were, to a large degree, priests without congregations. All of this made the extermination of a cult a fairly easy exercise for the empire. If the Romans thought a religion dangerous, they could remove its priests, demolish its shrines, and the cult would soon disappear, its devotees dispersed to other shrines, other gods.

But the Christian God made a jealous and total claim on every Christian, and Christians accepted His claims willingly. They would not worship other gods, most certainly not self-proclaimed divine emperors. And since they did not worship the emperor or the usual run of deities, they were often charged with atheism or treason, both capital crimes. Yet only occasionally were the empire's purges widely enforced against ordinary citizens and believers. Instead, the governors employed their proven tactic of eliminating the cult's high priests: the bishops. This failed, however, with Christianity, because for every bishop there were thousands of believers whose faith was personal, exclusive, and firm.

Some historians place the total number of martyrs in the hundreds of thousands. Others believe that the martyrs of the Roman Empire were relatively few in number, but that their testimony was considered so valuable that the Church has preserved the name of almost every one.

"Your cruelty is our glory,"[41] Tertullian wrote to the imperial authorities. And Rome could be ingenious in its cruelty. Thus, all the greater was the Church's glory. St. Irenaeus described the shock of pagans who witnessed the willingness of Christians to endure lingering tortures and "the games" rather than renounce the cult of Jesus. Tertullian taunted the pagans that their most noble philosophies offered them nothing comparable to die for. Testing Socrates' resignation, he found it wanting, when measured against the Christians' eager embrace of death. "The sword, the fire, the cross, the wild beasts, the torture — these surely are but trifling sufferings to obtain a celestial glory and a divine reward."[42]

One of the earliest known accounts of Christian martyrdom comes from the pagan historian Tacitus, an aristocrat of Rome, who reported Nero's execution of "vast numbers" in A.D. 64. "Ridicule accompanied their end," he wrote. "They were covered with wild beasts' skins and torn to death by dogs, or they were fastened on crosses and, when daylight failed, were burned to serve as torches by night."[43]

But martyrdom was the ultimate imitation of Christ: accepting a cruel and unjust death, as Jesus did. There could be no greater proof of one's faith than to choose death rather than apostasy. So the Christians recorded the trials and pains of the martyrs in almost unbearable detail. It was common teaching that the martyrs entered heaven immediately upon their death. Some Fathers taught that the confessors merited a sort of "priesthood" by their endurance and suffering.

This was true in a sense. A priest is one who offers sacrifice, and martyrs offered their lives in union with the sacrifice of Jesus on the cross. It is fascinating that two of the most celebrated early martyrs, St. Ignatius of Antioch and St. Polycarp of Smyrna, used eucharistic images to speak of their dying. "I am the wheat of God," St. Ignatius wrote to the Romans. "Let me be ground by the teeth of the wild beasts, that I may be found the pure bread of Christ."[44] From the pyre of his execution, St. Polycarp delivered an oration that reads like a eucharistic prayer, praying, in part: "I give You thanks that You have counted me worthy of this day and this hour, that I should have a part in the number of Your martyrs ... among whom may I be accepted this day before You as a rich and acceptable sacrifice, as You, the ever-truthful God, have foreordained."[45] Witnesses of Polycarp's execution reported that the smoke gave off not the odor of burning flesh, but the aroma of baking bread.[46]

Nevertheless, while Rome disdained Christianity, full-scale purges took place sporadically. Especially bloody persecutions occurred during the reigns of Domitian (81–95), Trajan (98–117), Antoninus Pius (138–161), Marcus Aurelius (161–180), Septimius Severus (193–211), Decius (249–251), Valerian (253–260), Diocletian (284–305), and Galerius (305–311). By the beginning of the fourth century, the failure of the persecutions was apparent even to the emperors: Christians, at that time, made up about half the citizens in the empire's major cities.

The emperor Galerius switched tactics and tried accommodation of the faith, issuing an Edict of Toleration in 311. Two years later, Constantine's Edict of Milan put an end to imperial persecution of Christians.

With the tapering off of persecutions, Christians still sought a heroic way to give their lives for Christ. So rose monasticism, sometimes called the "white martyrdom," a new witness to the power of Christ's sacrifice.

————————THE FATHERS' WAYWARD CHILDREN————————

As the Church revered martyrdom, so it mourned and reviled infidelity. And, like martyrdom, infidelity — in the form of heresy, apostasy, and schism — was with the Church from the beginning. We observed earlier that even the Apostles had to battle heretics in their midst. Some New Testament books make frontal assaults on Docetism and Gnosticism.

It only got worse. Among the Apostolic Fathers, St. Ignatius and St. Polycarp were preoccupied with the spread of heresies. In the next generations, St. Irenaeus, St. Hippolytus, and Tertullian each filled book after book with invective against "all heresies." But the heresies continued to multiply, and as soon as one seemed to flicker out, another blazed up. Epiphanius counted 80 varieties as the fourth century turned over to the fifth. At the close of the Patristic Era, St. John of Damascus drew up a catalog of heresies, and he counted 103, numbering among them the newly founded religion of Mohammed, as well as the very ancient sect of the Encratites, who were celibate vegetarians, and the more recent Pepuzians, whose priestesses purportedly made Communion hosts out of wheat flour and infants' blood.

Some heresies seem, in retrospect, mere justifications for immoral behavior, and the Fathers were quick to say so. Other heresies tantalized believers with the promise of magical power or visionary experience. Still others were quixotic attempts to rationalize mysteries that surpass human understanding, such as the Trinity or the Incarnation. Perhaps the most pitiable heretics were the moral reformers who had despaired, finding scandal in the sinners and slackers within the Church, and so sought to establish a newer, purer church elsewhere. Such was the sin of Tertullian and Hippolytus, and such was the sin so vigorously attacked, in the following generation, by Tertullian's sometime disciple, St. Cyprian of Carthage.

The Fathers abhorred infidelity wherever they perceived it, and they attacked it with whatever weapons they had at hand: tradition, philosophy, rhetoric, natural science, pleading, wit, sarcasm. When one heretic denied the perpetual virginity of Mary, St. Jerome insulted him personally at every turn — even questioning his masculinity — all the while making mincemeat of the man's arguments.

There were then, as there are now, many ways to be unfaithful. *Apostasy* is the renunciation of Christian faith. *Heresy* is the willful acceptance of incorrect doctrine. *Schism* is the attempt to preserve orthodoxy while breaking from union with the Church and the papacy. Individual Fathers — St. Irenaeus, for example, and St. John of Damascus — would sometimes categorize all instances of unfaithfulness together as *hairesis*, the Greek word for "choice" and the root of the modern English heresy. Pick-and-choose Catholicism, then as now, was the very definition of heresy.

Certain heresies are significant for the effects they had on history and for the activity they provoked in the Fathers:

- **Docetism** was the belief that Jesus only *seemed* to become a man, to suffer, and to die. Docetists taught that Jesus was really a pure spirit, who laughed from above the cross at his executioners' folly. Docetism was a common strain within Gnosticism. The term *docetism* comes from the Greek word for "seeming."

- **Gnosticism** was a widespread intellectual current in the ancient world, influencing pockets of Christianity, Judaism, and paganism. The term *gnostic* describes a great number of widely diverse movements, sects, and philosophical systems. If anything unites them, it is the emphasis of secret and pseudo-mystical knowledge (in Greek, gnosis). Gnostic sects tended to view themselves as an elite, whose special knowledge separated them from the rabble of ordinary Christians. Many held that ordinary Christians were incapable of discerning Jesus' real teaching, which was apparent only to "the elect." A common Gnostic tenet is the radical opposition of matter and spirit. Contrary to Christian orthodoxy, Gnostics believed that all matter was evil, including the human body, which they viewed as a prison for the spirit. Thus they believed the creator of this world was an evil "demiurge," whom Jesus came to vanquish. They denied the doctrines of the Trinity and the Incarnation. Their loathing of the body and creation led different sects to different conclusions about the moral life. Some concluded that, because all flesh was evil, the actions performed in the body did not matter, so everything was permitted: sexual license, theft, even murder. These Gnostics saw the commandments as arbitrary prohibitions imposed by a despotic creator. Others, however, concluded that, because all flesh was evil, the body's every desire must be severely repressed, and this led them to ascetical extremes: beyond celibacy and temperance to self-castration, rigorous fasting, and even suicide. Among the more famous Gnostic teachers were Simon Magus, Marcion, Valentinus, Basilides, and Mani.

- **Marcionism** held that Christianity should be a complete rejection of the heritage of Judaism. Marcion (born about 110) could not reconcile the revelation of Jesus with that of Yahweh, so he advocated the total elimination of the Old Testament and published an edited version of the New Testament, having removed all references to the Law and prophets. The Marcionite heresy persisted in some regions until the seventh century.

- **Montanism** was a pseudo-charismatic movement of the second century. Its founder, Montanus, claimed to be God's prophet and that his ecstatic revelations superseded the teachings of the Church. Montanists lived by a strict morality and asceticism, and shunned, without possibility of forgiveness, Christians who committed serious sins.

- **Donatism** held Christians to an uncompromisingly high standard of moral behavior. A North African, Donatus taught that sacraments were invalid if dispensed by a priest who had committed serious sin. Like the Montanists, Donatists taught that some sins were unforgivable. The Donatists persisted in North Africa until about 400.

- **Sabellianism** was a denial of the Trinity. Teaching in the early third century, Sabellius claimed that God the Father became man in Jesus Christ; that Jesus and the Father were the same and the only divine Person. Later Sabellians professed that Father, Son, and Holy Spirit were merely three aspects or elements of the same divine Person.

- **Manicheanism** was a Gnostic synthesis of several major world religions: Christianity, Zoroastrianism, Judaism, and Buddhism. Its founder, Mani, lived in the third century, teaching the radical opposition of matter and spirit. Manicheans disdained marriage and procreation. St. Augustine followed Manicheanism before he embraced Christianity.

- **Arianism** was the most notorious and most successful of the ancient heresies. The teachings of Arius, and the reactions they provoked, played a most crucial role in Church history and the development of doctrine. Teaching in Alexandria in the early fourth century, Arius denied that Jesus was coequal or co-eternal with God the Father. The heresy spread rapidly, winning over a succession of Byzantine emperors and many of the world's bishops. The heresy of Arius drew forceful opposition from the greatest minds and souls in the Church. The movement to oppose Arianism culminated in the teachings of St. Athanasius and of the Council of Nicaea in 325. Nicaea's creed refined the orthodox expression of fundamental doctrines such as the Trinity.

- **Nestorianism** arose in the aftermath of Arianism. Nestorius, a fifth-century patriarch of Constantinople, made such a distinction between the divine and human natures of Jesus as to suggest that they represented distinct persons. Nestorius also denied Mary the title "Mother of God," saying she gave birth only to Christ's human person. His teachings were condemned by the Council of Ephesus in 431 — a decision confirmed by the Second Council of Constantinople in 553 — but Nestorian communities have endured even to our own day.

- **Monophysitism** arose in reaction to Nestorianism. Proponents held that Christ had only one nature, a unique composite of divinity and humanity. The Monophysite heresy was condemned by the Council of Chalcedon in 451. Monophysite churches have persevered and are active today.

- **Monothelitism** was an abortive attempt to reconcile the Monophysites with orthodoxy. The Monothelites claimed that Jesus had two natures, but one will, His divine will. Monothelitism was condemned by the Third Council of Constantinople in 680.

- **Pelagianism** was a heresy that denied original sin, and claimed that man could avoid evil and win salvation by the power of his own free will; grace, then, was a merited reward, according to Pelagian doctrine.

THE COUNCILS AND CREEDS

With so many sects claiming the name "Christian" for such different and contradictory doctrines, it became necessary, almost from the start, to say precisely what one meant by one's "Christian faith." Thus, the Church professed concise statements of belief. Several are preserved for us in the New Testament. St. Paul wrote, for example, to the Corinthians: "For I delivered to you as of first importance what I also received, that Christ died for our sins in accordance with the scriptures, that he was buried, that he was raised on the third day in accordance with the scriptures, and that he appeared to Cephas, then to the twelve" (1 Cor 15:3-5). To the Romans, Paul taught an even briefer confession: "Jesus is Lord" (Rom 10:9). In the Acts of the Apostles, we see yet another: "I believe that Jesus Christ is the Son of God" (8:37). These are elementary creeds.

St. Cyril of Jerusalem, one of the greatest teachers among the Fathers, explained the creeds in this way:

This synthesis of faith was not made to accord with human opinions, but rather what was of the greatest importance was gathered from all the Scriptures, to present the one teaching of the faith in its entirety. And just as the mustard seed contains a great number of branches in a tiny grain, so too this summary of faith encompassed in a few words the whole knowledge of the true religion contained in the Old and New Testaments.[47]

The Catechism of the Catholic Church takes St. Cyril's fifth-century judgment as its own (see n. 186).

The two creeds most familiar to Catholics today are the Apostles' Creed and the Nicene Creed. Both come from the Patristic Era. The Apostles' Creed, according to legend, was assembled by the Twelve Apostles, who each contributed a single article, beginning with St. Peter's "I believe in God, the Father almighty." But there is no clear evidence of its use before the fourth century, so its apostolic authorship is unlikely. The Nicene Creed, used most often in the Mass of the Latin Rite, is the profession of faith compiled at the Council of Nicaea and completed at the Council of Constantinople in 381.

Both creeds seem to be descended from an early Roman baptismal creed described by St. Hippolytus around the year 200:

> I believe in God the Father almighty; and in Jesus Christ, Son of God, who, by the power of the Holy Spirit, was born of the Virgin Mary, was crucified under Pontius Pilate, died, and was buried; on the third day, He rose again to life from the dead; He ascended into heaven, and is seated at the right hand of the Father; from there He shall come to judge the living and the dead; I believe in the Holy Spirit, the holy Church, and the resurrection of the body.[48]

Such creeds became the foundation for the classic catechetical homilies of Fathers such as St. Cyril of Jerusalem in the East and St. Ambrose of Milan in the West.

Gradually, the creeds grew from the simple, single lines of the Apostolic Church to longer and more detailed professions of faith.

Heresy, apostasy, theological speculation, illiteracy — all these circumstances inspired the Fathers to greater doctrinal development and ever-clearer expression. Because the Montanists and Donatists taught that mortal sin was unforgivable, the Church saw the need to profess belief "in the forgiveness of sins." Because Arius denied Christ's divinity and co-eternity, the Church's creed would eventually proclaim Jesus "the Only Begotten Son of God, born of the Father before all ages. God from God, Light from Light, true God from true God, begotten, not made, consubstantial with the Father."

The Nicene formula was a masterpiece of clarity and brevity, poetically rhythmic and utterly memorable. Eventually, local churches required the chanting or singing of the creed in the Sunday liturgy. This repetition served as ongoing catechesis, boosting a congregation's immunity against error.

When the threat of a heresy was especially dire, or when a disputed question required the collaboration of many great minds and hearts, the Church would convene a council of bishops and theologians. The most authoritative councils, called "ecumenical councils," are those that involve the bishops of the whole Church in union with the pope. In the Patristic Era, there were six ecumenical councils, dealing, for the most part, with questions about the natures and person of Jesus Christ, and about the dogma of the Trinity. The fourth and fifth centuries — with the controversies surrounding Arius, Nestorius, and the Monophysites — produced the great "Christological councils": Nicaea I, Ephesus, Constantinople I, and Chalcedon. The debates and the conclusions of these councils marked some of the most subtle, profound, precise, and beautiful doctrinal expressions of the ancient Church, marshaling the skills of St. Athanasius, St. Cyril of Alexandria, St. Gregory of Nyssa, and St. Gregory of Nazianzus. This period is often called the "Golden Age of the Fathers."

The councils of the Patristic Era can be viewed as summaries of the Fathers' teachings, intended to last through the ages:

- **Nicaea I** (325). Convened by the emperor Constantine to settle the question of Arianism, which was threatening to destroy the peace of the Church and the unity of the empire.

The council ended by promulgating the anti-Arian Nicene Creed.

- **Constantinople I** (381). Settled the residual controversies surrounding Arianism, proclaimed the full deity of the Holy Spirit, and gave the Church of Constantinople precedence over all churches but Rome.
- **Ephesus** (431). Judged heretical the teachings of Nestorius regarding the person and natures of Jesus Christ. Confirmed the title of Mary as *Theotokos* ("God-bearer," or Mother of God).
- **Chalcedon** (451). Declared definitively that Jesus Christ is one person with two natures, settling almost two centuries of controversies involving several heresies.
- **Constantinople II** (553). Addressed lingering questions about Nestorianism.
- **Constantinople III** (680). Convened to settle the Monothelite controversy. The Monothelites claimed that Jesus had only one will, His divine will.

THE FATHERS TODAY

Those were graced moments, the sessions of the councils, the age of the Fathers. The judgments of the Fathers mark the boundaries of the faith we profess today. Thus, to know the Fathers is to know the truth summed up in the formula of St. Vincent of Lérins: the truth that has been taught everywhere, always, and by all. The Christ the Fathers preached is the very Christ we must know if we would know Him who is "God from God, Light from Light, true God from true God."

The Fathers teach with authority. Down to our own day, citation of the Fathers has remained the norm for doctrinal teaching in all the apostolic churches: the Catholic Church, the Orthodox Churches, and the other ancient Churches of the East. In the Protestant churches, the Fathers' authority has waxed and waned. The early reformers, such as Martin Luther and John Calvin, thought it necessary to cite the Fathers in justifying their innovations. Later, however, their followers,

Lutherans and Calvinists, would emphasize the Protestant doctrine of "Scripture alone" to the explicit exclusion of the Fathers of the Church.

Even today, the communities separated from Catholicism and Orthodoxy must confront the witness of the Fathers, and the apparent unity of the patristic experience with the experience of modern Catholic Christians. In order to dismiss the early witness of today's Catholic doctrines — for example, the Real Presence, the papacy, and the priesthood — Protestant scholars must posit a very early date when, they claim, the life of the Church went radically wrong, and then they must search out a subtle distinction between the witness of the Apostles in the New Testament and the seemingly identical witness of the Apostolic Fathers in the same century.

The Fathers are witnesses to the unbroken continuity of Catholic teaching. The Venerable John Henry Newman described the nature of their testimony: "They do not say, 'This is true because we see it in Scripture' — about which there might be differences in judgment — but, 'this is true because in matter of fact it is held, and has ever been held, by all the churches down to our times, without interruption, ever since the Apostles.'"[49]

It is true that the works of the Fathers, unlike the books of the Bible, are neither inspired nor inerrant; and, unlike the popes, the Fathers do not teach infallibly. The Fathers had their differences, some of them quite serious differences. What, then, is the Fathers' authority? The Church teaches that the "common doctrine of the Fathers" may not be opposed. This is especially true in matters of biblical interpretation. The First Vatican Council (1869–1870) confirmed the decision of the Council of Trent (1545–1563), saying that "it is not permissible for anyone to interpret Holy Scripture in a sense contrary to this, or indeed against the unanimous consent of the Fathers."[50] Newman wrote that this "consensus of the Fathers" is best discerned by the living Magisterium of the Church, since the Fathers themselves disagree on important matters. "We take them as honest informants, but not as sufficient authority in themselves, though they are an authority, too."[51]

The Second Vatican Council (1962–1965), in urging a return to Christian sources, repeatedly held the Fathers up as guides for the modern age:

"The words of the holy fathers witness to the presence of this living tradition, whose wealth is poured into the practice and life of the believing and praying Church. Through the same tradition the Church's full canon of the sacred books is known, and the sacred writings themselves are more profoundly understood and unceasingly made active in her." (*Dei Verbum*, 8)

"[T]here should be opened up to the students what the Fathers of the Eastern and Western Church have contributed to the faithful transmission and development of the individual truths of revelation." (*Optatam Totius*, 16)

"[S]uch theological speculation should be encouraged, in the light of the universal Church's tradition, as may submit to a new scrutiny the words and deeds which God has revealed, and which have been set down in Sacred Scripture and explained by the Fathers and by the Magisterium." (*Ad Gentes*, 22)

"The knowledge of the sacred minister ought to be sacred because it is drawn from the sacred source and directed to a sacred goal. Especially is it drawn from reading and meditating on the Sacred Scriptures, and it is equally nourished by the study of the Holy Fathers and other Doctors and monuments of tradition." (*Presbyterorum Ordinis*, 19)

The Fathers are abiding witnesses to the Church's "sacred tradition," which with the Scriptures is seen as a primary fount of Christian doctrine. The Second Vatican Council affirmed that "there exists a close connection and communication between sacred tradition and Sacred Scripture. For both of them, flowing from the same divine wellspring, in a certain way merge into a unity and tend toward the same end.... Therefore both sacred tradition and Sacred Scripture are to be accepted and venerated with the same sense of loyalty and reverence" (*Dei Verbum*, 9).

The *Catechism of the Catholic Church* shows this principle at work, and could justifiably be called a "catechism of the Fathers." In its opening pages, it admits as much, saying that its "principal sources are the Sacred Scriptures, the Fathers of the Church, the liturgy, and the Church's Magisterium" (n. 11). The *Catechism* invokes individual Fathers more than three hundred times, and the Fathers collectively many additional times. St. Augustine alone is cited almost ninety times, making him the most quoted individual in the book, aside from the writers of the Bible and the modern popes. Among the Fathers, St. Irenaeus finishes second, with over thirty citations. The *Catechism* echoes the Second Vatican Council in calling the faithful to a patristic revival: "Periods of renewal in the Church are also intense moments of catechesis. In the great era of the Fathers of the Church, saintly bishops devoted an important part of their ministry to catechesis. St. Cyril of Jerusalem and St. John Chrysostom, St. Ambrose and St. Augustine, and many other Fathers wrote catechetical works that remain models for us" (n. 8).[52]

This living relationship between the Fathers and Catholics of today the *Catechism* sums up neatly in number 688: "The Church, a communion living in the faith of the apostles which she transmits, is the place where we know the Holy Spirit ... in the Tradition, to which the Church Fathers are always timely witnesses...."

The Fathers, then, are ever "timely witnesses" to the sacred Tradition that comes from Jesus Himself — the Gospel entrusted to the Church and handed on even before the Gospels were written (see 2 Thess 2:14, 1 Tim 6:20, and 2 Tim 1:13). It is important for us to get this teaching right. The Fathers are witnesses to the Tradition, which predates them. They themselves are not the Tradition. The Fathers provide us a crucial link. They bear witness to the authenticity of our liturgy, our priesthood, our canon of sacred Scripture, and our structures of authority. They show us our Church's unbroken continuity with the Church of the Apostles. We share the same Tradition, though we have grown and developed in our understanding and expression of that Tradition.

Always timely witnesses. The Fathers are, even now, turning up anew to speak just the right word to their children. In the 1990s, researchers in Germany unearthed a long-lost transcription of one of St. Augustine's homilies. He exhorted his congregation: "Convert those who do not believe with the example of your life, so that your faith has a motive. If God's Word pleases you, act accordingly — not only God's Word in your heart, but in your life so that you will form God's family, united and pleasing to His eyes in all your actions. Don't doubt, brethren, that if your lives are worthy of God, unbelievers will find faith."[53]

Always timely witnesses. We should recall that the early Fathers especially were born into a culture that was beginning its moral decline, that the Roman Empire had all but abandoned the institutions of marriage and family, that divorce was common, as were abortion and contraception, that active homosexuality had become a norm for urban pagans, that euthanasia and suicide were unhappy endings to many life stories. You might call it a culture of death.

The Fathers await us with good counsel. Paternal, sure guides, they point the way beyond themselves, to God, "from whom all fatherhood in heaven and on earth receives its name" (Eph 3:15).

THE APOSTOLIC FATHERS

The Gospel's First Echo

The Apostolic Fathers are those teachers who lived during the generation of the Apostles or in its immediate aftermath. Most were bishops, and most, according to tradition, had some personal relationship with the Apostles. St. Clement, for example, was probably a disciple of St. Peter and St. Paul and was said to be consecrated a bishop by Peter himself. St. Polycarp was a disciple of St. John. According to one legend, St. Ignatius of Antioch made a cameo appearance in the Gospel according to Mark (14:51-52) as the youth on the Mount of Olives who ran away naked. And Papias of Hierapolis made it his business to seek out several of the original generation of disciples.

We see in the writings of these men a newness to the Good News. Primary among the Apostolic Fathers' concerns is Christian identity: What does it mean to be a believer, to belong to the Church? Related to this question were countless others: How is Christianity different from Judaism? What is the right way to conduct Christian worship? How does Christian morality apply to the everyday lives of citizens, merchants, and families? And who decides all of these matters, anyway — who is in charge of the Church?

These were important questions not only in the Fathers' own communities, which were already shaken from within by heresies, divisions, and disputes over authority. The questions arose also from the Christians' bewildered neighbors and worried governors, because Christianity's exclusive claims appeared to pose serious threats to the social order. Christians would not bow before the official gods; they would not worship the emperor or his "genius" or protector-god. Moreover, in a polymorphously pagan empire — an empire united by a somewhat cynical diversity in matters religious — the Christians were themselves publicly intolerant of pagan practices, condemning these as idolatry. Thus, to civil authorities in an empire just then at the height of its power, the new, fast-growing cult from Palestine seemed a disaster waiting to happen. And so persecutions followed, even from the earliest times. Most, if not all, of the Fathers we glimpse in this section died as martyrs.

ST. CLEMENT OF ROME

Almost all we know about St. Clement is the honor he received from the churches of the world. According to St. Irenaeus, Clement was the fourth pope, a Roman who had learned the faith from Sts. Peter and Paul during their years in the imperial capital. Tertullian reported that St. Peter himself had consecrated Clement a bishop.

But these few details are contested today as they were in ancient times. Even the years of Clement's reign are, at best, conjecture: 88-97 are the numbers some scholars have settled upon.

Some ancient writers identified Pope Clement with Titus Flavius Clemens, a cousin of the emperor Domitian who served at the imperial court. We know from pagan histories that this Clemens was executed late in the first century for "impiety" toward the gods and "atheism," charges often leveled at Christians. Evidence advanced for this identification is, however, shaky at best. Clement's only surviving text, his *Letter to the Corinthians*, includes a prayer for civil authorities and shows that the author possessed some knowledge of Roman military life. From the full text, it is clear, too, that the author was a deeply learned man, comfortably familiar with the whole of the Old Testament, as well as Stoic philosophy and Egyptian folklore.

What is most apparent from the *Letter to the Corinthians*, however, is the preeminence given to the Church of Rome, even in the first Christian century. St. Clement's opening paragraph indicates that people from Corinth had appealed to Rome to settle disputes within their church. His tone shows confidence in his paternal authority over that faraway community; he professes that his letter conveys words "written by us through the Holy Spirit," and he clearly expects to be obeyed. St. Clement seems to be completing a peacemaking mission undertaken by St. Paul more than a generation earlier and detailed in the Apostle's two New Testament letters to the Corinthians. The bishop of Rome's urgent concern is to heal the schisms in Corinth and restore unity to the Church.

Scholars ancient and modern have argued about the date when St. Clement wrote his letter. Some place it as early as A.D. 69 or early 70, since the author speaks as if the Jerusalem Temple is still standing. Such an early dating would likely place the letter before Clement's election to the papacy, but while he was serving as an "elder" of the Roman church. Other scholars place the letter around A.D. 96, during the years commonly accepted as Clement's pontificate.

St. Clement's *Letter to the Corinthians* received due reverence in Corinth, where, in 170, it was still read during liturgies along with a letter from the then-current pope, Soter. Eusebius related that other churches also revered St. Clement's letter, and we know that some even numbered it among the books of the New Testament. St. Polycarp quoted from this text in his own *Letter to the Philippians*. St. Clement of Alexandria was one of several Fathers who advocated the inclusion of St. Clement of Rome's letter in the canon of Scriptures.

One of the most striking passages in the letter is an effusion of praise for the natural order in the created world. A pope, a mystic, and a poet at heart, St. Clement saw a world charged with God's grandeur: Creation reflects the unity and harmony of the Godhead, and creation provides a model for unity and harmony in the Church.

To the Corinthians

The Letter to the Corinthians *is the only writing of St. Clement that has survived. A "Second Letter to the Corinthians" is attributed to him, but is probably spurious.*

The Church of God that sojourns at Rome, to the Church of God sojourning at Corinth, to them who are called and sanctified by the will of God, through our Lord Jesus Christ: Grace unto you, and peace, from Almighty God through Jesus Christ, be multiplied....

[W]e feel that we have been somewhat tardy in turning our attention to the points about which you consulted us; and especially to that shameful and detestable sedition, utterly abhorrent to the elect of God, which a few rash and self-confident persons have kindled to such a pitch of frenzy, that your venerable and illustrious name, worthy to be universally loved, has suffered grievous injury.…

It is right and holy, therefore, men and brothers, rather to obey God than to follow those who, through pride, have become the leaders of a detestable sedition. For we shall incur no slight injury, but rather great danger, if we rashly yield ourselves to the inclinations of men who aim at exciting strife and tumults, so as to draw us away from what is good. Let us be kind to one another after the pattern of the tender mercy and goodness of our Creator.…

Order in Creation

The heavens, revolving under His government, are subject to Him in peace. Day and night run the course appointed by Him, without hindering each other. The sun and moon, with the companies of the stars, roll on in harmony according to His command, within their prescribed limits, and without any deviation. The fruitful earth, according to His will, brings forth food in abundance, at the proper seasons, for man and beast and all the living beings upon it, never hesitating, nor changing any of the ordinances that He has fixed. The unsearchable places of abysses, and the indescribable arrangements of the lower world, are restrained by the same laws. The vast immeasurable sea, gathered together by His working into various basins, never passes beyond the bounds placed around it, but does as He has commanded. For He said, "Thus far shall you come, and no farther, and here shall your proud waves be stayed" (Job 38:11).

The ocean, impassible to man, and the worlds beyond it, are regulated by the same enactments of the Lord. The seasons of spring, summer, autumn, and winter peacefully give place to one another. The winds in their several quarters fulfill, at the proper time, their service without hindrance. The ever-flowing fountains, formed both for enjoyment and health, fill without fail their breasts for the life of men. The very smallest of living beings meet together in peace and concord. All these the great Creator and Lord of all has appointed to exist in peace and harmony; while He does good to all, but most abundantly to us who have fled for refuge to His compassion through Jesus Christ our Lord, to whom be glory and majesty for ever and ever. Amen....

Order in the Church

Let us reflect how near He is, and that none of the thoughts or reasonings in which we engage are hid from Him. It is right, therefore, that we should not leave the post which His will has assigned us.... Let us, men and brothers, with all energy, act as soldiers, in accordance with His holy commandments. Let us consider those who serve under our generals, with what order, obedience, and submissiveness they perform the things which are commanded them. All are not prefects, nor commanders of a thousand, nor of a hundred, nor of fifty, but each one in his own rank performs the things commanded by the king and the generals. The great cannot subsist without the small, nor the small without the great....

Let every one of you, brethren, give thanks to God in his own order, living in all good conscience, with becoming gravity, and not going beyond the rule of the ministry prescribed to him.... The Apostles preached the Gospel to us from the Lord Jesus Christ; Jesus Christ has done so from God. Christ therefore was sent forth by God, and the Apostles by Christ. Both these appointments, then, were made in an orderly way, according to the will of God. Having therefore received their orders, and being fully assured by the resurrection of our Lord Jesus Christ, and established in the word of God, with full assurance of the Holy Spirit, they went forth proclaiming that the kingdom of God was at hand. And thus preaching through countries and cities, they appointed the first-fruits of their labors (having first proved them by the Spirit) to be bishops and deacons of those who should afterwards believe....

Our Apostles also knew, through our Lord Jesus Christ, that there would be strife on account of the bishop's office. For this reason,... they appointed those already mentioned, and afterwards gave instructions that when these should fall asleep, other approved men should succeed them in their ministry....

A Time for Healing

Why, then, are there strifes, tumults, divisions, schisms, and wars among you? Have we not one God and one Christ? Is there not one Spirit of grace poured out upon us? And have we not one calling in Christ? Why do we divide and tear to pieces the members of Christ, and raise up strife against our own body, and have reached such a height of madness as to forget that "we are members one of another" (Eph 4:25)? Remember the words of our Lord Jesus Christ, how He said, "Woe to that man by whom offenses come! It were better for him that he had never been born, than that he should cast a stumbling-block before one of my elect. Yea, it were better for him that a millstone should be hung about his neck, and he should be sunk in the depths of the sea, than that he should cast a stumbling-block before one of my little ones" (cf. Mt 18:6-7). Your schism has subverted the faith of many, has discouraged many, has given rise to doubt in many, and has caused grief to us all. And still your sedition continues.

Take up the epistle of ... Paul.... It is disgraceful, beloved, highly disgraceful, and unworthy of your Christian profession, that such a thing should be heard of as that the most steadfast and ancient Church of the Corinthians should, on account of one or two persons, engage in sedition against its priests. And this rumor has reached not only us, but those also who are unconnected with us; so that, through your infatuation, the name of the Lord is blasphemed, while danger is also brought upon yourselves.

Let us therefore, with all haste, put an end to this state of things.... Let us implore forgiveness for all those transgressions which through any suggestion of the adversary we have committed.... Let us also pray for those who have fallen into any sin, that meekness and humility may be given to them, so that they may submit, not to us, but to the will of God.... You, therefore, who laid the foundation of this sedition, submit yourselves to the priests, and receive correction so as to repent, bending the knees of your hearts. Learn to be subject, laying aside the proud and arrogant self-confidence of your tongue....

Send back speedily — and in peace and with joy — our messengers, Claudius Ephebus and Valerius Bito, with Fortunatus, that they may sooner announce to us the peace and harmony we so earnestly desire and long for among you, and that we may more quickly rejoice over the good order reestablished among you.

—ANF 1:5, 8, 10-11, 15, 16-21

ST. IGNATIUS OF ANTIOCH

St. Ignatius, bishop of Antioch at the end of the first century, took as his surname Theophorus, "God-carrier." He would live up to that name in a literal way as he bore the Gospel across a continent and then across the sea.

According to his earliest biographers, St. Ignatius was a convert, a disciple of the Apostle John. Fourth-century histories report that Ignatius served as bishop of Antioch for forty years, having been installed there by the Apostles Peter and Paul. Antioch, one of the first and most important Christian communities (see Acts 11:26), claimed St. Peter himself as its first bishop.

Yet we know practically nothing of Bishop Ignatius's acts while he held office. He would perform his greatest work on the long voyage to his execution in Rome, as he "carried God" to the people and churches in Asia Minor.

St. Ignatius was condemned during the persecution of the emperor Trajan (reigned 98–117). As Roman purges went, Trajan's was not particularly ambitious or intense, so scholars believe either that St. Ignatius did something publicly to provoke the authorities, or that he was betrayed by heretics. But perhaps that was not necessary. His prestige alone may have been enough to make him a target. Antioch was a major metropolitan area; it was the capital of the Roman province of Syria and the second city of the empire. And the Antiochene church, with its apostolic roots, was esteemed by Christians everywhere. If St. Ignatius was indeed Antioch's bishop for four of Christianity's most formative decades, he was surely, by the end of his life, a man of tremendous fame.

Moreover, imperial Rome, early on, tended to target the Church's bishops rather than laymen. Rome assumed that the public torture and execution of Christianity's leaders would frighten and disperse their congregations. Finally, St. Ignatius's eloquence and profound learning, both evident in his letters, probably earned him celebrity status far from his home diocese. The Romans must have found this bishop, in every way, to be the ideal exemplary victim.

For his part, the bishop was a willing victim. His eagerness to die for Christ is a recurring theme in his letters. He urged the Roman Christians, for example, not to intercede with the emperor on his behalf: "I beg you not to show an unseasonable goodwill toward me. Let me become food for the wild beasts, through whose favor it will be granted me to attain to God."

He was arrested and interrogated in Antioch. Unreliable legends have the questioning carried out by the emperor Trajan himself. Condemned, St. Ignatius, like St. Paul before him, was transported under military guard to his execution in Rome.

At the stops along his route, he received visitors from the nearby churches. Impending martyrdom brought even greater fame and veneration for Antioch's bishop, and his caravan seems to have become something of a pilgrimage destination. Bishops traveled to pay homage to him.

Condemnation elevated St. Ignatius's authority within the universal Church. During two of his layovers, in Smyrna and Troas (both in modern-day Turkey), he composed six letters to churches in Asia Minor and Europe: Ephesus, Magnesia, Troas, Rome, Philadelphia, and Smyrna. (A seventh letter is a personal missive to St. Polycarp, the bishop of Smyrna.) His epistles are compact and to the point, pastoral in manner, doctrinal in content, encouraging in tone. St. Ignatius testifies to early Christian teaching about marriage, the Trinity, the Incarnation, the Real Presence of Jesus in the Eucharist, the primacy of the Roman Church, and the authority of priests and bishops. He is much concerned with the proliferation of heresies, especially Docetism, and with the gradual backsliding of those Christians who retained Jewish practices.

An effective teacher, St. Ignatius could summarize profound truths with memorable images. He was also master of the art of coining concise professions of faith, or creeds.

St. Ignatius arrived in Rome, according to legend, on the last day of the public games, perhaps in the year 107. He was whisked to the amphitheater, where he was torn apart by lions. Immediately after his death, his letters were venerated everywhere, and even considered canonical Scriptures by some churches. St. Polycarp testifies, in his own *Letter to the Philippians,* that St. Ignatius's letters were much in demand throughout the Church even before Ignatius's martyrdom.

THE EFFECTS OF HERESY

St. Ignatius's Letter to the Smyrnaeans is a valuable record of the ancient Church's beliefs regarding the Eucharist, the priesthood, and the Church hierarchy. It records the earliest surviving use of the term "Catholic Church" to describe the worldwide body of the Christian faithful. The bishop is especially concerned about the deadly effects of the heresy of the Docetists, who taught that Jesus was not truly human and that He only seemed to possess a body, to suffer, and to die.

Now, [Christ] suffered all these things for our sakes, that we might be saved. And He suffered truly, even as also He truly raised Himself up, not, as certain unbelievers maintain, that He only seemed to suffer, as they themselves only seem to be Christians. As they believe, so shall it happen to them, when they shall be divested of their bodies, and be mere evil spirits.

For I know that after His resurrection, too, He still had flesh, and I believe that He has flesh now. When, for instance, He came to those who were with Peter, He said to them, "Lay hold, handle me, and see that I am not a ghost" (cf. Lk 24:39). And immediately they touched Him and believed, being convinced both by His flesh and spirit. For this reason, they despised death, and vanquished it. And after His resurrection He ate and drank with them, as having flesh, although spiritually He was united to the Father.

I give you these instructions, beloved, sure that you hold the same opinions as I do. I guard you from those beasts in the shape of men, whom you must not receive, and if possible, not even meet with. Still, you must pray to God for them, that they may be brought to repentance. That will be difficult, but Jesus Christ, who is our true life, has the power to accomplish it....

Some ignorantly deny Him,... not confessing that He truly had a body. But he who does not acknowledge this has in fact altogether denied Him, being enveloped in death.... Such persons are unbelievers. Far be it from me to mention them, until they repent and return to a true belief in Christ's passion, which is our resurrection....

But consider those who hold a different opinion with respect to the grace of Christ that has come unto us, how opposed they are to the will of God. They have no regard for love; no care for the widow, or the orphan, or the oppressed; of the bond, or of the free; of the hungry, or of the thirsty.

They abstain from the Eucharist and from prayer, because they confess not the Eucharist to be the flesh of our Savior Jesus Christ, which suffered for our sins, and which the Father, of His goodness, raised up again. Those, therefore, who speak against this gift of God, incur death in the midst of their disputes....

See that you all follow the bishop, even as Christ Jesus does the Father, and the priests as you would the Apostles. Reverence the deacons as those who carry out the appointment of God. Let no man do anything connected with the Church without the bishop. Let that be deemed a proper Eucharist which is administered either by the bishop or by one to whom he has entrusted it. Wherever the bishop shall appear, there let the multitude also be; even as wherever Jesus Christ is, there is the Catholic Church. It is not lawful without the bishop either to baptize or to celebrate a love-feast; but whatsoever he shall approve of, that is also pleasing to God, so that everything done may be secure and valid.

— ANF 1:39-41

The Desire for Martyrdom

To the Romans St. Ignatius revealed his deep desire to die as a martyr, a witness for the Christian faith. For the Christian, there could be no greater honor, no closer imitation of Jesus Christ than to die as He had died, at the hands of persecutors. In this letter, St. Ignatius identifies himself with the bread of the eucharistic sacrifice. His deference to the Roman Church, an attitude he shows toward none of the other churches, is early, though indirect, evidence of the primacy of the Roman See.

Ignatius, who is also called Theophorus,
to the Church which has found mercy,
through the majesty of the Most High Father,
and Jesus Christ, His only-begotten Son;
the Church that is beloved and enlightened ...
the Church that presides in the capital of the Romans,
worthy of God, worthy of honor,
worthy of the highest happiness, worthy of praise,
worthy of obtaining her every desire,
worthy of being deemed holy,
the Church that presides in love,
named from Christ and from the Father....

Do Not Try to Save Me

Through prayer to God I have won the privilege of seeing your most worthy faces, and have even been granted more than I asked; for I hope as a prisoner in Christ Jesus to salute you, if indeed it is the will of God that I am worthy of persevering to the end. The beginning has been well ordered. Now may I win grace to cling to my lot without hindrance to the end. For I am afraid of your love, lest it should injure me. For it is easy for you to accomplish what you please; but it is difficult for me to attain to God, if you spare me under the pretense of fleshly affection.

It is not my wish to please man, but to please God, even as you, too, please Him. For perhaps I will never have such another opportunity of attaining to God; nor will you, if you would now be silent, ever be entitled to the honor of a better work. For if you are silent concerning me, I shall become God's; but if you show your love to my flesh, I shall again have to run my race. Pray, then, do not seek to confer any greater favor upon me than that I be sacrificed to God while the altar is still prepared; that, being gathered together in love, you may sing praise to the Father, through Christ Jesus, that God has deemed me, the bishop of Syria, worthy to be sent for from the East unto the West. It is good to set from the world unto God, that I may rise again to Him.

The Pure Bread of Christ

You have never envied anyone; you have taught others. Now I desire that those things may be confirmed by your conduct, which in your instructions you urge on others. Only ask, on my behalf, both inward and outward strength, that I may not only speak, but truly will; and that I may not merely be called a Christian, but may really prove to be one. For if I prove myself a Christian, I may also be called one, and then be deemed faithful when I shall no longer appear to the world. Nothing visible is eternal. "For the things that are seen are transient, but the things that are unseen are eternal" (2 Cor 4:18). For our God, Jesus Christ, now that He is with the Father, is all the more revealed in His glory. Christianity is not a thing of silence only, but also of manifest greatness.

I write to the churches to impress upon them all that I shall willingly die for God, unless you hinder me. I beg you not to show an unseasonable goodwill toward me. Let me become food for the wild beasts, through whose favor it will be granted me to attain to God. I am the wheat of God, so let me be ground by the teeth of the wild beasts, that I may be found the pure bread of Christ. Rather, entice the wild beasts, that they may become my tomb, and may leave nothing of my body; so that when I have fallen asleep in death, I may be no trouble to anyone. Then shall I truly be a disciple of Christ, when the world shall not see so much as my body. Pray to Christ for me, that by these instruments I may be found a sacrifice to God. I do not, as Peter and Paul, issue commandments unto you. They were Apostles; I am but a condemned man: they were free, while I am, even now, a servant. But when I suffer, I shall be the freedman of Jesus, and shall rise again emancipated in Him. And now, being a prisoner, I learn not to desire anything worldly or vain.

The Journey Home

From Syria to Rome, I fight with beasts, both by land and sea, by night and day, being bound to ten leopards (I mean a band of soldiers), who, even when they receive benefits, show themselves all the worse. But I am the more instructed by their injuries to act as a disciple of Christ; "but I am not thereby acquitted" (1 Cor 4:4). May I enjoy the wild beasts that are prepared for me; and I pray they may be found eager to rush upon me, when I will entice them to devour me speedily, and not deal with me as with some, whom, out of fear, they have not touched. But if they be unwilling to assail me, I will compel them to do so.

Pardon me: I know what is for my benefit. Now I begin to be a disciple. And let no one, visible or invisible, envy me that I should attain to Jesus Christ. Let fire and the cross; let the crowds of wild beasts; let tearings, breakings, and dislocations of bones; let cutting off of members; let shatterings of the whole body; and let all the dreadful torments of the devil come upon me: only let me attain to Jesus Christ.

All the pleasures of the world, and all the kingdoms of this earth, shall profit me nothing. It is better for me to die in behalf of Jesus Christ than to reign over all the ends of the earth. "For what does it profit a man, to gain the whole world and forfeit his life?" (Mk 8:36). I seek Him who died for us; I desire Him who rose again for our sake. This is the reward that is laid up for me. Pardon me, brothers: do not hinder me from living, do not wish to keep me in a state of death; and while I desire to belong to God, do not give me over to the world. Let me obtain pure light: when I have gone there, I shall indeed be a man of God. Allow me to be an imitator of the suffering of my God. If anyone has Him within himself, let him consider what I desire, and let him have sympathy with me, as knowing how I am bound.

My Love Has Been Crucified

The prince of this world would rather carry me away, and corrupt my disposition toward God. Let none of you, therefore, who are in Rome help him; rather be on my side, that is, on the side of God. Do not speak of Jesus Christ and yet set your desires on the world. Do not let envy find a dwelling-place among you; nor even should I, when present with you, exhort you to it, if you are persuaded to listen to me, but rather give credit to those things that I now write to you. For though I am alive while I write, yet I am eager to die. My love has been crucified, and there is no fire in me desiring to be fed; but there is within me a water that lives and speaks, saying to me inwardly, "Come to the Father." I have no delight in perishable food, nor in the pleasures of this life. I desire the bread of God, the heavenly bread, the bread of life, which is the flesh of Jesus Christ, the Son of God, from the seed of David and Abraham; and I desire the drink of God, namely His blood, which is incorruptible love and eternal life....

Remember in your prayers the Church in Syria, which now has God for its shepherd, instead of me. Jesus Christ alone will oversee it, and your love will also regard it. But, as for me, I am ashamed to be counted one of them; for indeed I am not worthy, for I am the very last of them, born out of due time. But I have obtained mercy to be somebody, if I shall attain to God. My spirit salutes you, and the love of the churches that have received me in the name of Jesus Christ, and not as a mere passerby. For even those churches which were not near to me in the way, I mean according to the flesh, have gone before me, city by city, to meet me....

Farewell, to the end, in the patience of Jesus Christ. Amen.

— ANF 1:73-77

ST. POLYCARP OF SMYRNA

St. Polycarp (c. 69–c. 155) could be called the most well-connected man in the ancient Church. At one end of his long life, he was a young disciple of St. John the Apostle. At middle age, he was a bishop-colleague of St. Ignatius of Antioch. As an old man, he was master to the young boy who would grow up to be St. Irenaeus of Lyons. By his longevity, St. Polycarp was able to teach many how to live as the Apostles had taught him to live. By his death as a martyr, at age eighty-six, he taught generations of persecuted Christians after him how to die.

From his one letter that has survived (actually, many scholars believe it is two letters combined as one), we can see that St. Polycarp, like his master St. John, was much concerned about persecution and heresy in the Church of Smyrna (see Rev 2:8-11). St. Polycarp's letter specifically addresses Docetic teaching and the pain caused by the infidelity of a priest named Valens. He alludes to other heresies, but does not mention them by name or telltale doctrine.

From St. Irenaeus, we know that St. Polycarp took particular interest in eradicating the errors of the heretics Marcion and Valentinus. St. Irenaeus tells of St. Polycarp meeting Marcion during a visit to Rome. Marcion, proud of his own celebrity, asked if the bishop recognized him. Polycarp replied: "Of course I recognize the offspring of Satan."

St. Polycarp exhorts the Philippians to virtue, whatever their state in life. He includes specific advice and encouragement for married couples, young people, consecrated virgins, widows, priests, and deacons. "Teach your wives to walk in the faith given to them, and in love and purity, tenderly loving their own husbands in all truth, and loving all others equally in all chastity; and to train up their children in the knowledge and fear of God. Teach the widows to be discreet as respects the faith of the Lord, praying continually for all, being far from all slandering, evil-speaking, false-witnessing, love of money, and every kind of evil; knowing that they are the altars of God.... Let the young men also be blameless in all things, being especially careful to preserve purity, and keeping themselves, as with a bridle, from every kind of evil. For it is well that they should be cut off from the lusts that are in the world."[54]

Because of his connections to the Apostles, the great bishop of Smyrna was esteemed by Christians everywhere. When he was eighty, he was called to Rome by Pope Anicetus to help resolve the dispute over the date when Christians should celebrate Easter. St. Polycarp claimed to follow the Apostles, who marked Easter on a fixed date every year. The pope favored marking it as a movable feast, always on Sunday. The two met as brothers, but failed to make a conclusive decision. They agreed to disagree, and parted with great affection.

On St. Polycarp's return to Smyrna (in what is today Turkey), there was a persecution against Christians. Refusing to worship the emperor, the bishop was condemned and was executed about 155. It is his persecutors who are first on record as naming St. Polycarp a Father. In his trial, they derided him as "the great teacher of Asia, the father of the Christians."

THE MARTYRDOM OF POLYCARP

Within months of Polycarp's death, the Church of Smyrna published an account of his martyrdom as a circular letter to the entire Catholic Church. This anonymous report launched the literary genre of "acts of the martyrs." It was the first of its kind, was widely reproduced, and gave encouragement to persecuted Christians for many centuries afterward.

The most admirable Polycarp, when he first heard that he was sought for, was not disturbed, but resolved to remain in the city. However, in deference to the wish of many, he was persuaded to leave. He departed, therefore, to a country house not far from the city....

His pursuers then set out, along with horsemen ... as if going out against a robber. About evening, they found him lying down in the upper room of a certain little house, from which he might have escaped; but he refused, saying, "The will of God be done." So when he heard that they had arrived, he went down and spoke with them. And as those that were present marveled at his age and constancy, some of them said, "Was so much effort made to capture such a venerable man?" Immediately, he ordered that something to eat and drink should be set before them, as much as they cared for, while he asked them to allow him an hour to pray without disturbance.

Now, as soon as he had ceased praying,... they set him upon an ass, and conducted him into the city.... And the Irenarch Herod, accompanied by his father Nicetes (both riding in a chariot), met him, and taking him up into the chariot, they seated themselves beside him, and tried to persuade him, saying, "What harm is there in saying, 'Lord Caesar,' and in sacrificing, with the other ceremonies observed on such occasions, and so gain safety?" At first he gave them no answer; and when they continued to urge him, he said, "I shall not do as you advise me." Having no hope of persuading him, they began to speak bitter words to him, and cast him so violently out of the chariot that he dislocated his leg by the fall. But without being disturbed, and as if suffering nothing, he went eagerly forward with all haste, and was conducted to the stadium, where the tumult was so great that there was no possibility of being heard.

Away with the Atheists

Now, as Polycarp was entering into the stadium, there came to him a voice from heaven, saying, "Be strong, and show thyself a man, Polycarp!" No one saw who it was that spoke to him; but those of our brothers who were present heard the voice. And as he was brought forward, the tumult became great when they heard that Polycarp was captured.

The proconsul approached and asked him if he was Polycarp. On his confessing that he was, the proconsul tried to persuade him to deny Christ, saying, "Have respect for your old age" and "Swear by the fortune of Caesar; repent, and say, 'Away with the atheists.'" But Polycarp, gazing with a stern expression on all the crowd of the wicked heathen then in the stadium, and waving his hand toward them — while with groans he looked up to heaven — said, "Away with the atheists." Then the proconsul urged him, "Swear, and I will set you at liberty. Reproach Christ." Polycarp declared, "Eighty-six years have I served Him, and He never did me any injury: how then can I blaspheme my King and my Savior?"

When the proconsul pressed him yet again, and said, "Swear by the fortune of Caesar," he answered, "Since you are so intent that I should swear by the fortune of Caesar, and since you pretend not to know who and what I am, hear me declare with boldness, I am a Christian. And if you wish to learn what the doctrines of Christianity are, appoint me a day, and you shall hear them." The proconsul replied, "Persuade the people." But Polycarp said, "To you I have thought it right to offer an account of my faith; for we are taught to give all due honor (which entails no injury upon ourselves) to the powers and authorities ordained of God. But as for these, I do not deem them worthy of receiving any account from me."

The proconsul then said to him, "I have wild beasts at hand; to these will I throw you unless you repent." But he answered, "Call them then, for we are not accustomed to repent of what is good in order to adopt what is evil; and it is well for me to be changed from what is evil to what is righteous." But again the proconsul said to him, "If you are not afraid of the wild beasts, I will cause you to be consumed by fire, if you will not repent." But Polycarp said, "You threaten me with fire that burns for an hour, and after a little is extinguished, but you are ignorant of the fire of the coming judgment and of eternal punishment, reserved for the ungodly. But why do you delay? Bring forth what you wish."

Uncontrollable Fury

The proconsul was astonished, and sent his herald to proclaim three times in the midst of the stadium, "Polycarp has confessed that he is a Christian." This proclamation having been made by the herald, the whole crowd both of the heathen and Jews who lived in Smyrna, cried out with uncontrollable fury, and in a loud voice, "This is the great teacher of Asia, the father of the Christians, and the destroyer of our gods, he who has been teaching many not to sacrifice, or to worship the gods."

The multitudes immediately gathered together wood ... and when the funeral pile was ready, Polycarp, laying aside all his garments, and loosing his girdle, sought also to take off his sandals — something he was not used to doing, because every one of the faithful had always been eager to touch his skin. For, on account of his holy life, he was, even before his martyrdom, adorned with every kind of good. Immediately then they surrounded him with those substances which had been prepared for the funeral pile. But when they were about to fix him with nails, he said, "Leave me as I am; for He who gives me strength to endure the fire, will also enable me, without your securing me by nails, to remain without moving in the pile."

They did not nail him then, but simply bound him. And, placing his hands behind him, he was bound like a distinguished ram chosen from a great flock for sacrifice, and prepared to be an acceptable burnt-offering unto God.

The Prayer of Polycarp

He looked up to heaven, and said, "O Lord God Almighty, the Father of Your beloved and blessed Son, Jesus Christ, by whom we have received the knowledge of You, the God of angels and powers, and of every creature, and of the whole race of the righteous who live before You, I give You thanks that You have counted me worthy of this day and this hour, that I should be counted in the number of Your martyrs, in the cup of Your Christ, to the resurrection of eternal life, both of soul and body, through the incorruption given by the Holy Spirit. Among them may I be accepted this day before You as a rich and acceptable sacrifice, as You, the ever-truthful God, have foreordained, have revealed beforehand to me, and now have fulfilled. I praise You for all things, I bless You, I glorify You, along with the everlasting and heavenly Jesus Christ, Your beloved Son; with Him, to You and the Holy Spirit, be glory now and forever. Amen."

When he had pronounced this amen, and so finished his prayer, those who were appointed for the purpose kindled the fire. And as the flame blazed forth in great fury, we ... beheld a great miracle.... For the fire, shaping itself into the form of an arch, like the sail of a ship when filled with wind, encircled the body of the martyr. And he appeared within not like flesh that is burnt, but as bread that is baked, or as gold and silver glowing in a furnace. Moreover, we smelled a sweet odor, as if frankincense or some other precious spices had been smoking there.

When those wicked men saw that his body could not be consumed by the fire, they commanded an executioner to go near and pierce him through with a dagger. This done, there came forth a dove, and a great quantity of blood, so that the fire was extinguished; and all the people wondered that there should be such a difference between the unbelievers and the elect, of whom this most admirable Polycarp was one, having in our own times been an apostolic and prophetic teacher, and bishop of the Catholic Church that is in Smyrna. For every word that went out of his mouth either has been or shall yet be accomplished.

— ANF 1:40-42

HERMAS

Among the most widely distributed Christian books in the second century was *The Shepherd*, written by a Roman man named Hermas. A visionary work, *The Shepherd* was used in catechesis — and even counted among Scripture by some notable Christians (Irenaeus of Lyons, Clement of Alexandria, Origen). Fragments have survived in many languages.

The Shepherd is an apocalypse, similar in form to the biblical Book of Revelation. The word apocalypse means "revelation" or "unveiling"; and *The Shepherd*, like some other early Christian texts, claims to record divine teachings revealed to the author in extraordinary visions.

Most of what we know about Hermas himself is what we can glean from his one writing that has survived and from passing comments made by other authors.

In the document itself, we learn that Hermas was a Greek, who arrived in Rome as a slave, sold to a woman named Rhoda. He was quite fond of her. Eventually, she freed him; and he grew prosperous in business, but slack in the practice of his faith. He married and raised children; but his family life was dysfunctional. His wife was a gossip, and Hermas himself was dishonest.

Years passed, and he renewed his contact with Rhoda and "began to love her as a sister." He confesses, though, that once, as he saw her bathe in Rome's Tiber River, he longed to have a wife like Rhoda.

More time passed, and presumably Rhoda died. For Hermas had a vision of her as he traveled on a business trip to Cumae. Rhoda informed him that she had become his accuser in heaven, and she led him to understand the sinfulness of his long-ago desire for her (see Mt 5:28).

The accusation provoked a crisis for Hermas, and he began to doubt his salvation. His crisis was resolved by subsequent visions and revelations. In these he was first instructed by a matronly woman, representing the Church (she grows younger as the narrative proceeds). Next, and for the remaining visions, he encountered a man identified as "The Shepherd." It is from that apparition that the work drew its name.

Hermas's account was probably set down over the course of many years. He refers to contemporary events that seem to have taken place decades apart. His children fell away from the practice of the faith, and during persecution even denounced their parents to the authorities. In the end, however, they returned to the fold.

The Shepherd is structured according to its contents: five Visions, twelve Mandates (or Commandments), and five Similitudes (or Parables). Its dominant concern is the problem of sins committed after baptism. Could they be forgiven? It was a lively debate in the early Church, a debate that would continue for centuries, sometimes threatening to divide the Church. *The Shepherd* makes the case for the forgiveness of post-baptismal sin, provided the sinner does penance — but such forgiveness could be granted only once. As an apocalyptic text, it claims divine authority for its contents.

Judged by later standards, *The Shepherd* is sometimes described as "severe" or "rigorist," because it limits a sinner to one chance at repentance. Seen in its historical context, however, *The Shepherd* is remarkable for granting even that much mercy. It was history's first strong hint that perhaps God, too, will forgive seventy times seven times (see Mt 18:21-22).

Its hopeful message made it a runaway best seller. Its revelatory claims made some people want to count it among the books of Scripture. St. Irenaeus, writing around 180, quoted it as such. The anonymous document known as the *Muratorian Canon* acknowledges that some people held *The Shepherd* to be divinely inspired, but rejects that claim because Hermas wrote his work long after the era of the Apostles: "Hermas wrote *The Shepherd* very recently, in our times, in the city of Rome, while Pius, his brother, was bishop, occupying the chair of the Church of the city of Rome." Pope Pius I reigned from (approximately) 140 to 154.

Some scholars, a minority, have argued for a much earlier composition of the text. Even in antiquity, Origen believed *The Shepherd* was written by the Hermas mentioned by St. Paul in his Letter to the Romans (16:14). And in *The Shepherd* itself Hermas makes mention of St. Clement of Rome, a first-century pope and one of the Apostolic Fathers, as if he too is a contemporary.

The seeming contradictions are probably impossible to sort out, given what we currently know, or even what we're likely to know this side of heaven. This has led others to conclude that the work is entirely a fiction, and a sloppy one at that.

The Shepherd is an odd document, in both style and content. Its theology is simple and sometimes muddled. Its doctrine of Christ suggests Adoptionism — the belief that Christ was a merely mortal man elevated by God — a view that was later condemned as heresy. *The Shepherd's* influence waned over time. By the end of the second century, rigorists such as Tertullian vehemently rejected it (though he had spoken warmly of it in his Catholic phase). In the early fourth century, Eusebius noted that the work remained controversial, revered by some, spurned by others. A hundred years later, St. Jerome observed that the work was practically unknown in the Western Church.

Hermas Tells His Story
With the first chapters of his work, Hermas gives the background to his visions.

He who had brought me up sold me to one Rhoda in Rome. Many years after this I recognized her, and I began to love her as a sister. Some time after, I saw her bathe in the river Tiber; and I gave her my hand, and drew her out of the river. The sight of her beauty made me think to myself, "I should be a happy man if I could but get a wife as beautiful and good as she is." This was the only thought that passed through me: this and nothing more.

A short time after this, as I was walking on my road to the villages, and wondering at God's creatures, and thinking how magnificent, and beautiful, and powerful they are, I fell asleep. And the Spirit carried me away, and took me through a pathless place, through which a man could not travel, for it was situated in the midst of rocks; it was rugged and impassible on account of water. Having passed over this river, I came to a plain. I then bent down on my knees, and began to pray to the Lord, and to confess my sins.

And as I prayed, the heavens were opened, and I see the woman whom I had desired saluting me from the sky, and saying, "Hail, Hermas!"

And looking up to her, I said, "Lady, what are you doing here?"

And she answered me, "I have been taken up here to accuse you of your sins before the Lord."

"Lady," said I, "are you to be the subject of my accusation?"

"No," said she; "but hear the words that I am going to speak to you. God, who dwells in the heavens, and who made out of nothing the things that exist, and multiplied and increased them on account of His holy Church, is angry with you for having sinned against me."

I answered her, "Lady, have I sinned against you? How or when did I speak an unseemly word to you? Did I not always think of you as a lady? Did I not always respect you as a sister? Why do you falsely accuse me of this wickedness and impurity?"

With a smile she replied to me, "The desire of wickedness arose within your heart. Is it not your opinion that a righteous man commits sin when an evil desire arises in his heart? There is sin in such a case, and the sin is great," said she, "for the thoughts of a righteous man should be righteous. For by thinking righteously his character is established in the heavens, and he has the Lord merciful to him in every business. But those who entertain wicked thoughts in their minds are bringing upon themselves death and captivity; and especially is this the case with those who set their affections on this world, and glory in their riches, and look not forward to the blessings of the life to come. For many will their regrets be; for they have no hope, but have despaired of themselves and their life. But pray to God, and He will heal your sins, and the sins of your whole house, and of all the saints."

After she had spoken these words, the heavens were shut. I was overwhelmed with sorrow and fear, and said to myself, "If this sin is assigned to me, how can I be saved, or how shall I make amends to God for my sins, which are of the grossest character? With what words shall I ask the Lord to be merciful to me?"

While I was thinking over these things, and discussing them in my mind, I saw opposite to me a chair, white, made of white wool, of great size. And there came up an old woman, arrayed in a splendid robe, and with a book in her hand; and she sat down alone, and saluted me, "Hail, Hermas!"

And in sadness and tears I said to her, "Lady, hail!"

And she said to me, "Why are you downcast, Hermas? For you were accustomed to be patient and temperate, and always smiling. Why are you so gloomy, and not cheerful?"

I answered her and said, "O Lady, I have been reproached by a very good woman, who says that I sinned against her."

And she said, "Far be such a deed from a servant of God. But perhaps a desire after her has arisen within your heart. Such a wish, in the case of the servants of God, produces sin. For it is a wicked and horrible wish in an all-chaste and already well-tried spirit to desire an evil deed; and especially for Hermas so to do, who keeps himself from all wicked desire, and is full of all simplicity, and of great guilelessness.

"But God is not angry with you on account of this, but that you may convert the members of your household, who have committed iniquity against the Lord, and against you, their parents. And although you love your sons, yet did you not warn your house, but permitted them to be terribly corrupted. On this account is the Lord angry with you, but He will heal all the evils that have been done in your house. For, on account of their sins and iniquities, you have been destroyed by the affairs of this world. But now the mercy of the Lord has taken pity on you and your house, and will strengthen you, and establish you in His glory. Only do not be careless, but be of good courage and comfort your house. For as a blacksmith hammers out his work, and accomplishes whatever he wishes, so shall righteous daily speech overcome all evil. So do not cease to admonish your sons; for I know that, if they will repent with all their heart, they will be enrolled in the Books of Life with the saints."

Having ended these words, she said to me, "Do you wish to hear me read?"

I say to her, "Lady, I do."

"Listen then, and give ear to the glories of God." And then I heard from her, magnificently and admirably, things that my memory could not retain. For all the words were terrible, such as man could not endure. The last words, however, I did remember; for they were useful to us, and gentle. "Lo, the God of powers, who by His invisible strong power and great wisdom has created the world, and by his glorious counsel has surrounded His creation with beauty, and by His strong word has fixed the heavens and laid the foundations of the earth upon the waters, and by His own wisdom and providence has created His holy Church, which He has blessed — lo! He removes the heavens and the mountains, the hills and the seas, and all things become plain to His elect, that He may bestow on them the blessing that He has promised them, with much glory and joy, if only they keep the commandments of God that they have received in great faith."

When she had ended her reading, she rose from the chair, and four young men came and carried off the chair and went away to the east. And she called me to herself and touched my breast, and said to me, "Have you been pleased with my reading?"

And I say to her, "Lady, the last words please me, but the first are cruel and harsh."

Then she said to me, "The last are for the righteous: the first are for heathens and apostates." And while she spoke to me, two men appeared and raised her on their shoulders, and they went to where the chair was in the east. With joyful countenance did she depart; and as she went, she said to me, "Behave like a man, Hermas."

— ANF 2:9-11

THE ANTE-NICENE FATHERS

The Church Finds a Voice

Through the writings of the second- and third-century Fathers, we can identify a growing emphasis on the sustained, disciplined study of the revealed truths of Christianity. What, today, we call theology was just then emerging. Heretics and pagans forced the Church and its teachers to be ever clearer in their expression of faith. To this end, the Fathers struggled to find an appropriate vocabulary and method. For some, like St. Justin and St. Clement of Alexandria, the language of Greek philosophy, especially Platonism, suited their purposes adequately well. Others, such as Tertullian, believed the pagan science had nothing to offer Christians, and so resisted the movement toward "Hellenization." What indeed, demanded Tertullian, has Athens to do with Jerusalem?

The Hellenizers prevailed, for several reasons. First, because Greek was the common language of the educated and merchant classes in the eastern empire, and these classes needed to be evangelized. But perhaps the most pressing reason was the inadequacy of any terminology — outside of the most rarefied philosophical language — in dealing with the basic facts of Christianity. How was God one and yet three? How could Jesus be both God and man? How can grace coexist with free will? To address these questions, teachers needed to define what they meant by person, substance, will, essence, and nature, a task that Greek philosophers had already done remarkably well.

St. Justin Martyr undertook the task of making Christianity intelligible to philosophically oriented Greeks. Others followed in his path. But some went too far in Hellenizing and merely layered Greek thought, of Pythagoras or Plato, with a veneer of Christianity. To this latter group, "knowledge" (in Greek, *gnosis*) was the real subject of religion. To some of these "Gnostics," the goal was magical power or

81

pseudo-mystical knowledge; to others, mere rationalism. St. Irenaeus made it his great work to correct the errors of those who over-Hellenized and made their "Christianity" a sort of Platonism run amok.

Theology increasingly became the province of the schools, especially those that arose in Alexandria, Egypt; Antioch, Syria; and Caesaria in Palestine. From the late second century on, many of the outstanding Fathers were associated with these three schools as alumni or faculty.

Persecution continued intermittently through the second and third centuries, and many controversies arose over how Christians should respond. Should believers turn themselves in? Should they seek martyrdom? When is it legitimate to flee persecution? Should the Church forgive those who give in under torture and renounce their Christian faith? Gradually, the Church came to understand and teach that Christians were not obligated to seek martyrdom; in fact, those who, at first, actively sought to die often failed in their courage at the moment of crisis.

The more acrimonious debate was over forgiveness for the lapsi, those who had renounced their faith but later repented their failure. Some Christians, especially those who themselves had been tortured, thought that the lapsi should be most severely punished — denied the sacraments until the moment of their death. Others thought that the lapsi should never be readmitted, that they had committed the unforgivable sin, the sin against the Holy Spirit, and so had permanently removed themselves from the source of salvation. The Church, again gradually, came to accept the lapsi back into the fold, after a time of penance.

ST. ARISTIDES OF ATHENS

The *Apology of Aristides* is the earliest surviving work that attempts to explain Christianity to a Greco-Roman pagan audience and defend Christians against the outrageous accusations leveled against them (orgies and incest, for example).

In most surviving manuscripts, the *Apology* is addressed to the Emperor Hadrian, which would place it around A.D. 125. In the fourth century, Eusebius reported that Aristides' work was presented along with the *Apology of Quadratus*. In the Syriac translation, however, the *Apology* is addressed to the Emperor Antoninus Pius, whose reign began in the late 130s. It is possible that the same text was adapted and repurposed for more than one occasion.

Later historians (Eusebius and Jerome) tell us that Aristides was a philosopher in the city of Athens, and his work seems to bear this out. He reasons from creation to the Creator, and he presents God in terms that anticipate the creeds and theology of a much later date: "God is not born, not made, an ever-abiding nature without beginning and without end, immortal, perfect, and incomprehensible." His summary treatment of Jesus' life also seems a harbinger of later creeds and an echo of the earliest preaching.

We know nothing more about Aristides' life.

He looked at the world around him and divided its people into four "races": Greeks, Barbarians, Jews, and Christians. In his *Apology* he examines the religious history and beliefs of each of these peoples. He emphasizes the absurdity of idolatry, which is the worship of handicrafts and natural elements. His descriptions show a familiarity with not only Greek myths and rituals, but also those of the Egyptians, Romans, Babylonians, and primitive tribes. He compares all of these to Christianity, which appears more sober, credible, and compatible with a philosophical temperament (though he singles the Jews out favorably for their monotheism and morals). Only at the end of his work does he bring up the accusations of Christian immorality, which he dismisses as nonsense, and with only the briefest mention, directing the accusations back at Christianity's opponents, especially the Greeks.

From Creation to Creator

At the beginning of his Apology, Aristides establishes the terms for his discussion. He will proceed as a philosopher and demonstrate the reasonableness and superiority of Christian faith, answering those who accused Christians of superstition and atheism.

All-powerful Cæsar Titus Hadrianus Antoninus, venerable and merciful, from Marcianus Aristides, an Athenian philosopher.

I, O King, by the grace of God came into this world; and when I had considered the heaven and the earth and the seas, and had surveyed the sun and the rest of creation, I marveled at the beauty of the world. And I perceived that the world and all that is in it are moved by the power of another; and I understood that He who moves them is God, who is hidden in them, and veiled by them. And it is manifest that that which causes motion is more powerful than that which is moved.

But it would be vain for me to search out the nature of this Mover of all; for it seems to me, He is indeed unsearchable in His nature. And it would be vain to argue as to the constancy of His government, and try to grasp it fully; for it is impossible for a man to comprehend it fully. I say, however, concerning this mover of the world, that He is God of all, who made all things for the sake of mankind. And it seems to me that this is reasonable, that one should fear God and should not oppress man.

I say, then, that God is not born, not made, an ever-abiding nature without beginning and without end, immortal, perfect, and incomprehensible. Now when I say that He is "perfect," this means that there is not in Him any defect, and He is not in need of anything but all things are in need of Him. And when I say that He is "without beginning," this means that everything which has beginning has also an end, and that which has an end may be brought to an end. He has no name, for everything that has a name is kindred to things created. He has no form, nor any assembly of parts; for whatever possesses these is kindred to things fashioned. He is neither male nor female. The heavens do not limit Him, but the heavens and all things, visible and invisible, receive their bounds from Him. He has no adversary, for there exists no one stronger than He. He possesses neither wrath nor indignation, for there is nothing that is able to stand against Him. Ignorance and forgetfulness are not in His nature, for He is altogether wisdom and understanding; and in Him stands fast all that exists. He requires neither sacrifice nor libation, nor anything visible; He requires not anything from any, but all living creatures stand in need of Him.

Since, then, we have addressed you concerning God, so far as our discourse can bear upon Him, let us now come to the race of men, that we may know which of them participate in the truth of which we have spoken, and which of them go astray from it.

This is clear to you, O King, that there are four classes of men in this world: Barbarians and Greeks, Jews and Christians. The Barbarians, indeed, trace the origin of their kind of religion from Kronos and from Rhea and their other gods; the Greeks, however, from Helenos, who is said to be sprung from Zeus. And by Helenos there were born Aiolos and Xuthos; and there were others descended from Inachos and Phoroneus, and lastly from the Egyptian Danaos and from Kadmos and from Dionysos.

The Jews, again, trace the origin of their race from Abraham, who begot Isaac, of whom was born Jacob. And he begot twelve sons who migrated from Syria to Egypt; and there they were called the nation of the Hebrews, by him who made their laws; and at length they were named Jews.

The Christians, then, trace the beginning of their religion from Jesus the Messiah; and He is named the Son of God Most High. And it is said that God came down from heaven, and from a Hebrew virgin assumed and clothed himself with flesh; and the Son of God lived in a daughter of man. This is taught in the gospel, as it is called, which a short time ago was preached among them; and you also if you will read therein, may perceive the power that belongs to it. This Jesus, then, was born of the race of the Hebrews; and He had twelve disciples in order that the purpose of His incarnation might in time be accomplished. But He himself was pierced by the Jews, and He died and was buried; and they say that after three days He rose and ascended to heaven. Thereupon the twelve disciples went forth throughout the known parts of the world, and kept showing His greatness with all modesty and uprightness. And hence also those of the present day who believe that preaching are called Christians, and they have become famous.

— ANF 9:263-265

ST. JUSTIN MARTYR

The first Christians were signs of contradiction. They prayed for the emperor, but refused to burn incense before him. They loved everyone, even as they taught that all men were sinners. Turned out by pious Jews, they claimed to be heirs to a spiritual Israel.

Thus, they were misunderstood by both pagans and Jews, both of whom accused Christians of a variety of crimes, including atheism, cannibalism, infanticide, and sedition. The most hysterical charges spread through the empire, reaching the capital. The Roman emperors and Senate responded with decrees that Christians should be persecuted.

Yet much of Rome's "received wisdom" on Christianity was gossip and hearsay. At the beginning of the second century, a movement of Christian teachers spoke up to set the record straight. They are known as the "apologists," and perhaps the greatest of their first generation was St. Justin (c. 100–c. 165).

The apologists set out to give reasoned explanations of Christian doctrines. They were not so much preachers as debaters. Amid a hostile and confused culture, they methodically explained and defended all that Christians really believed.

Justin was well prepared for this task. As a young man, a pagan of Samaria, he was an intense seeker looking for wisdom in all the usual places in the ancient world. He studied philosophy, rhetoric, history, and poetry. He was, by turns, a Stoic, a Peripatetic, a Pythagorean, and a Platonist. He pushed his inquiries to ultimate questions, to first principles, but no master was able to satisfy him. (Justin abandoned one sage who demanded cash in advance from his disciples.)

One day during his Platonist phase, he was walking along a beach, where he met an old man. The young Justin engaged the man in conversation, and before long, like Plato before him, Justin found himself taken up into a dialogue. Justin identified himself as a philosopher.

"Does philosophy, then, make happiness?" asked the old man.

"Surely," said Justin, "and only philosophy."

"What, then, is philosophy?" the man asked. "And what is happiness?"

"Philosophy," replied Justin, "is the knowledge of what really exists, and a clear perception of the truth; and happiness is the reward of such knowledge and wisdom."

"But what do you call God?" said the old man.

From there, the old man led Justin to see that, if he sincerely sought truth and sought the God who really exists, he needed to consult the prophets. "They alone," said the mysterious stranger, "both saw and announced the truth to men..., not influenced by a desire for glory, but filled with the Holy Spirit. Their writings are still extant, and he who reads them gains much in his knowledge of ... all a philosopher ought to know."[55]

Justin lit out at once to find these books, and on reading he found much more: "Immediately a flame was kindled in my soul; and I was possessed by a love of the prophets, and of those men who are friends of Christ ... I found this philosophy alone to be safe and profitable." Tradition indicates that he was baptized in Ephesus.

Studying Christian doctrine, he discovered that much of what he had learned about Christianity — in his days as a Stoic, a Platonist, and so on — was utterly false. He was further distressed that these rumor campaigns were leading to the persecution of Christians. So he dedicated himself to the refutation of these errors, explaining and defending his adopted faith before pagans and Jews. Two of his defenses, or "apologies," are addressed to the emperor Antoninus Pius and the Roman Senate. Another is a dialogue concerning Jesus' fulfillment of the Jewish law and prophets.

St. Justin continued to identify himself as a philosopher, wearing the traditional cloak. He saw everything that was good and true in pagan philosophy as a glimpse of the truth and goodness of God revealed in Jesus Christ. St. Justin traveled to Rome, where he established a school of Christian philosophy. In the capital city, he was charged with impiety toward the gods and, with six companions, was scourged and beheaded about the year 165.

To the Emperor Antoninus Pius

The following passages come from the longer of Justin's two famous "Apologies." Here, Justin challenges the emperor to live up to Rome's high ideals of justice. We can see implicit in Justin the teaching of the Second Vatican Council: "Whatever good is in the minds and hearts of men, whatever good lies latent in the religious practices and cultures of diverse peoples, is not only saved from destruction but is also cleansed, raised up and perfected unto the glory of God" (Lumen Gentium, 17).

By the mere application of a name, nothing is decided, either good or evil.... For, from a name, neither praise nor punishment could reasonably spring, unless some excellent or base action may be proved ...; but in our case you receive the name as proof against us.... If anyone acknowledges that he is a Christian, you punish him on this account.

Justice requires that you inquire into the life of him who confesses and of him who denies. Thus, by deeds it may be apparent what kind of man each is. For some who have been taught by the Master, Christ, not to deny Him, give encouragement to others when they are put to the question, and so, in all probability, do those who lead wicked lives [encourage] those who ... accuse all Christians of impiety and wickedness.

This is not right. For some assume the name and the garb of philosopher who do nothing worthy of their profession; and you know that the ancients, whose opinions and teachings were quite diverse, still share the one name "philosopher." And some of them taught atheism; and the poets who have flourished among you raise a laugh out of the impurity of Jupiter with his own children. Those who now take such instruction are not restrained by you; on the contrary, you bestow prizes and honors upon those who beautifully insult the gods.

Why should this be? In our case — who pledge ourselves to do no wickedness, nor to hold these atheistic opinions — you do not examine the charges made against us; but, yielding to unreasoning passion, and to the instigation of evil demons, you punish us without consideration or judgment. For the truth shall be spoken: for ages, these evil demons, making apparitions of themselves, defiled women, corrupted boys, and showed such fearful sights to men, that those who did not use their reason in judging the actions done were struck with terror; and, carried away by fear, and not knowing that these were demons, they called them gods, and gave to each the name that each demon had chosen for himself. When Socrates tried, by reason and examination, to bring these things to light, and deliver men from the demons, then the demons themselves, by means of men who rejoiced in evil, brought about his death, as an atheist and a blasphemer, on the charge that "he was introducing new divinities." In our case, they act in a similar way. For ... in obedience to [Christ], we not only deny that those who did such things are gods, but we insist that they are wicked and impious demons, whose actions do not compare even with men who desire virtue.

Hence are we called atheists. And we confess that we are atheists, so far as gods of this sort are concerned, but not with respect to the most true God, the Father of righteousness, temperance, and the other virtues, who is free from all impurity. But Him, and the Son — who came forth from Him and taught us these things ... — and the prophetic Spirit, we worship and adore, knowing them in reason and truth, declaring them to everyone, without exception, who wishes to learn as we have been taught.

— ANF 1:163-164

To the Roman Senate

After the beheading of three Christians, Justin wrote his "Second Apology," from which the following is taken, this time addressing the imperial Senate.

Our doctrines, then, appear to be greater than all human teaching; because Christ, who appeared for our sakes, became the whole rational being — body, reason, and soul. For whatever lawgivers or philosophers said well, they elaborated by finding and contemplating some part of the Word. But since they did not know the whole of the Word, which is Christ, they often contradicted themselves. And those who by human birth were more ancient than Christ, when they attempted to consider and prove things by reason, were brought before the tribunals as impious persons and busybodies.

Socrates, who was more zealous in this way than all of them, was accused of the very same crimes as we are. For they said that he was introducing new divinities, and did not consider as gods those recognized by the state. But he cast out from the state both Homer and the rest of the poets, and taught men to reject wicked demons and those who did the things the poets related; and he exhorted them to become acquainted with the God who was to them unknown, by means of the investigation of reason, saying, "That it is neither easy to find the Father and Maker of all, nor, having found Him, is it safe to declare Him to all."

But our Christ did these things through His own power. For no one trusted in Socrates to the point of dying for his doctrine. But in Christ, who was partially known even by Socrates — for He was and is the Word who is in every man ... — not only philosophers and scholars believed, but also craftsmen and people entirely uneducated, despising glory, fear, death; since He is a power of the ineffable Father, and not the mere instrument of human reason.

— ANF 1:191-192

———————ST. MELITO OF SARDIS———————

St. Melito of Sardis was one powerful preacher — who has been woefully misunderstood in modern times.

Most of his words were, in fact, lost to most of Christian history. Only in the mid-twentieth century was an almost-complete text of Melito found — in the manuscript collections of the University of Michigan, of all places. The rediscovered text was titled *Peri Pascha* — which means both "On Passover" and "On Easter," since in the ancient languages both holidays share the same name.

The manuscript preserves a rhetorical masterpiece. Scholars are divided over whether Melito composed the text as a homily or as a liturgical text. In any event, it is stunning: a rich, poetic meditation on salvation history, from creation to Christ, and on the metaphysical and theological underpinnings of that history.

Who was St. Melito, who preached up this rhetorical storm? He was a bishop in Sardis, a city in Asia Minor (modern-day Turkey), whose church merits its own letter and angel in the Bible's Book of Revelation (Rev 3:1-6). History records that Melito consecrated himself to virginity at an early age and lived an exemplary and holy life. Shortly after Melito's death (around the year 190), the bishop of Ephesus wrote to the pope saying that Melito's "entire walk was in the Holy Spirit." St. Jerome and Tertullian testified that many Christians considered Melito a prophet.

Melito was a prolific author and, though most of his works have vanished, Eusebius gives us the names of his books and even a few precious quotations. In the ancient Church, Melito was best known for his *Apology for the Christian Faith* (written around 175), which was an examination of the false accusations against Christians, addressed to the Roman emperor Marcus Aurelius.

Today, however, all we have is *Peri Pascha*, which is itself a remarkable legacy. It is the work of a virtuoso in the classical rhetorical methods of Greek-speaking Asia. It is also the work of a man steeped in the history of Israel.

Some modern readers have misunderstood and condemned Melito as "anti-Jewish" — an accusation that probably would have stunned and horrified Melito himself. For it is likely that he was himself a convert from Judaism. He was, in any event, a profound student of the Hebrew Scriptures. And he lived in a time when rabbinic Judaism and Christianity presented two different, newly emerging responses to the destruction of Jerusalem and its temple in A.D. 70. It was a time of crisis. Both the ancient rabbis and the Church Fathers saw their respective traditions as a continuation of the tradition and history of Israel. Both the rabbis and the Fathers recognized that the old order was giving way to something new. Where Christians and Jews differed was on the nature and form of the new order.[56]

Like the rabbis (and the prophets before them), Melito sometimes exhorted the Jews to repentance. Yet — again like the rabbis and prophets — he called upon the Jews not as a foreign people, but as his people, family members who were estranged. Yes, he saw the fall of Jerusalem as a chastisement for the sins of Jews; but so did the ancient rabbis. Melito saw the disputes between Jews and Christians as essentially a family quarrel. This does not mean it was always a courteous quarrel. As any policeman can tell you, domestic disputes are the most volatile and prone to violence.

Eusebius records that Melito had a profound interest in the Hebrew Bible. He journeyed to Palestine to study Scripture on its home turf and in its native tongue.[57] When Melito addressed the emperor on the subject of the "philosophy" of the Christians, he says that this philosophy "flourished first" among the Jews. We know, too, that Melito was among the most ardent advocates of the ancient practice (called "quartodecimian") of observing Easter on the same day as the Jewish Passover, rather than on the Sunday following. All of these facts seem to belie the modern charge of anti-Judaism, and testify instead that Melito was a "Jewish Christian" and a man of his time.

His *Peri Pascha* is a poetic presentation of the Fathers' "typological" reading of biblical history. The *Catechism of the Catholic Church* (nn. 128 and 130) explains this method in clear terms.

> The Church, as early as apostolic times,[58] and then constantly in her Tradition, has illuminated the unity of the divine plan in the two Testaments through typology, which discerns in God's works of the Old Covenant prefigurations of what he accomplished in the fullness of time in the person of his incarnate Son.... Typology indicates the dynamic movement toward the fulfillment of the divine plan when "God [will] be everything to everyone."[59] Nor do the calling of the patriarchs and the exodus from Egypt, for example, lose their own value in God's plan, from the mere fact that they were intermediate stages.

In Melito's life, and in *Peri Pascha*, we see these principles at work. He saw the special dignity of the old, even as he evangelized for the new.

THE OLD PASSOVER AND THE NEW
Melito offers analogies to explain the unfolding of biblical typology. This passage from Peri Pascha *has been adapted from the translation of*

Campbell Bonner, in The Homily on the Passion *(London: Christophers, 1940), pages 171-173.*

A pattern of something to come,
a pattern of wax or clay or wood,
is made for this reason:
that the thing to come —
loftier in height, and mightier in power,
beautiful in form, and rich in adornment —
may be seen through the small, perishable pattern.
But when the thing foretold arises,
the pattern is destroyed as useless,
yielding to the truth of nature the image of that truth.
What was once precious becomes useless,
when the naturally precious is revealed.

To each thing its own time:
for the type its own time, for the fulfillment its own time.
Of the truth you make the prototype —
You want to, because in it you see the image of what is to come.
You fashion the material according to the pattern;
You want to, because of what is to arise in it.
You prepare the work; this alone you love,
in it alone beholding the type and the truth.

Therefore, as it is with corruptible models,
so also with things incorruptible;
as in earthly things, so with things in the heavens.
For indeed the salvation and truth of the Lord
were foreshadowed in the people,
and the ordinances of the Gospel
were proclaimed beforehand by the Law.
So the people became the pattern of the Church,
and the Law the writing of a parable,
and the Gospel the setting-forth and fulfillment of the Law,
and the Church the reservoir of truth.

The type, then, was precious before the truth came,
the parable was wondrous before its interpretation.
The people were held in honor before the Church arose,
and the Law was wondrous before the light of the Gospel was
    shed abroad.
But since the Church arose
and the Gospel was shed abroad upon men on earth,
the type is made void,
giving over the image to the natural truth,
and parables are fulfilled,
being made clear by the interpretation.
So then the Law, too, was fulfilled
when the light of the Gospel was spread abroad,
and the people became of no account
when the Church was raised on high,
and the type was done away
when the Lord was made manifest.

Today things once precious are become worthless,
since those things which are truly precious are revealed.
Once the sacrifice of the sheep was held in honor;
now it is worthless because of the life of the Lord.
Honored was the death of the sheep,
but now it is worthless because of the Lord's salvation.
Precious was the blood of the sheep,
now of no worth because of the Spirit of the Lord.
Precious was the dumb lamb,
but now of no worth because of the unblemished Son.
Precious the temple here below,
now worth nothing because of the Christ above.
Precious was the Jerusalem here below,
but now of no esteem because of the Jerusalem above.
Precious the new inheritance,
now of no value because of encompassing grace.
For the glory of God is not established in one place,

nor in a paltry form,
but His grace is poured out to all the ends of the world,
and there almighty God has taken up His dwelling,
through Christ Jesus, to whom be glory for the ages. Amen.

ST. THEOPHILUS OF ANTIOCH

The work of Theophilus of Antioch marks a shift in the attention of the Church at the end of the second century. He is known today for his only work that has survived to modern times, his apology in three books, *To Autolycus*, a defense of Christianity addressed to a pagan friend. In ancient times, however, Theophilus was most revered for his arguments against Christian heretics, teachers attempting to corrupt doctrine from within the Church. Thus, in Theophilus's lifetime we see the concerns of the early apologists as well as those of the later anti-heretical authors.

An adult convert to Christianity, Theophilus was bishop of Syrian Antioch around 170–181. From references in the works of Eusebius and Jerome, we gather that he was a prolific author, writing books in several genres.

In explaining Christianity to Autolycus, Theophilus exposes the absurdities of the practice of idolatry as well as the scandalous morality of the gods as they appear in popular myths. He contrasts the myths of the Greeks with the history contained in the Old Testament. The testimony of the Scriptures is more valuable, he says, because it was set down by eyewitnesses, whereas the myths were proclaimed by poets who admittedly had lived many centuries after the events they described. History is very important to Theophilus, and he shows himself to be familiar with the books of both Greek and Jewish historians.

In his final argument he presents a detailed chronology that begins with the first man, Adam, and continues to the time of the Emperor Marcus Aurelius, who had recently died. (Thus the work can be dated around A.D. 180.) While acknowledging the good that pagans have accomplished, Theophilus traces much of it back to the influence of

Moses and the prophets, whom he claims were plagiarized by the later Greek philosophers.

Theophilus is the first to use the Greek word *Trias* ("Triad") to describe the God of Christian worship. He speaks of this triad as God, the divine Word, and the divine Wisdom.

THE BLINDNESS OF SIN

Theophilus opens his argument by explaining a basic principle of Christianity: sin darkens the intellect and weakens the will. The sinner cannot behold God.

A fluent tongue and elegant style give pleasure and the sort of praise that pleases the vanity of wretched men who have been corrupted in mind. The lover of truth does not listen to fancy speeches, but examines the real matter of the speech — what it is, and what kind it is.

You have attacked me with empty words, my friend, boasting of your gods of wood and stone, hammered and cast, carved and graven, which neither see nor hear, for they are idols, and the works of men's hands. Moreover, you call me a Christian, as if this were a damning name to bear. I, for my part, avow that I am a Christian, and I bear this name beloved of God, hoping to be serviceable to God. For it is not the case, as you suppose, that the name of God is hard to bear; but possibly you entertain this opinion of God, because you are yourself yet unserviceable to Him.

But if you say, "Show me your God," I would reply, "Show me yourself, and I will show you my God." Show, then, that the eyes of your soul are capable of seeing, and the ears of your heart able to hear.

Those who look with the eyes of the body perceive earthly objects and what concerns this life, and they distinguish between things that differ, whether light or darkness, white or black, deformed or beautiful, well proportioned and symmetrical or disproportioned and awkward, or monstrous or mutilated. So, too, by the sense of hearing, we discriminate either sharp, or deep, or sweet sounds.

The same holds good regarding the eyes of the soul and the ears of the heart. It is by them that we are able to behold God. God is seen by those who are enabled to see Him when they have the eyes of their soul opened: for all have eyes, but in some they are covered over and do not see the light of the sun. Yet it does not follow, because the blind do not see, that the light of the sun does not shine; but let the blind blame themselves and their own eyes. So also you, O man, have the eyes of your soul covered over by your sins and evil deeds. Like a burnished mirror, a man ought to have his soul pure. When there is rust on the mirror, a man's face cannot be seen in it; so also when there is sin in a man, such a man cannot behold God.

Show me yourself, then — whether you are not an adulterer, a fornicator, a thief, a robber, or a purloiner; whether you do not corrupt boys; whether you are not insolent, a slanderer, or passionate, envious, proud, or supercilious; whether you are not a brawler, covetous, or disobedient to parents; and whether you do not sell your children. For to those who do these things God is not manifest, unless they have first cleansed themselves from all impurity. All these things, then, involve you in darkness, as when a filmy discharge on the eyes prevents one from beholding the light of the sun. So, too, do sins, O man, involve you in darkness, so that you cannot see God.

— ANF 2:89

---------------ST. ATHENAGORAS OF ATHENS---------------

All we know of Athenagoras is what we find in his two writings that have survived, his *Plea for the Christians* and *On the Resurrection of the Dead*. Of all the Christian apologists, Athenagoras is the most disciplined philosopher. He has a method, and he sticks to it in a most orderly way. He spells out his principles and presuppositions. He anticipates objections and presents reasoned responses. He writes as if following an outline, resisting digressions. He is professorial in style, dispassionate and direct.

He addresses his *Plea* to the Emperors Marcus Aurelius and Commodus. The titles he uses for them indicate that the work was completed in A.D. 177.

Christianity was still very new at that time and practiced by only a tiny minority. A foreign cult, it proposed a way of life that had revolutionary implications for individuals, families, and communities. Moreover, the Church was secretive about its rituals; and its liturgy was closed to nonbelievers. This led to wild speculation. Urban legends arose and spread throughout the empire, sometimes inciting mobs to violence and moving authorities to initiate persecutions.

In his *Plea*, Athenagoras answers charges that the Christians were atheists, that they were cannibals, and that they were sexual libertines — atheists, because they refused to worship the gods of Greece and Rome; cannibals, because they held banquets closed to the public where they "ate the flesh" and "drank the blood" of a man named Jesus; libertines, because they called their secret banquets by the suggestive name "love feast" (agape). Athenagoras counters rumor with fact, informing his emperor-audience that the Christians do not approve of any of those actions. In fact, they consider all of them to be sins, whose punishment is an eternity in hell.

In his defense of the resurrection, he speaks to the Christians' most outlandish claim: that the dead will rise again in their bodies, and indeed that Jesus Christ already has. He addresses objections systematically and thoroughly, concluding that bodily resurrection is not only reasonable, but necessary.

His works are the first to employ Trinitarian language, making clear distinctions among the Father, Son, and Holy Spirit.

In all antiquity, we find few references to Athenagoras's life, and only in works written much later. They add nothing to the minimal details that are evident from his own writings — that Athenagoras was a philosopher who had once been an unbeliever; he converted to Christianity after intensive study of the Scriptures.

The Church venerates him as a saint. In his work he identified himself by name, place of residence, vocation, and profession: "Athenagoras the Athenian, philosopher and Christian."

ARGUMENTS FOR THE DEFENSE
An eminently methodical man spells out his method, at the beginning of his book On the Resurrection of the Dead.

Alongside every opinion and doctrine that agrees with the truth of things, there springs up some falsehood; and it does so, not because it arises naturally from some fundamental principle, or from some cause peculiar to the matter in hand, but because it is invented on purpose by men who value the spurious seed for its tendency to corrupt the truth.

This is apparent, in the first place, from those who, in former times, addicted themselves to such inquiries, and their lack of agreement with their predecessors and contemporaries. It is apparent also in the very confusion that marks the discussions that are now going on. For such men have left no truth free from their calumnious attacks — not the being of God, not His knowledge, not His operations, not those books that follow by a regular and strict sequence from these, and delineate for us the doctrines of piety. On the contrary, some of them utterly, and once for all, give up in despair the truth concerning these things, and some distort it to suit their own views, and some are determined to doubt even things that are palpably evident.

Hence I think that those who give attention to such subjects should adopt two lines of argument, one in defense of the truth, another concerning the truth — in defense of the truth, for disbelievers and doubters; concerning the truth, for those who are candid and who readily receive the truth. It is good for those who wish to investigate these matters to keep in view whatever the necessity of each case requires, and to regulate their discussion by this. They should also accommodate the order of their treatment of these subjects to what is suitable for the occasion, and not for the sake of appearing always to preserve the same method, to disregard fitness and the place that properly belongs to each topic. As far as proof and the natural order are concerned, discussions concerning the truth always take precedence of those in defense of it. But, for the sake of greater usefulness, the order must be reversed, and arguments in defense should precede those concerning it. For the farmer could not properly cast the seed into the ground unless he first removed the wild wood and whatever would be harmful to the good seed. Nor could the physician introduce any wholesome medicines into the body that needed his care, if he did not previously remove the disease within, or stay that which was approaching. Neither surely can he who wishes to teach the truth persuade any one by speaking about it, so long as there is a false opinion lurking in the mind of his hearers, barring the entrance of his arguments.

Therefore, for the sake of greater usefulness, I myself sometimes place arguments in defense of the truth before those concerning the truth; and on the present occasion it appears to me, looking at the requirements of the case, advantageous to follow the same method in treating of the resurrection. For in regard to this subject we find some utterly disbelieving, and some others doubting, and — even among those who have accepted the first principles — some who are as much at a loss what to believe as those who doubt. The most unaccountable thing of all is that they are in this state of mind without having any ground whatsoever in the matters themselves for their disbelief, or finding it possible to assign any reasonable cause why they disbelieve or experience any perplexity.

—ANF 2:149-150

Consistent Ethic of Life

Defending Christians against charges of ritual murder and cannibalism, Athenagoras responded, in his Plea, *that believers rejected all forms of homicide, even those that were legal and socially acceptable.*

What man of sound mind would say that we are murderers? For we cannot eat human flesh till we have killed someone. The former charge, therefore, is false. In regard to the second: if any one should ask them whether they have seen what they assert, not one of them would be so barefaced as to say that he had. And yet we have slaves, some more and some fewer, by whom we could not help being seen; but not even one of these has been found to invent even such things against us. For they know that we cannot endure even to see a man put to death, though justly. Then who among them can accuse us of murder or cannibalism?

Who does not reckon among the things of greatest interest the contests of gladiators and wild beasts, especially those that are given by you [the emperor]? But we say that to watch a man put to death is much the same as killing him, and so we swear off such spectacles. We do not even look on, lest we should contract guilt and pollution. How then could we put people to death?

We say also that women who use drugs to bring about abortion commit murder, and they will have to give an account to God for the abortion. So, on what principle should we commit murder? The same person could not simultaneously regard the very fetus in the womb as a created being — and therefore an object of God's care — and yet kill it when it has passed into life. Nor could one refuse to expose an infant — because those who expose them are guilty of child-murder — and yet destroy it when it has grown up.

We are in all things constant and consistent, submitting ourselves to reason, and not overruling it.

— ANF 2:147

ST. IRENAEUS OF LYONS

St. Irenaeus (c. 125–c. 202) was a pivotal figure in the history of the Church's intellectual life. Some scholars count him among the apologists; others call him "the Father of theology." Actually, his work seems to mark a transition from one movement to another, or from one phase to another, a deepening of the Church's consideration of God.

Irenaeus did write apologetics. His most hefty work, and most famous, is his great defense *Against the Heresies*, also called *Against Those Falsely Called 'Gnostics.'* Yet in this defense, he goes further than the apologists before him in his consideration of the nature of God, the workings of Providence, and the interrelation among the Persons of the Blessed Trinity.

Perhaps the Church can "thank" the Gnostic heretics for creating an urgent need for the science of theology. The Gnostics were famous for their wild speculation about God, cosmology, the soul, and human redemption. One historian called the Gnostic phenomenon, "Platonism run amok." Valentinus, Marcion, Basilides, Simon — and many others — all spun intricate systems of thought, fantastic mythologies. They made extravagant promises of visionary experience, not just faith but gnosis, real knowledge, an immediate experience of the divine. Often, the Gnostic teachers did all of this in the name of "Jesus Christ" — not a Jesus recognizable by orthodox Christians, but rather a "savior" designed to appeal to the intellectual and esthetic sensibilities of a leisured and bored elite class.

Gnostic claims demanded the response of a trained, disciplined, subtle mind. And, in due time, Providence sent Irenaeus to Lyons.

He had been born in Smyrna about the year 125, and spent a spiritually privileged childhood in the presence of men who had lived with the Apostles. He received much of his formation from St. Polycarp, and would spend his adulthood meditating on the venerable bishop's intimate recollections of his own master, St. John the Apostle. Some traditions tell us that it was St. Polycarp who sent Irenaeus, then a young priest, away to the mission territory of Gaul (modern-day France).

Once in Gaul, Irenaeus lived up to his name, which means "peace," by trying to settle disputes among Christians. He pleaded with the popes for clemency for the Montanists, who, though misguided in their emphasis on ecstasies, still held to the apostolic faith, and for those Christians who held to the "Eastern" tradition of celebrating Easter on a fixed date.

But in his opposition to the Gnostics he was unstinting. For their errors were not only schismatic — violating the unity of the Church — but heretical. They attacked the very nature and identity of God and Jesus Christ. They denied the goodness of the Creator and declared all creation a prison. Against them, he marshaled all the forces at his command: sustained arguments, sharp satire, open ridicule, and chains of authority reaching back to the Apostles.

St. Irenaeus wrote volumes of doctrinal works, even as he administered the Church of Lyons. Later Fathers wrote that he died a martyr, but there is no early testimony to substantiate that claim.

Union with God

In a brief space at the beginning of Book 5 of Against the Heresies, *St. Irenaeus defends the doctrines of Creation and Fall, Trinity and Incarnation, prophecy and Eucharist. In doing so, he reveals the great dignity of our redemption in Christ: It is true "divinization," a sharing of God's life in a communion of real flesh and blood.*

We could never have learned the things of God unless our Teacher, existing as the Word, had become man. No other being had the power to reveal to us the things of the Father, except His very own Word. What other person "knew the mind of the Lord," or who else "has been his counselor" (Rom 11:34)? We could have learned in no other way than by seeing our Teacher and hearing His voice with our own ears. Then, when we have become imitators of His works and doers of His words, we may have communion with Him, receiving growth from the perfect One, from Him who exists before all creation.

We were but lately created by Him who is most excellent and good, who has the gift of immortality. We have been formed after His likeness — when we did not exist, we were predestined, according to the foreknowledge of the Father, to come into being and become the first-fruits of creation. We now have received, in the times known beforehand, the blessings of salvation, according to the ministry of the Word, who is perfect in all things, as both the mighty Word and true man. He redeemed us by His own blood in a reasonable way. He gave Himself as a redemption for those who had been led into captivity....

The Lord has redeemed us through His own blood, giving His soul for our souls, His flesh for our flesh. He has poured out the Spirit of the Father for the union and communion of God and man. He has truly given God to men by means of the Spirit. And He has brought man to God by His own incarnation. At His coming, he has given us lasting and true immortality by means of communion with God. Before these truths, all the doctrines of the heretics fall to ruin.

Empty indeed are those who say that He only seemed to appear. For these things did not merely seem to happen; they really happened. If He was not a man when He appeared to be a man, the Holy Spirit could not have rested upon Him — an occurrence which did actually take place — as the Spirit is invisible. Nor, if He wasn't what He seemed to be, was there any measure of truth in Him.

But I have already remarked that Abraham and the other prophets beheld Him in a prophetic way, foreseeing in a vision what would happen in the future. If such a being has now appeared in this way, but is not what He seems to be, then there has been another prophetical vision made to the people; and we should expect another coming, in which He shall be the fulfillment of these latter prophecies.

It is the same thing to say that He merely seemed to appear and to say that He received nothing at all from Mary. For He would not have truly had flesh and blood — by which He redeemed us — unless He had summed up in Himself the ancient form of Adam.

Empty, then, are the disciples of Valentinus, who put forth this opinion, in order that they may exclude all flesh from salvation, and cast aside what God Himself has fashioned.

Empty, too, are the Ebionites, who do not receive by faith into their soul the union of God and man, but who remain in the old leaven of the natural birth. They choose not to believe that the Holy Spirit came upon Mary, and that the power of the Most High overshadowed her, so that what was born of her was something holy, the Son of the Most High God. The Father of all caused the incarnation of this being, and showed forth a new kind of birth. By the old birth we inherited death, but by this new birth we inherit life.

For the same reason these men reject the mingling of water with the heavenly wine. They wish instead for the cup to hold only worldly water. Thus they do not receive God so as to have union with Him. Instead they remain in that Adam who had been conquered and was expelled from Paradise. They do not see that the same breath of life that proceeded from God at the beginning of our formation in Adam gave life to man because it was united to what God had fashioned. So, too, in these end times, the Word of the Father and the Spirit of God, having become united with the ancient substance of Adam's formation, have rendered man living and perfect, receptive of the perfect Father. As in the natural Adam we all were dead, so in the spiritual man we may all be made alive. For never at any time did Adam escape those hands of God, which the Father speaks of when He says, "Let us make man in our image, after our likeness" (Gen 1:26). This is why, in these last times, His hands formed a living man not by the will of the flesh, nor by the will of man, but by the good pleasure of the Father, in order that Adam might be created again after the image and likeness of God.

— *ANF 1:526-527*

AGAINST THE HERETICS: A SATIRE OF GNOSTICISM

In a lighter moment in his screed Against the Heresies, *Irenaeus offers readers ironic guidance for fabricating their own Gnostic mythology.*

Since certain men have set aside the truth, to favor lying words and pointless genealogies — which, as the Apostle says, "promote speculations rather than the divine training that is in faith" (1 Tim 1:4) — and since, by means of their cleverly crafted speculation, they lure away the minds of the inexperienced and take them captive, I have felt constrained, dear friend, to write the following, in order to expose and counteract their plots.

These men falsify the oracles of God, and prove themselves evil interpreters of the good word of revelation. They overthrow the faith of many, luring them away, under a pretense of superior knowledge, from Him who rounded and adorned the universe; as if they had something more excellent and sublime to reveal than God, who created heaven and earth and all things within....

Let us now look at the inconsistent opinions of those heretics.... The first of them, Valentinus, adapted the principles of the heresy called "Gnostic" to the peculiar character of his own school, and taught as follows: He maintained that there is a certain Dyad (twofold being), who is inexpressible by any name, of whom one part should be called Arrhetus (unspeakable), and the other Sige (silence). But of this Dyad a second was produced, one part of whom he names Pater, and the other Aletheia. From this Tetrad, again, arose Logos and Zoe, Anthropos and Ecclesia. These constitute the primary Ogdoad. He next states that from Logos and Zoe ten powers were produced, as we have before mentioned. But from Anthropos and Ecclesia proceeded twelve — one, separating from the rest and falling from its original condition, produced the rest of the universe. He also supposed two beings of the name of Horos, the one of whom has his place between Bythus and the rest of the Pleroma, and divides the created Aeons from the uncreated Father, while the other separates their mother from the Pleroma. Christ also was not produced from the Aeons within the Pleroma, but was brought forth by the mother who had been excluded from it, in virtue of her remembrance of better things, but not without a kind of shadow. He, indeed, as being masculine, having severed the shadow from himself, returned to the Pleroma; but his mother being left with the shadow, and deprived of her spiritual substance, brought forth another son, namely, the Demiurge [or Creator], whom he also styles the supreme ruler of all those things which are subject to him.... Sometimes, again, he maintains that Jesus was produced from him who was separated from their mother.... And he declares that the Holy Spirit was produced by Aletheia for the inspection and fructification of the Aeons, by entering invisibly into them, and that, in this way, the Aeons brought forth the plants of truth....

Phew! Well may we exclaim at his unabashed boldness in coining names for his system of falsehood.... It is obvious that he speaks of things of his own invention, and that he himself has given names to his scheme of things.... It is obvious, too, since he alone has had the boldness to coin such names, that, unless he had appeared in the world, the truth would still have been deprived of a name! But, in that case, nothing keeps anyone else from giving such names as the following:

"There is a certain Proarche, royal, surpassing all thought, a power existing before every other substance, and extended into space in every direction. But along with it there exists a power which I term a Gourd; and along with this Gourd there exists a power which again I term Utter-Emptiness. This Gourd and Emptiness, since they are one, produced (and yet did not simply produce, so as to be apart from themselves) a fruit, everywhere visible, eatable, and delicious, which fruit-language calls a Cucumber. Along with this Cucumber exists a power of the same essence, which again I call a Melon. These powers, the Gourd, Utter-Emptiness, the Cucumber, and the Melon, brought forth the remaining multitude of the delirious melons of Valentinus." ... If anyone may assign names at his pleasure, who shall prevent us from adopting these names? They are much more credible than the others.

— ANF 1:315-318

MARY, THE NEW EVE

Again from Irenaeus's Against the Heresies, *these are the Church's classic statements considering Mary as the "new Eve."*

In accordance with design, Mary the Virgin is found obedient, saying, "Behold, I am the handmaid of the Lord; let it be to me according to your word" (Lk 1:38). But Eve was disobedient; for she did not obey when as yet she was a virgin.... Thus it was that the knot of Eve's disobedience was loosed by the obedience of Mary. For what the virgin Eve had bound fast through unbelief, this did the virgin Mary set free through faith....

For just as the former was led astray by the word of an angel — so that she fled from God when she had transgressed His word — so did the latter, by an angelic communication, receive the glad tidings that she should bear God, being obedient to His word. And if the former did disobey God, yet the latter was persuaded to be obedient to God, in order that the Virgin Mary might become the patroness of the virgin Eve.

Thus, as the human race fell into bondage to death by means of a virgin, so is it rescued by a virgin. Virginal disobedience was balanced in the opposite scale by virginal obedience. For in the same way the sin of the first created man receives amendment by the correction of the First-begotten, and the coming of the serpent is conquered by the harmlessness of the dove, unloosing those bonds by which we had been bound to death.

— ANF 1:455, 547

THE EUCHARIST, PLEDGE OF OUR RESURRECTION

In a passage of Against the Heresies *evocative of John 6:54, Irenaeus speaks of the Holy Eucharist as a pledge of the resurrection of the body, a doctrine denied by many Gnostic sects.*

Directing His disciples to offer God the first-fruits of His own creation — not because He stood in need of them, but that they themselves might be neither unfruitful nor ungrateful — He took that created thing, bread, and gave thanks, and said, "This is my body" (Mt

26:26). And the cup likewise, which is part of that creation to which we belong, He confessed to be His blood, and taught the new oblation of the new covenant. This the Church has received from the Apostles, and offers now to God throughout all the world.…

Then how can they say that the flesh, which is nourished with the Body of the Lord and with His Blood, goes to corruption and does not partake of life? Let them, therefore, either alter their opinion or cease from offering the things just mentioned. But our opinion is in accordance with the Eucharist, and the Eucharist in turn establishes our opinion. For we offer to Him His own, announcing consistently the fellowship and union of the flesh and Spirit. For as the bread, which is produced from the earth, when it receives the invocation of God, is no longer common bread, but the Eucharist, consisting of two realities, earthly and heavenly, so also our bodies, when they receive the Eucharist, are no longer corruptible, having the hope of the resurrection to eternity.

— ANF 1:484, 486

TERTULLIAN

No one ever accused Tertullian of excessive tact. Though, like St. Justin before him, he wrote apologetical works, he showed no interest in accommodating Christian doctrine to the categories of pagan philosophy. On the contrary, he gloried in all that was scandalous in his adopted religion: that God is three and yet one; that Christ is man and yet God; that God, eternal and omnipotent, could suffer and die. One of his most quoted lines might serve as a summary of his faith: "It is to be believed because it is absurd."[60]

Though himself a learned man, perhaps the most renowned lawyer in the empire, Tertullian (c. 155–c. 222) judged his rich classical culture of little use in propagating or defending the Gospel. "What indeed," he asked, "has Athens to do with Jerusalem?… Away with all attempts to produce a mottled Christianity of Stoic, Platonic, and Dialectic composition. We want no curious disputation after possessing Christ Jesus, no research after enjoying the Gospel!"[61] St. Justin could argue persuasively that Roman persecutions violated the established legal rights of Christians who were Roman citizens. Tertullian would rather call his persecutors inhuman, godless, and damned, taunting them, moreover, to kill more Christians, if they dared. The persecutions, he pointed out, merely increased the Church's numbers: "The blood of Christians is seed."[62]

Pithy lines like that gave his arguments remarkable rhetorical force. His style was explosive and confrontational. He once wrote a tract on patience, and joked along the way that he was like an invalid writing about health. He was constitutionally unsuited to suffering fools or obstinate pagans.

Inspired by the courage of Christian martyrs, Tertullian converted to the faith when he was in his late thirties. Even by then, his fame as a legal scholar had spread far beyond his home in North Africa. Once in the Church, he wielded his pen like a blazing brand, to expose error by the light of truth (one of his favorite words), and to immolate falsehood with the flames of his invective. It was Tertullian who first used the Latin word *Trinitas* (Trinity) to describe God.[63]

Problems arose when he encountered infidelities, apostasy, cowardice, lukewarmness, and immorality among his own people. He came, more and more, to excoriate those who called themselves Christian but who fell into mortal sin. Calling for a purer Church, he fell under the influence of the schismatic Montanus, who claimed to speak by the power of the Holy Spirit. In time, Tertullian came to invent a distinction between the "spiritual church" and the "church of a bunch of bishops."[64] He joined the Montanist sect — though, ultimately, he would find even them unsatisfactory. He then founded his own sect, the Tertullianists, which would survive till St. Augustine's day. Tertullian died about 222, separated from the Catholic Church he had spent passionate years to build up.

THE LOVE OF CHRISTIANS

The following passage comes from Tertullian's Apology *addressed to the Roman governors, who were then directing severe persecutions of Christians in their provinces. The* Apology *contains perhaps the most frequently quoted description of the ancient Church: "See those Christians, how they love one another."*

We are the same to emperors as to our ordinary neighbors. For we are equally forbidden to wish ill, do ill, speak ill, think ill of all men. The thing we must not do to an emperor, we must not do to anyone else: what we would not do to anybody, perhaps we should not do to him whom God has been pleased to exalt so highly. If we are enjoined to love our enemies, whom have we to hate? If injured, we are forbidden to retaliate, lest we become as bad ourselves. Who can suffer injury at our hands?

Think about your own experiences. How often you inflict gross cruelties on Christians, partly because it is your own inclination, and partly in obedience to the laws! How often, too, the hostile mob, paying no regard to you, takes the law into its own hand, and assails us with stones and flames! With the frenzy of Bacchanalia, they do not even spare the Christian dead, but tear them, now sadly changed, no longer entire, from the rest of the tomb, from the asylum we might say of death, cutting them in pieces, rending them asunder.

Yet, banded together as we are — ever so ready to sacrifice our lives — what single case of revenge for injury are you able to point to, though, if we believed it right to repay evil by evil, a single night with a torch or two could achieve an ample vengeance?

But away with the idea of a divine sect avenging itself by human fires, or shrinking from the sufferings in which it is tried....

One All-Embracing Commonwealth

Ought not Christians, therefore, to receive not merely a somewhat milder treatment, but to have a place among law-abiding societies, since they are not chargeable with any crimes?... For, unless I mistake the matter, the prevention of such associations is based on a prudential regard for public order, that the state may not be divided into parties, which would naturally lead to disturbance in the electoral assemblies, the councils, the courts, the special conventions, even in the public shows by the hostile collisions of rival parties — especially when now, in pursuit of gain, men have begun to consider their violence an article to be bought and sold.

But as those in whom all ardor in the pursuit of glory and honor is dead, we have no pressing need to take part in your public meetings; nor is there anything more foreign to us than affairs of state. We acknowledge one all-embracing commonwealth — the world. We renounce all your spectacles.... Among us nothing is ever said, or seen, or heard, which has anything in common with the madness of the circus, the immodesty of the theater, the atrocities of the arena, the useless exercises of the wrestling-ground. Why do you take offense at us because we differ from you in regard to your pleasures? If we will not partake of your enjoyments, the loss is ours, not yours — if there is any loss. We reject what pleases you. You, on the other hand, have no taste for what is our delight. The Epicureans were allowed by you to decide for themselves one true source of pleasure — I mean equanimity. The Christian, on his part, has many such enjoyments — what harm in that?...

See Those Christians

We are a body knit together as such by a common religious profession, by unity of discipline, and by the bond of a common hope. We meet together as an assembly and congregation, that, offering up a united prayer, we may wrestle with Him in our supplications. This violence God delights in. We pray, too, for the emperors, for their ministers and for all in authority, for the welfare of the world, for the prevalence of peace, for the delay of the final consummation.... In the same place also exhortations are made, rebukes and sacred censures are administered. For with a great seriousness is the work of judging carried on among us, as is proper to those who are sure they are in the sight of God. And you have the most notable example of judgment to come when anyone has sinned so grievously as to require his severance from us in prayer, in the congregation and in all sacred worship.

The tried men of our elders preside over us, gaining that honor not by purchase, but by established character. There is no buying and selling of the things of God. Though we have our treasure chest, it is not made up of purchase-money, as of a religion that has its price. On the monthly day, if he likes, each puts in a small donation; but only if he wishes it, and only if he is able: for there is no compulsion; all is voluntary. These gifts are piety's deposit fund. For they are not taken thence and spent on feasts and drinking bouts, but to support and bury poor people, to supply the wants of boys and girls destitute of means and parents, and of old persons confined now to the house; those who have suffered shipwreck; and any who are in the mines, or banished to the islands, or shut up in the prisons for nothing but their fidelity to the cause of God's Church. They become the nurslings of their confession.

But it is mainly the deeds of a love so noble that lead many to put a brand upon us. "See," they say, "how they love one another," for they themselves are animated by mutual hatred; "how they are ready even to die for one another," for they themselves will sooner put to death.

— ANF 3:45-46

ATHENS AND JERUSALEM

Tertullian wrote a comprehensive Prescription Against Heretics. *To him, "heresy" included all non-Christian thought, including classical philosophy. Tertullian represents the extreme of Christian resistance to the influence of Greek philosophy and culture. Other Fathers, such as St. Clement of Alexandria and Origen, eagerly applied the methods and language of "pagan" science to their understanding of the Christian faith.*

These are the doctrines of men and of demons, produced for itching ears of the spirit of this world's wisdom! This the Lord called folly, and "chose what is foolish in the world" (1 Cor 1:27) to confound even philosophy itself. For philosophy is the material of the world's wisdom, the rash interpreter of the nature and the dispensation of God. Indeed heresies are themselves instigated by philosophy. From this source came the Aeons, and I know not what infinite forms, and the trinity of man in the system of Valentinus, who was of Plato's school. From the same source came Marcion's better god, with all his tranquility; he came of the Stoics. Then, again, the opinion that the soul dies is held by the Epicureans; while the denial of the restoration of the body is taken from the aggregate school of all the philosophers.

Also, when matter is made equal to God, then you have the teaching of Zeno; and when any doctrine is alleged touching a god of fire, then Heraclitus comes in.

The same subject matter is discussed over and over again by the heretics and the philosophers; the same arguments are involved. Whence comes evil? Why is it permitted? What is the origin of man? And in what way does he come? Besides the question which Valentinus has very lately proposed — Whence comes God? Which he settles with the answer: From *enthymesis* and *ectroma*.

Unhappy Aristotle, who invented for these men dialectics, the art of building up and pulling down, an art so evasive in its propositions, so farfetched in its conjectures, so harsh in its arguments, so productive of contentions — embarrassing even to itself, retracting everything, and really treating of nothing! Whence spring those "myths and endless genealogies" (1 Tim 1:4), and "unprofitable" questions (Ti 3:9), and talk that will "eat its way like gangrene" (2 Tim 2:17)? From all these, when the Apostle would restrain us, he expressly names philosophy as that which he would have us be on our guard against. Writing to the Colossians, he says, "See to it that no one makes a prey of you by philosophy and empty deceit, according to human tradition" (Col 2:8) and contrary to the wisdom of the Holy Spirit. He had been at Athens, and had in his interviews (with its philosophers) become acquainted with that human wisdom which pretends to know the truth, while it only corrupts it, and is itself divided into its own manifold heresies, by the variety of its mutually repugnant sects.

What indeed has Athens to do with Jerusalem? What concord is there between the Academy and the Church? What between heretics and Christians? Our instruction comes from the Portico of Solomon (see Acts 3:11), who had himself taught that the Lord should be sought in simplicity of heart (see Wis 1:1). Away with all attempts to produce a mottled Christianity of Stoic, Platonic, and dialectic composition! We want no curious disputation after possessing Christ Jesus, no inquisition after enjoying the Gospel! With our faith, we desire no further belief.

— ANF 3:246

ST. HIPPOLYTUS OF ROME

An old saying goes that "the Church is not a hotel for saints, but a hospital for sinners." To modern Christians, the statement might seem self-evident. But in the time of the Fathers, it was a disputed point. In fact, the Fathers themselves argued vigorously over whether the Church should dispense forgiveness freely or sparingly, and whether priests should impose heavy or light penances.

Hippolytus of Rome most certainly stood in the "hotel for saints" camp.

Hippolytus was a Greek-speaking priest, perhaps from Egypt, serving in Rome during the late second and early third century. Early histories tell us that he was a sometime student of St. Irenaeus.

He became a noted theologian in his own right. He wrote biblical commentaries and a comprehensive Refutation of Heresies. The great prodigy Origen traveled from Egypt to Rome to sit at the feet of this cranky master.

Hippolytus seems to have thrived in Rome. Yet he was not pleased with the way the Church was administered. Eventually, in fact, he concluded that Pope St. Callistus I (217–222) had invalidated his authority by excessive leniency toward heretics and sinners.

Well, if Callistus's papacy was invalid, the Church was in dire need of a pope. And who might that be?

Hippolytus had himself elected "pope" by a group of influential Roman priests. He extended his claim through the reign of three legitimate popes. Thus, history knows him as the first "antipope."

Persecution, however, brings together strange cellmates. In 235, the imperial authorities sentenced both Hippolytus and the recently resigned Pope St. Pontian to exile on the island of Sardinia. While working side by side in the salt mines, Hippolytus and Pontian reconciled, and Hippolytus made his peace with the Church. The two men died in exile, and their bodies were transferred together to Rome for burial.

It seems that the Church venerated Hippolytus almost immediately. A third-century monument honors him with an allegorical representation of wisdom and a listing of many of his literary works.

Hippolytus's life, though it ended violently, had been long and productive. He is best known today for his liturgical manual, *The Apostolic Tradition*. When the Catholic Church was revising its rites after the Second Vatican Council, it drew much from the Mass set down by Hippolytus. Eucharistic Prayer II in today's missal is based on the central prayer in *The Apostolic Tradition*.

St. Hippolytus's feast day, which he shares with Pope St. Pontian, is August 13.

Milk and Honey

Every now and then, the Fathers give us a precious glimpse of liturgical customs that vanished long ago. During the Easter Vigil Mass, for example, the Roman Church would dispense a chalice of milk and honey along with the eucharistic elements. This symbolized the newly baptized Christian's entrance into the true promised land through the sacraments. The following passage is adapted from Gregory Dix's translation of The Apostolic Tradition *by St. Hippolytus (London: SPCK, 1937), pages 40-42.*

The deacons immediately bring the offering to the bishop, who, by giving thanks, shall make the bread into an antitype of the body of Christ, and the cup of wine mixed with water into the likeness of His blood, which is shed for all who believe in Him. Milk and honey shall be mixed together in fulfillment of the promise given to the patriarchs, of a land flowing with milk and honey. This is Christ's flesh, which He gave, by which those who believe are nourished like babies. He sweetens the bitterness of the heart by the gentleness of His word. Water is brought as a sign of the washing, in order that the inner part of man, which is spiritual, may receive the same as the body. The bishop shall explain the reason of all these things to those who partake. And when he breaks the bread and distributes the fragments he shall say: "The heavenly bread in Christ Jesus." And the recipient shall say, "Amen."

The priests — or if there are not enough priests, the deacons — shall hold the cups, and stand with reverence and dignity; first the one who holds the water, next the milk, then the wine. The recipients shall taste three times from each. He who gives the cup shall say: "In God the Father Almighty" And the recipient shall say, "Amen." Then: "In the Lord Jesus Christ." And he shall say, "Amen." Then: "In the Holy Spirit and Holy Church." And he shall say, "Amen." So it shall be done to each. And when these things are completed, let each hasten to do good and please God and live rightly, devoting himself to the Church, practicing what he has learned, advancing in the service of God.

WISDOM'S HOUSE AND WISDOM'S BANQUET

In a Scripture commentary, Hippolytus depicted the Eucharist as Wisdom's banquet, foreshadowed allegorically in the Old Testament.

"Wisdom has built her house, she has set up her seven pillars" (Prov 9:1). This means Christ, the wisdom and power of God the Father, has built His house, His nature in the flesh derived from the Virgin. It is just as John said: "And the Word became flesh and dwelt among us" (Jn 1:14). So the wise prophet also testifies: Wisdom that was before the world, and is the source of life, the infinite Wisdom of God, has built her house, by a mother who knew no man — that is, as He assumed the temple of the body.

"She has set up her seven pillars," and these are the fragrant grace of the all-holy Spirit, as Isaiah says: "And the seven spirits of God shall rest upon him" (cf. Is 11:2). But others say that the seven pillars are the seven divine orders that sustain creation by His holy and inspired teaching: the prophets, the Apostles, the martyrs, the bishops, the hermits, the saints, and the righteous....

The passage goes on to say, "She has mixed her wine, she has also set her table" (Prov 9:2). "She has mixed her wine" means that the Savior, uniting His Godhead, like pure wine, with the flesh in the Virgin, was born of her. He was simultaneously God and man, without confusion of the one in the other. "She has also set her table": This denotes the promised knowledge of the Holy Trinity; it also refers to his honored and undefiled body and blood, which day by day are administered and offered sacrificially at the spiritual divine table, as a memorial of that first and ever-memorable table of the spiritual divine supper.

It goes on: "She has sent out her maids." Wisdom has done so — Christ has done so — "to call from the highest places in the town, 'Whoever is simple, let him turn in here!'" So she says, in an obvious reference to the holy Apostles, who traveled the whole world, summoning the nations, with their lofty and divine preaching, to the knowledge of Him in truth.

The passage continues, "To those who want understanding she says" — to those, that is, who have not yet received the power of the Holy Spirit — "Come, eat of my bread and drink of the wine I have mixed." By this is meant that He gave His divine flesh and precious blood to us, to eat and to drink for the remission of sins.

— ANF 5:175-176

───────ST. CYPRIAN OF CARTHAGE───────

Is it right for the Church to welcome prodigal children home again … and again? And, if so, how many times? Is there a limit to the mercy the Church should dispense in the name of Jesus Christ?

For North African Christians of the second and third centuries, those were essential questions. An individual's answer placed him either with the Catholic Church or with one of the fast-multiplying schismatic sects: the Montanists, Tertullianists, and many others who taught that Christians who lapsed into mortal sin should not be readmitted to the Church, even if they were repentant.

The persecutions of Decius and Valerian forced the issue to a crisis. Some Christians proved unable or unwilling to withstand the tortures, or even the threat of torture. Caving in to Roman pressure, they agreed to renounce their faith and offer sacrifice to the gods. Such weak believers were termed lapsi, "the lapsed."

Yet most of the lapsi had given in reluctantly and were immediately filled with regret. Their anguish was only heightened as they watched more courageous Catholics persevering under torture, even to death. Repentant, they wanted to return to the Church, to be fortified by the sacraments and preaching, should they need to face the torturers again.

Should they be allowed to return? Christians were divided on the question. Some said no; the lapsi had committed the sin against the Holy Spirit, the unforgivable sin. Others said yes, but the lapsi should only be readmitted once; repeat offenders should be shut out.

St. Cyprian (c. 200–258), as bishop of Carthage, stood ready to welcome any Christian who was willing to confess his sins and do penance. Born to a wealthy pagan family, a successful lawyer, he gave all his fortune to the poor when he accepted Christianity. He considered Tertullian his master in theology, but looked to Jesus as his master in charity.

In short order, he was ordained to the priesthood, and about 248 was elected bishop by the people. (In the early Church, it was the custom, when a bishop died, for the local people or local clergy to choose his successor.) When the emperor Decius decreed a persecution in 250, Bishop Cyprian faced a decision: Should he face martyrdom as an exemplar for his flock? Or should he go into hiding, so that, through the time of trial, he might continue to lead the Christians of Carthage? He chose to flee, a decision bitterly resented by some of his priests.

After the Decian persecution, which had claimed Pope Fabian, the Church of Rome called Bishop Cyprian to account for his action. He replied, dutifully and admirably, sending the Roman clergy copies of all the many pastoral letters he had written during his years in hiding.

When peace returned to Carthage, St. Cyprian tried mightily to restore unity to a flock divided over suspicions and allegations of treachery committed during the persecution. Some who had undergone torture were reluctant to forgive the lapsi. To aggravate the situation, heretical sects made inroads with both groups, with some offering welcome to the lapsi, while others offered congregational purity to the steadfast.

St. Cyprian surmised that the interlude between persecutions would be brief, and he knew that a divided Church could not well withstand such a trial. He wrote voluminously — to settle the squabbles, to convert heretics — and his mildness won over many of his most defiant foes.

He also won praise from the pagans, as, during the devastating worldwide epidemic of 251, he exhorted his flock to serve Christians and non-Christians alike.

This was not enough, however, to stave off Valerian's persecution, which came in 257, as St. Cyprian was in the midst of a rather intense disagreement with Pope Stephen. Within a year, their differences would not matter. Pope Stephen was executed and Cyprian exiled. St. Cyprian was beheaded near Carthage in 258.

To Pope Cornelius

Pope Cornelius was a longtime correspondent and great supporter of St. Cyprian. Both men would die as martyrs. In the following letter, Cyprian consults with the pope in preparation for a coming persecution.

We had decided some time ago, dearest brother, after consulting each other, that those who, in the fierceness of persecution, had been overthrown by the adversary and had lapsed, and had polluted themselves with unlawful sacrifices, should undergo a long and full repentance; and if the risk of sickness should be urgent, should receive peace on the very point of death. For it was not right — neither did the love of the Father nor divine mercy allow — that the Church should be closed to those who knock, or the help of the hope of salvation be denied to those who mourn and entreat, so that when they pass from this world, they should be dismissed to their Lord without communion and peace; since He Himself who gave the law, that things which were bound on earth should also be bound in heaven, allowed, moreover, that things might be loosed there which were here first loosed in the Church.

But now we see the day of trouble again drawing near. And we are admonished by often-repeated intimations that we should be prepared and armed for the struggle that the enemy announces to us, that we should also prepare the people committed to us ... by our exhortations, and gather together from all parts all the soldiers of Christ who desire arms, anxious for the battle within the Lord's camp. Compelled by this need, we have decided that peace is to be given to those who have not withdrawn from the Church of the Lord, but have not ceased from the first day of their lapse to repent, and to lament, and to beseech the Lord; and we have decided that they ought to be armed and equipped for the battle which is at hand....

For, in days of peace and tranquility, it was reasonable to prolong the repentance of the mourners for a lengthier time, and to give help only to the sick in their departure.... But now peace is necessary, not for the sick, but for the strong.... And, as the Eucharist is appointed a safeguard to those who receive, we need it in order to arm, with the protection of the Lord's abundance, those whom we wish to be safe against the adversary. For how do we teach or provoke them to shed their blood in confession of His name, if we deny to those who are about to enter warfare the Blood of Christ? How do we make them fit for the cup of martyrdom, if we do not first admit them to drink, in the Church, the cup of the Lord by the right of Communion?

We should make a distinction, dearest brother, between — on the one hand — those who either have apostatized and ... are living heathenish lives, or have become deserters to the heretics ... and — on the other hand — those who do not depart from the Church's threshold, who, constantly and sorrowfully imploring divine and paternal consolation, profess that they are now prepared for the battle, and ready to stand and fight bravely for the name of their Lord and for their own salvation.

In these times we grant peace, not to those who sleep, but to those who watch. We grant peace, not amid indulgences, but amid arms. We grant peace, not for rest, but for the field of battle. If, according to what we hear, and desire, and believe of them, they shall stand bravely, and shall overthrow the adversary with us in the encounter, we shall not repent of having granted peace to men so brave.

— ANF 5:336-337

ON THE UNITY OF THE CHURCH
Controversy over the reconciliation of lapsed Catholics led to schisms in the Church of Carthage. In 251, Cyprian convened a council to settle the matter, and there he read his famous tract On the Unity of the Church, *from which the following is taken.*

The office of bishop is one, and each part of it is held by each one for the whole. The Church also is one, though spread far and wide into a multitude by an increase of fruitfulness. As there are many rays of the sun, but one light; and many branches of a tree, but one strength, based in its tenacious root; and since from one spring flow many streams, although the multiplicity seems diffused in the generosity of an overflowing abundance, yet the unity is still preserved in the source.

Separate a ray of the sun from its body of light, its unity does not allow a division of light; break a branch from a tree — when broken, it will not be able to bud; cut off the stream from its fountain, and that which is cut off dries up. Thus also the Church, shone over with the light of the Lord, sheds forth her rays over the whole world, yet it is one light that is everywhere diffused; nor is the unity of the body separated. Her fruitful abundance spreads her branches over the whole world. She broadly expands her rivers, liberally flowing, yet her head is one, her source one; and she is one mother, plentiful in the results of fruitfulness: from her womb we are born, by her milk we are nourished, by her spirit we are animated.

The spouse of Christ cannot be adulterous; she is uncorrupted and pure. She knows one home; she guards with chaste modesty the sanctity of one couch. She keeps us for God. She appoints the sons whom she has borne for the kingdom. Whoever is separated from the Church and is joined to an adulteress is separated from the promises of the Church; nor can he who forsakes the Church of Christ attain to the rewards of Christ. He is a stranger; he is profane; he is an enemy. He can no longer have God for his Father, who has not the Church for his mother....

The Lord says, "I and the Father are one" (Jn 10:30). Again, it is written of the Father, and of the Son, and of the Holy Spirit, "And these three agree" (1 Jn 5:8). Does anyone believe that this unity, which thus comes from the divine strength and coheres in celestial sacraments, can be divided in the Church and can be separated by the parting asunder of opposing wills? He who does not hold this unity does not hold God's law, does not hold the faith of the Father and the Son, does not hold life and salvation....

Unanimity formerly prevailed among the Apostles; and thus the new assembly of believers, keeping the Lord's commandments, maintained its charity. Divine Scripture proves this when it says, "Now the company of those who believed were of one heart and soul" (Acts 4:32). And again: "All these with one accord devoted themselves to prayer, together with the women and Mary the mother of Jesus, and with his brethren" (Acts 1:14). And thus they prayed with effectual prayers; thus they were able with confidence to obtain whatever they asked from the Lord's mercy.

— *ANF 5:423, 429*

————————ST. CLEMENT OF ALEXANDRIA————————

"Knowledge" had a nasty reputation among some Christians by the end of the second century. The heretical Gnostics used the term to mean secret *gnosis* reserved for a spiritual elite, and the Gnostic sects kept a stubborn presence, especially in intellectual circles.

Christian teachers and pastors tended to react in one of two ways. One might be called the anti-intellectual approach, favored by polemicists like Tertullian. Those who took this approach declared that Jerusalem had nothing to do with Athens, and that faith had nothing to do with knowledge. They were suspicious of philosophy, which seemed only to lead to trouble. Faith was superior to reason and, therefore, superseded any need for philosophy.

The second way, favored by St. Clement of Alexandria (150–215), was to make distinctions. The *gnosis* of the heretics was bogus, yes, but there was a gnosis, a knowledge, that could prepare the mind for revelation. "Greek philosophy purifies the soul," Clement wrote, "and prepares it to receive the faith on which truth constructs knowledge." What is more, philosophy gave Christians a language for articulating their more elevated doctrines. How else to describe the incarnation of the Word without mastery of metaphysical concepts such as time, eternity, being, and substance? Clement's attitude is best summed up in the later axiom that secular philosophy is "theology's handmaid."

Clement, presiding over the famous school at Alexandria, tried to rescue *gnosis* from its heretical associations. "God is love," he wrote, "and He is knowable to those who love Him." Clement put to use his encyclopedic knowledge of the Scriptures, as well as of pagan poetry, philosophy, and the sciences. He wrote many theological, spiritual, and catechetical works, as well as his own works of philosophy and poetry, which were influential among the later Fathers. Clement was one of the tutors of the boy genius Origen.

Clement fled Alexandria during the persecution of Septimus Severus, early in the third century. He died abroad, possibly in Cappadocia.

He was subject to occasional disfavor throughout the Patristic Era, partly because of his perceived Gnostic associations.

TRUE GNOSTICS AND FALSE GNOSTICS

In this passage taken from his Stromata, *or "Carpets," St. Clement contrasts the true knowledge of the Christian with the false gnosis of the heretic. The Christian is the true Gnostic, and the heretic is not even worthy to be called a "knower." The Christian Gnostic enjoys true freedom, even as he is bound to the witness of Scripture and the rule of the Church.*

The [Christian] Gnostic receives the closest likeness to the mind that the Master possessed and which He commanded and recommended to His disciples and to the prudent. Understanding this as the Teacher wished, and receiving it in all its greatness, he teaches worthily from "the housetops" (Mt 10:27) those who are capable of being built to a lofty height. He begins to live by what is spoken, in accordance with the example of life. For Christ commanded only what is possible. And, in truth, the kingly man and Christian ought to be a ruler and a leader. For we are commanded to be lords over not only the wild beasts around us, but also over the wild passions within ourselves.

Knowing the difference between a bad and a good life, the Gnostic is saved, understanding and executing "[more than] the scribes and Pharisees" (Mt 5:20)....

But the things that cooperate in the discovery of truth are not to be rejected. The kind of philosophy, for example, that proclaims a providence, and the reward of a life lived well, and the punishment of a life of misery, teaches a comprehensive theology. Still, it does not preserve accuracy and particular points. For neither respecting the Son of God, nor respecting the economy of providence, does it treat similarly with us; for it did not know the worship of God.

The same goes for the heresies of barbarian philosophy. Although they speak of one God and they sing the praises of Christ, they speak without accuracy, not in line with the truth. They discover another

God, and receive Christ not as the prophecies deliver. Their false dogmas are against us and opposed to conduct that accords with the truth.

Consider Paul, who circumcised Timothy because of the Jews who believed, so that those who had been trained in the law might not revolt from the faith because he broke such points of the law as were understood in a more fleshly way. He knew quite well that circumcision does not justify; for he professed that "all things were for all" by conformity, preserving those of the dogmas that were essential, "that he might win all" (cf. 1 Cor 9:19). Similarly, Daniel, under the king of the Persians, wore "the chain" (Dan 5:7), though he had sympathy for the afflictions of the people.

The real liars, then, are not those who for the sake of the scheme of salvation conform, nor those who err in small points, but those who are wrong in essentials, and reject the Lord, and do their best to deprive the Lord of the true teaching. They do not quote or deliver the Scriptures in a manner worthy of God and of the Lord; for the deposit rendered to God, according to the teaching of the Lord by His Apostles, is the understanding and the practice of the godly Tradition. "What I tell you in the dark" — that is, in a hidden manner, and in a mystery — "proclaim," He says, "upon the housetops." That is, understand them sublimely, and deliver them in a lofty way, and according to the rule of the truth explaining the Scriptures. For neither prophecy nor the Savior Himself announced the divine mysteries simply so that they could be easily apprehended by everyone. They spoke, instead, in parables.

The Apostles say that the Lord told all things "to the crowds in parables; indeed he said nothing to them without a parable" (Mt 13:34).... "All [things are] straight," says the Scripture, "to him who understands (Prov 8:9)" — that is, to those who receive and observe, according to the Church's rule, the interpretation of the Scriptures explained by Him. And the Church's rule is the concord and harmony of the law and the prophets in the covenant delivered at the coming of the Lord.

Knowledge is then followed by practical wisdom, and practical wisdom by self-control. It may be said that practical wisdom is divine knowledge, and exists in those who are deified; but that self-control is mortal, and subsists in those who philosophize, and are not yet wise. But if virtue is divine, so is also the knowledge of it, while self-control is a sort of imperfect wisdom that aspires after wisdom, with laborious exertion, and is not contemplative. Human righteousness is a common thing, subordinate to holiness, which subsists through the divine righteousness; for the righteousness of the perfect man does not rest on civil contracts, or on the prohibition of law, but flows from his own spontaneous action and his love to God.

— ANF 2:507-509

A Hymn to Christ the Savior
Clement was a versatile writer, capable of high degrees of abstraction and sublime poetry. His poetry, in translation, is still found in hymnals today.

I.
Bridle of colts untamed,
Over our wills presiding;
Wing of unwandering birds,
Our flight securely guiding.
Rudder of youth unbending,
Firm against adverse shock;
Shepherd, with wisdom tending
Lambs of the royal flock:
Thy simple children bring
In one, that they may sing
In solemn lays
Their hymns of praise
With guileless lips to Christ their King.

II.
King of saints, almighty Word
Of the Father highest Lord;
Wisdom's head and chief;
Assuagement of all grief;
Lord of all time and space,
Jesus, Savior of our race;

Shepherd, who dost us keep;
Husbandman, who tillest,
Bit to restrain us, Rudder
To guide us as Thou willest;
Of the all-holy flock celestial wing;
Fisher of men, whom Thou to life dost bring;
From evil sea of sin,
And from the billowy strife,
Gathering pure fishes in
Caught with sweet bait of life:
Lead us, Shepherd of the sheep,
Reason-gifted, holy One;
King of youths, whom Thou dost keep,
So that they pollution shun:
Steps of Christ, celestial Way;
Word eternal, Age unending;
Life that never can decay;
Fount of mercy, virtue-sending;
Life august of those who raise
Unto God their hymn of praise,
Jesus Christ!

III.

Nourished by the milk of heaven,
To our tender palates given;
Milk of wisdom from the breast
Of that bride of grace exprest;
By a dewy spirit filled
From fair Reason's breast distilled;
Let us sucklings join to raise
With pure lips our hymns of praise
As our grateful offering,
Clean and pure, to Christ our King.
Let us, with hearts undefiled,
Celebrate the mighty Child.
We, Christ-born, the choir of peace;

We, the people of His love,
Let us sing, nor ever cease,
To the God of peace above.
— *ANF 2:295-296*

ORIGEN

Origen (185–254) lived with an intensity matched by few figures in history, and it drove him to most remarkable achievements.

The child of Christian parents, Origen was educated at home and at the famous school of Alexandria, receiving a comprehensive classical and Christian training. At seventeen, he lost his father to the persecution of the emperor Severus. Origen himself was spared only because his mother had hidden his clothing, so that he could not go outside to present himself to the authorities, as indeed he wanted to do. The example of his father remained with him all his life, in a burning desire for martyrdom.

With his father's arrest, the state confiscated the family's property, and Origen was forced to take up teaching to support his mother and many younger siblings. This he did masterfully, and he soon attracted many students. At age eighteen, he was appointed rector of the school of Alexandria, which was then the most prestigious Christian institute in the world.

Alexandria had, in the first century, been home to the great Jewish philosopher Philo, a Greek-speaking Platonist who interpreted the Old Testament allegorically. As Christianity arose in that city, Christian scholars took up the method of Philo and applied it to the Christian Scriptures, discerning both "literal" and "spiritual" senses. The spiritual sense was sometimes seen as operating on several levels; a text could simultaneously relate a historical event, foretell a truth about the Messiah, teach a moral lesson, and make a promise about heaven. Origen is usually credited with developing this method of scriptural interpretation into a science. Some scholars also number him among the first systematic theologians.

He excelled in many academic disciplines, but his greatest love was Scripture. He gave himself over to the most exacting, word-by-word study of the books of the Bible. He learned the original languages and brought together the first critical edition of the Bible, including six versions in parallel columns. He studied philology, history, philosophy, and physics, all so that he could apply these sciences to Holy Writ.

And he could teach. We know this from the surviving testimonies of his students. Origen gained such a reputation for pedagogy that the emperor's mother summoned him to tutor her, as did the Roman governor of Arabia and the bishops of Palestine. One of his students was a wealthy man who had been a heretic. Grateful to Origen for steering him right, he wished many more people the same grace, so he pledged to fund seven stenographers to serve Origen, along with seven copyists and several calligraphers. This remarkable secretarial pool helped to make Origen phenomenally productive. When all was said and done, Origen had, with the help of his stenographers, written more than six thousand books.

Being a pioneer in any field has its dangers, however; being first in speculative theology and the scientific study of Scripture is perhaps most perilous of all. Origen's speculations sometimes took him into uncharted waters, and he did not always sail as surely as those who came after him. Though he always sought to think and write only with the Church, subsequent generations would judge him to have fallen into serious error on several points.

Contrary to Church teaching that was only later expressed explicitly, he taught the Platonic doctrine that the soul existed before the creation of the body; and that all creatures, even Satan and the demons, would be restored in Christ at the end of time. Later Fathers would make an important distinction here: that, though Origen had taught error, he himself was not a heretic, because he had never wished to teach heresy; he had spoken his errors in ignorance.

Once, while he was in Palestine teaching the clergy there, the bishops got carried away with their enthusiasm and ordained him a priest. This infuriated his bishop back in Alexandria, who issued sharp and swift disciplinary actions; he called a synod that removed Origen from the priesthood and banished him from the Egyptian Church.

Origen responded by establishing a school in Caesarea, Palestine, where the bishops were friendlier to him. It was there that he taught many future bishops, future martyrs like St. Pamphilus, and future missionaries like St. Gregory the Wonderworker.

Origen spent his later years in frequent transit, partly because he was in demand as a teacher, and partly because he was hounded by envious clerics who charged him with all manner of infidelity. The situation was complicated by the most bizarre action of his life. Taking Matthew 19:12 far too literally — "There are eunuchs who have made themselves eunuchs for the sake of the kingdom of heaven" — Origen castrated himself. (He would surely have been better served by an allegorical reading.) Some priests rightly charged that such mutilation was a grave offense against the body; they even argued that the action invalidated Origen's ordination.

Taken prisoner during the persecution of the emperor Decius, Origen suffered the most excruciating tortures. From the effects of these, the good Christian whom Eusebius later called the "Man of Steel" died in 254, a martyr, as he had wished.

Origen worked with a singular passion. But his passion does not manifest itself in oratorical flourishes. He wrote many volumes of highly technical scholarship in careful though colorless prose. In style, he is most unlike the Fathers who were rhetoricians, Tertullian and St. Augustine, and more like that much later master-builder of theology, St. Thomas Aquinas. He will be more appreciated for his accomplishments — the breadth, depth, and volume of his writing — than read for entertainment.

TO A YOUNG CHRISTIAN INTELLECTUAL
In an affectionate letter, Origen offers advice to a star pupil, who would one day be canonized and deemed a Church Father, St. Gregory of Pontus, often called "the Wonderworker."

Greetings in God, my most excellent sir, and venerable son Gregory, from Origen…. Your natural good qualities might make you a finished Roman lawyer or a Greek philosopher of one of the schools in high reputation. But I am anxious that you should devote all the strength of your natural good qualities with Christianity as your goal; and so I wish to ask you to extract from Greek philosophy what may serve as a course of study or a preparation for Christianity, and from geometry and astronomy what will serve to explain the sacred Scriptures, so that all that the sons of the philosophers say about geometry and music, grammar, rhetoric, and astronomy, as fellow-helpers to philosophy, we may say about philosophy itself in relation to Christianity.

Perhaps something of this kind is foreshadowed in what is written in Exodus. From the mouth of God, the children of Israel were commanded to ask from their neighbors, and those who dwelt with them, vessels of silver and gold, and raiment, in order that, by depriving the Egyptians, they might have material to fashion things pertaining to the service of God. For from all the things the children of Israel took from the Egyptians, the vessels in the holy of holies were made — the ark with its lid, and the cherubim, and the mercy seat, and the golden coffer, where was the manna, the angels' bread. These things were probably made from the best of the Egyptian gold....

My son, diligently apply yourself to the reading of the sacred Scriptures. Apply yourself, I say. For we who read the things of God need much application, lest we should say or think anything too rashly about them. And applying yourself thus to the study of the things of God, with faithful prejudgments that are well pleasing to God, knock at its locked door, and it will be opened to you by the porter, of whom Jesus says, "To him the gatekeeper opens" (Jn 10:3). And applying yourself thus to the divine study, seek aright, and with unwavering trust in God, the meaning of the holy Scriptures, which so many have missed. Do not be satisfied with knocking and seeking; for prayer is of all things indispensable to the knowledge of the things of God. For to this the Savior exhorted, and said not only, "Knock, and it will be opened to you" and Seek, and you shall find," but also, "Ask, and it will be given you" (Mt 7:7).

My fatherly love to you has made me bold; but whether my boldness be good, God will know, and His Christ, and all partakers of the Spirit of God and the Spirit of Christ. May you also be a partaker, and be ever increasing your inheritance, that you may say not only, "for we share in Christ" (Heb 3:14), but also in God.

— ANF 9:295-296

THE SENSES OF SCRIPTURE

In his work On First Principles, *Origen set out his method for discerning the "senses" of Scripture — both the literal-historical sense and the spiritual (or mystical) sense. In later writers, like St. John Cassian, this interpretive method would be fleshed out as Scripture's "fourfold sense," including the literal, allegorical, moral, and anagogical senses.*

Having spoken briefly on the divine inspiration of the holy Scriptures, it is necessary to proceed to the manner in which they should be read and understood. Many fall into error because they have not discovered the method by which the holy documents ought to be examined. For both the hardened in heart and the ignorant persons who belong to the circumcision have not believed in our Savior, thinking that they are following the *language* of the prophecies respecting Him, and not perceiving in a manner *palpable to their senses* that He had proclaimed liberty to the captives, nor that He had built up what they truly consider the city of God, nor cut off the chariots of Ephraim, and the horse from Jerusalem, nor eaten butter and honey, and before knowing or preferring the evil, had selected the good. Thinking, moreover, that it was prophesied that the wolf — the four-footed animal — was to feed with the lamb, and the leopard to lie down with the kid, and the calf and bull and lion to feed together, being led by a little child ... and seeing none of these things visibly accomplished during the advent of Him who is believed by us to be Christ, they did not accept our Lord Jesus. Instead, believing that He called himself Christ improperly, they crucified Him....

Now the cause, in all these points listed, of the false opinions, and of the impious statements or ignorant assertions about God, appears to be nothing more than the lack of understanding of the Scripture according to its *spiritual* meaning, favoring instead its merely *literal* interpretation....

Now, everyone — even the most simple of those who adhere to the word — believes that there are certain mystical economies made known by holy Scripture. But honest and modest individuals confess that they do not know what these are. If, then, one were to be perplexed about the intercourse of Lot with his daughters, and about the two wives of Abraham, and the two sisters married to Jacob, and the two handmaids who bore him children, they can return no other answer than this: that these are mysteries we do not understand. Also, when they read the description of the construction of the tabernacle, they believe that what is written is a prototype and seek to adapt what they can to each particular related about the tabernacle. Now, they are not wrong in believing that the tabernacle is a type of something, but they err sometimes as they seek to apply the description ... to some special thing in a manner worthy of Scripture....

We consider the following to be the way that seems correct for the understanding of Scriptures and for the investigation of their meaning.... In the Proverbs of Solomon we find the following rule laid down for consideration of holy Scripture: "Describe these things to yourself in a threefold manner, in counsel and knowledge, that you may show what is right and true, that you may give a true answer to those who sent you" (cf. Prov 22:20-21).

Each one, then, ought to describe in his own mind, in a threefold manner, the understanding of the divine words:

—First, by the very *body* of Scripture, or what we would call that *common* and *historical* sense, so that all the more simple individuals may be edified.

—If some have begun to make considerable progress, and are able to see something more, they may be edified by the very *soul* of Scripture.

—Finally, those who are mature — who resemble those of whom the Apostle says, "among the mature we do impart wisdom, although it is not a wisdom of this age or of the rulers of this age, who are doomed to pass away. But we impart a secret and hidden wisdom of God, which God decreed before the ages for our glorification" (1 Cor 2:6-7). These may be edified by the spiritual law itself, which has a shadow of good things to come, as if by the Spirit.

As man is said to consist of *body, soul,* and *spirit,* so also does sacred Scripture, which has been granted by the divine bounty for the salvation of man....

— ANF 4:355-356, 359

A SNIPPET OF ALLEGORY
Origen sometimes finds the literal reading of the Gospels problematic, as when Jesus violently drives the moneychangers from the Jerusalem Temple. And so he finds many allegorical and symbolic ways to understand the event. This is one of many he offers in his Commentary on John.

The natural temple is the soul skilled in reason. Because of its inborn reason, it is higher than the body, to which Jesus ascends from Capernaum, the lower-lying place of less dignity. There, before Jesus' discipline is applied to it, are found earthly, senseless, and dangerous tendencies — things that have the name but not the reality of beauty — things that are driven away by Jesus with His word plaited out of doctrines of demonstration and rebuke. All this takes place so that His Father's house may no longer be a house of merchandise but may receive, for its own salvation and that of others, the service of God performed according to heavenly and spiritual laws. The ox is symbolic of earthly things, for he is a husbandman. The sheep, of senseless and brutal things, because it is more servile than most of the creatures without reason. The dove is a symbol of empty and unstable thoughts. The small change is a symbol of things that are thought good but are not.

— ANF 9:394

WHEN IT'S TOUGH TO READ THE BIBLE
Even the third century's most brilliant Scripture scholar knew that Bible reading can sometimes be arduous. He offered advice for just such occasions. This passage was preserved by Sts. Basil and Gregory in their anthology, The Philocalia of Origen, *translated by George Lewis (Edinburgh: T. & T. Clark, 1911), page 156.*

If any of you have ever seen an asp or some other venomous creature under the spell of the charmer, I would have you take that as an illustration of the Scripture. If it is read and not understood, the hearer sometimes grows listless and weary. Yet let him believe that the asps and vipers within him are weakened through the charms of the charmers — that is to say, by wise Moses, wise Joshua, the wise and holy prophets.

Let us not grow weary when we hear Scriptures that we do not understand; but let it be unto us according to our faith (see Mt 9:29), by which we believe that all Scripture is inspired by God and profitable (see 2 Tim 3:16). For you must admit one of two things about these Scriptures: either they are not inspired because they are not profitable, as an unbeliever might suppose; or, as a believer, you must allow that because they are inspired they are profitable.

We must, however, know that we often profit without perceiving it. This happens, for example, when we go on a special diet to improve our eyesight. We do not, while we are eating, notice that our eyesight is getting better, but after two or three days, when the beneficial food is assimilated, experience convinces us of the fact. And the same remark applies to other foods that benefit other parts of the body.

Well, then, have the same faith with regard to divine Scripture. Believe that your soul profits from the mere reading, even though your understanding does not receive the fruit of profiting from these passages. Our inner nature is charmed; its better elements are nourished; the worse are weakened and brought to nothing.

St. Gregory of Pontus: On Origen, My Teacher
At the end of his school days in Caesarea, Gregory paid tribute to his most influential tutor.

How shall I give account of what he did for us, in instructing us in theology and devout character? And how shall I enter into the real disposition of the man, and show with what judiciousness and careful preparation he would have us familiarized with all discourse about the Divinity, guarding us sedulously against any peril with respect to what is the most necessary thing — namely, the knowledge of the Cause of all things?

For he deemed it right for us to study philosophy this way: that we should read with utmost diligence all that has been written, both by the philosophers and by the poets of old, rejecting nothing, and repudiating nothing (for, indeed, we did not yet possess the power of critical discernment), except only the productions of the atheists, who, in their conceits, lapse from the general intelligence of man and deny that there is either a God or a providence. From these he would have us abstain, because they are not worthy of being read, and because the soul within us, which is meant for piety, might be defiled by listening to words contrary to the worship of God....

He did not introduce us to any one exclusive school of philosophy; nor did he judge it proper for us to go away with any single class of philosophical opinions, but he introduced us to all, and determined that we should be ignorant of no kind of Grecian doctrine. And he himself went on with us, preparing the way before us, and leading us by the hand, as if on a journey, whenever anything tortuous and unsound and delusive came in our way. And he helped us like a skilled expert who has had long familiarity with such subjects.... Thus did he deal with us, selecting and setting before us all that was useful and true in all the various philosophers, and putting aside all that was false. And this he did for us, both in other branches of man's knowledge, and most especially in all that concerns piety.

— ANF 6:33-36

———————————ST. DIONYSIUS THE GREAT———————————

It seems there were no slow-news days in Alexandria during the years when Dionysius was bishop (248–265). Egypt's Christians endured repeated eruptions of mob violence against believers; a bloody civil war; plague; doctrinal disputes about the Trinity and the sacraments; a schism, which had begun in Rome and threatened to rend the Church in two; and brutal persecution under the emperors Valerian and Decius. The bishop himself was abducted, exiled, rescued, restored, denounced, vindicated, and ultimately venerated.

Dionysius had converted to Christianity when he was young. He became a student of Origen at Alexandria's famed catechetical school. Some say he was Origen's most gifted pupil. A voracious reader, he had, according to his own account, received from the Lord a supernatural gift for discerning true doctrine. He read everything he could lay hands on, whether the author was orthodox or heretical, and he became an expert in the refutation of error.

When Origen was expelled, Heraclas assumed the leadership of the school. Later, when Heraclas was chosen as bishop of Alexandria, he entrusted the school to Dionysius.

In time, Dionysius was himself appointed bishop, and even then it seems he continued to teach at the school. He produced many theological and spiritual tracts to shore up the faithful in trying times, but only a few of his letters have survived, along with fragments of his longer works. (Most of these are preserved in Eusebius's *Church History*.) Early in life, Dionysius published a refutation of current materialist philosophies. He wrote a tract on temptation. He also produced biblical commentaries.

He was best known, however, as a pastor of souls. Dionysius guided his people through a succession of crises, and sometimes many crises simultaneously. He recognized, moreover, the prominence and influence of the Church of Alexandria, and so he played an active role in the wider Catholic Church. He corresponded with bishops from all over the map.

At the time there were heated debates over how — or even if — the Church should reconcile members who had committed apostasy under torture. There were deep disagreements, too, about whether the Church should recognize the validity of baptism performed by heretics — or just have converted heretics rebaptized. In Dionysius's own orbit, there was serious dissension even about the doctrine of God.

As a bishop, he had to contend with "modalist" heresies: those that sought to preserve God's unity by saying He merely operated in three different modes. He also confronted heretics on the opposite end of the spectrum: those who sought to preserve God's monarchy by declaring the Son and Holy Spirit to be creatures.

Dionysius's own Trinitarian theology was called into question on one occasion. His adversaries accused him, before the pope in Rome, of subordinationism. So much did Dionysius respect the pope that he immediately penned a lengthy response in two parts: a refutation of his opponents, and a defense of his own orthodoxy. A half-century later, St. Athanasius the Great told the story in detail in a work titled *On the Opinion of Dionysius.*

Dionysius' respect for the Roman pontiff shines through in another letter, this one to Novatian, a heretic and a pretender to the papal throne. Novatian had written to Dionysius asking for his support. The Alexandrian replied with a firm but heartfelt plea for Novatian's repentance.

> Dionysius to Novatian, a brother: greetings.
>
> If it was against your will, as you say, that you were promoted, you should prove this by retiring of your own accord. It is good to suffer anything and everything to avoid dividing the Church of God. And martyrdom to avoid schism is no less glorious than martyrdom to avoid idolatry. No, it is to my mind greater! In one case a man is a martyr for his own single soul's sake. But this is for the whole Church.
>
> Even now if you should persuade or constrain the brethren to come to one mind, your true deed would be greater than your fall. The fall will not be reckoned to you; the other deed will be praised. And if you should be powerless to sway disobedient spirits, save, save your own soul.
>
> I pray for your health and your steadfast cleaving to peace in the Lord.[65]

Dionysius endured a long exile during the persecution of Valerian, but eventually was able to return to his see in relatively peaceful times. Though he died in his bed, his contemporaries counted him a martyr because of all he had suffered. From antiquity he has been called by the honorific "the Great."

THE CHRISTIAN DIFFERENCE

In Church History *7.22, Eusebius preserves a letter of Dionysius dramatically recounting the Alexandrian Christians' heroic behavior in times of plague.*

To other men the present might not seem to be a suitable time for a festival. Nor indeed is this or any other time suitable for them; neither sorrowful times, nor even such as might be thought especially cheerful. Now, indeed, everything is tears and everyone is mourning, and wailings resound daily through the city because of the multitude of the dead and dying. As it was written of the firstborn of the Egyptians, so now again there has been "a great cry in Egypt, for there was not a house where one was not dead" (Exodus 12:30). And if only that was all!

For many terrible things have happened already. First, they drove us out; and when we were alone and persecuted and put to death by all, even then we kept the feast. And every place of affliction was for us a place of festival: field, desert, ship, inn, prison; but the perfected martyrs kept the most joyous festival of all, feasting in heaven.

After these things war and famine followed, which we endured in common with the heathen. But we bore alone those things with which they afflicted us, and at the same time we experienced also the effects of what they inflicted upon and suffered from one another; and again, we rejoiced in the peace of Christ, which he gave to us alone.

But after both we and they had enjoyed a very brief season of rest, this pestilence assailed us — to them more dreadful than any dread, and more intolerable than any other calamity. One of their own writers has called it the only thing that prevails over all hope. To us this was not so, but no less than the other things was it an exercise and probation. For it did not keep aloof even from us, but the heathen it assailed more severely....

Most of our brethren were unsparing in their exceeding love and brotherly kindness. They held fast to each other and visited the sick fearlessly, and ministered to them continually, serving them in Christ. And they died with them most joyfully, taking the affliction of others, and drawing the sickness from their neighbors to themselves, and willingly receiving their pains. And many who cared for the sick and gave strength to others died themselves, having transferred to themselves their death.... Truly the best of our brethren departed from life in this manner, including some priests and deacons and those of the people who had the highest reputation; so that this form of death, through the great piety and strong faith it exhibited, seemed to lack nothing of martyrdom.

And they took the bodies of the saints in their open hands and to their breast, and closed their eyes and their mouths; and they bore them away on their shoulders and laid them out; and they clung to them and embraced them; and they prepared them suitably with washings and garments. And after a little they received like treatment themselves, for the survivors were continually following those who had gone before them.

But with the heathen everything was quite otherwise. They deserted those who began to be sick, and fled from their dearest friends. And they cast them out into the streets when they were half dead, and left the dead like refuse, unburied. They shunned any participation or fellowship with death; which yet, with all their precautions, it was not easy for them to escape.

—NPNF2 1:306-307

THE COURAGE OF THE MARTYRS

Dionysius also recounted the heroism of contemporary martyrs, victims of mob violence in and near Alexandria. This portion of a letter to Fabius, bishop of Antioch, is preserved in Eusebius's History *6.41.*

The persecution among us did not begin with the royal decree, but preceded it by an entire year. The prophet and author of evils to this city, whoever he was, previously moved and aroused against us the masses of the heathen, rekindling among them the superstition of their country. And being thus excited by him and finding full opportunity for any wickedness, they considered this the only pious service of their demons, that they should slay us.

They seized first an old man named Metras, and commanded him to utter impious words. But as he would not obey, they beat him with clubs, and tore his face and eyes with sharp sticks, and dragged him out of the city and stoned him.

Then they carried to their idol temple a faithful woman named Quinta, so that they might force her to worship. And as she turned away in detestation, they bound her feet and dragged her through the entire city over the stone-paved streets, and dashed her against the millstones, and at the same time scourged her; then, taking her to the same place, they stoned her to death.

Then all with one impulse rushed to the homes of the pious, and they dragged forth whomsoever any one knew as a neighbor, and robbed and plundered them. They took for themselves the more valuable property; but the poorer articles and those made of wood they scattered about and burned in the streets, so that the city appeared as if taken by an enemy.

But the brethren withdrew and went away, and joyfully accepted the plundering of their property, like those to whom Paul bore witness (see Hebrews 10:34). I know of no one unless possibly someone who fell into their hands, who, up to this time, denied the Lord …

Then they seized Serapion in his own house, and tortured him with harsh cruelties, and having broken all his limbs, they threw him headlong from an upper story. And there was no street, nor public road, nor lane open to us, by night or day; for always and everywhere, all of them cried out that if any one would not repeat their impious words, he should immediately be dragged away and burned.

And matters continued thus for a considerable time. But a sedition and civil war came upon the wretched people and turned their cruelty toward us against one another. So we breathed for a little while as they ceased from their rage against us.

—NPNF2 1:283

ST. METHODIUS OF OLYMPUS

What we know of Methodius we know from his published works and from the fact of his martyrdom. He holds a special place in history, however, because he launched the first sustained and disciplined critique of Christianity's gigantic intellectual figure of that period: Origen. The movement Methodius began at the end of the third century would gain momentum in the fourth — and become immensely important at the beginning of the fifth century.

Early in life, Methodius was an avid reader of Origen. Like his master, he drew inspiration from the philosophical works of Plato, and he shared Origen's fondness for allegorical interpretation of Scripture.

At some point, however, he parted intellectual company with Origen's books and launched a major critique of the Alexandrian's more speculative notions: the pre-existence of the soul, for example, the eternity of matter, and the purely spiritual nature of the resurrected body. Against these hypotheses of Origen, Methodius staked what would be accepted as the orthodox doctrine: that the human being is created, composite of body and soul, in the womb of his or her mother; that matter is created out of nothing; and that the resurrected body will be glorified and perfected, but still identical with the physical, earthly body.

Probably because of his vehement rejection of Origen, Methodius is ignored in the most exhaustive account of the writers of his time, the *Church History* of the bishop-historian Eusebius. (Eusebius was a devoted disciple of Origen's Palestinian pupil and successor, Pamphilus.) Thus we know little about Methodius's activity, apart from a few writings and fragments that have survived, and his brief entry in Jerome's biographical encyclopedia.

Jerome confirms for us that Methodius was bishop of Olympus in Lycia. He adds that he was later bishop of Tyre, though that detail is confirmed nowhere else in the ancient records and is contested by historians. He wrote scriptural commentaries, a refutation of the anti-Christian Platonist philosopher Porphyry, and philosophical dialogues in imitation of Plato. His most famous dialogue is *The Banquet*, a discussion of consecrated virginity and the ascetical life. Methodius celebrates the virginal life offered to God, yet sees it in the context of all the ways God blesses. He compares the Church "to a flower-covered and variegated meadow, adorned and crowned not only with the flowers of virginity, but also with those of child-bearing" (*The Banquet* 2.7).

Methodius died a martyr in the last, most savage persecution, that of Diocletian, around 311.

THE CHURCH PREFIGURED AND FULFILLED
In his dialogue The Banquet, *Methodius writes this allegorical flight in the voice of a virgin named Thallousa. She presents the Church as an intermediate stage between the shadows of the Old Law and the realities of heaven.*

If the law, according to the Apostle, is spiritual, containing the image "of the good things to come" (Hebrews 10:1), then let us strip off the veil of the letter which is spread over it, and consider its naked and true meaning.

The Hebrews were commanded to decorate the Tabernacle as a type of the Church, that they might be able, by means of sensible things, to announce beforehand the image of divine things. For Moses was shown a pattern on the Mount (see Exodus 25:40), and he was to use this in fashioning the Tabernacle. It was an accurate representation of the heavenly dwelling, which we now perceive more clearly than through types, yet more darkly than if we saw the reality. For not yet, in our present condition, has the truth arrived unmixed. While here, we are unable to bear the sight of pure immortality, just as we cannot bear to look upon the rays of the sun.

The Jews declared that the shadow of the image (of the heavenly things which was given to them) was the third step from the reality. But we clearly behold the image of the heavenly order; for the truth will be accurately made manifest after the resurrection, when we shall see the heavenly tabernacle — the city in heaven "whose builder and maker is God" (Hebrews 11:10) — "face to face," and not "dimly" and "in part" (1 Corinthians 13:12).

The Jews prophesied our state, but we foretell the heavenly, since the Tabernacle was a symbol of the Church, and the Church a symbol of heaven. Therefore, since the Tabernacle is a type of the Church, as I said, it is fitting that the altars should signify some of the things in the Church. And we have already compared the brazen altar to the company and order of widows; for they are a living altar of God, to which they bring calves and tithes, and free-will offerings, as a sacrifice to the Lord.

But the golden altar within the Holy of Holies, before the presence of the testimony, on which it is forbidden to offer sacrifice and libation, has reference to those in a state of virginity. They have their bodies preserved pure, like unalloyed gold, from bodily intercourse. Now, gold is commended for two reasons: first, because it does not rust; and second, because in its color it seems to resemble the rays of the sun; and thus it is suitably a symbol of virginity, which does not admit any stain or spot, but ever shines forth with the light of the Word.

Therefore, also, it stands nearer to God within the Holy of Holies, and before the veil, with undefiled hands, like incense, offering up prayers to the Lord, acceptable as a sweet aroma; as also John indicated, saying that the incense in the vials of the twenty-four elders were the prayers of the saints.

This, then, I offer to you, O Arete, on the spur of the moment, according to my ability, on the subject of chastity.

— *ANF 6:28*

LACTANTIUS

Born around A.D. 250 and raised in a pagan family in North Africa, Lactantius studied rhetoric under Arnobius of Sicca. This respected professor converted to Christianity late in life, and this event may eventually have exercised an influence on his gifted student.

So gifted was Lactantius that he was invited, by the Emperor Diocletian himself, to become professor of Latin rhetoric in Nicomedia, which was then the newly declared capital of the eastern empire. He took the job, which gave him access to very powerful circles, though it earned him little money. As a Latin professor in a Greek city, he attracted few students, so he turned instead to writing. When he converted to Christianity, in the earliest years of the fourth century, he resigned from his official post.

His timing was fortuitous. Soon afterward, Diocletian purged all Christians from his direct employment, blaming them for angering the gods when they made the Sign of the Cross during a session of divination at the imperial court. Things got very bad, very quickly.

Diocletian promulgated his "Edict Against the Christians" early in 303, and so began the most bloody of the Roman persecutions.

Lactantius eluded capture, but suffered extreme poverty as a result of this turn of events. He took to writing Christian apologetic works, earnestly trying to overcome the prejudice of the Roman establishment, presenting Christianity as a reasonable philosophy and a sound source of morality. While the persecution raged, he composed his book *On the Works of God*.

His most famous work, the *Divine Institutes*, was begun during the persecution, but completed under the peace of Constantine. It is a positive exposition of basic Christian doctrines in their most elementary form, like a catechism. He would later publish an abridged version that was easier to master.

Renowned for his beautiful Latin style, Lactantius was called "the Christian Cicero." Rhetoricians studied and imitated his work for a millennium and more. His theology, however, is often dismissed as crude, ill-informed, and shallow.

He survived the last persecution and was able to preserve an invaluable record of the beginning of the ruthless slaughter. His is an insider's view, and it presents details that would otherwise be unknown. His historical work, *Of the Deaths of the Persecutors* — an extended indulgence of righteous schadenfreude — dwells mostly on the events that took place during his own lifetime, events he sets down with breathtaking drama.

In old age, he achieved a measure of fame. He was a hero of the age of persecution, an intellectual who bridged two worlds and two eras. Constantine, on becoming emperor, summoned Lactantius to be tutor to his teenage son, Crispus. It is then that history loses track of him.

Many of his works have survived and been translated. Several long poems have been attributed to him, and two of these are almost certainly genuine. His long allegorical poem *The Phoenix*, on the mythical bird, was influential on Christian art and literature down the ages.

Just Deserts

In his history Of the Deaths of the Persecutors, *Lactantius described the divine vengeance in gory detail. Most of the work is devoted to very recent events, of which he was a witness. The (more manageable) excerpts included here recount the horrible ends of the previous generation's villains, Decius and Valerian.*

The Lord has heard those supplications which you, my most beloved Donatus, pour forth in his presence all the day long, and the supplications of the rest of our brethren, who by a glorious confession have obtained an everlasting crown, the reward of their faith…. Those who insulted the Divinity lie low. Those who cast down the holy temple are fallen with more tremendous ruin. The tormentors of the just have poured out their guilty souls amidst plagues inflicted by heaven, and amidst deserved tortures. For God delayed to punish them, that, by great and marvelous examples, he might teach posterity that He alone is God, and that with fit vengeance He executes judgment on the proud, the impious, and the persecutors.

Of the end of those men I have thought good to publish a narrative, that all who are afar off, and all who shall arise hereafter, may learn how the Almighty manifested His power and sovereign greatness in rooting out and utterly destroying the enemies of His name. And this will become evident, when I relate who were the persecutors of the Church from the time of its first constitution, and what were the punishments by which the divine Judge, in his severity, took vengeance on them….

Decius appeared in the world, an accursed wild beast, to afflict the Church — and who but a bad man would persecute religion? It seems as if he had been raised to sovereign eminence, at once to rage against God, and at once to fall; for, having undertaken an expedition against the Carpi, who had then taken possession of Dacia and Moefia, he was suddenly surrounded by the barbarians, and slain, together with great part of his army; nor could he be honored with the funeral rites, but, stripped and naked, he lay to be devoured by wild beasts and birds — a fit end for the enemy of God.

And then Valerian, in a mood just as frantic, lifted up his impious hands to assault God, and, although his time was short, shed much righteous blood. But God punished him in a new and extraordinary manner, that it might be a lesson to future ages that the adversaries of heaven always receive the just recompense of their iniquities. Having been made prisoner by the Persians, he lost not only that power which he had exercised without moderation, but also the liberty of which he had deprived others; and he wasted the remainder of his days in the vilest condition of slavery.

Shapur, the king of the Persians, kept him prisoner; and whenever the king chose to get into his chariot or to mount on horseback, he commanded the Roman to stoop and present his back. Then, setting his foot on Valerian's shoulders, he said, with a smile of reproach, "This is the truth, and not what the Romans paint on canvas or plaster."

Valerian lived for a considerable time under the well-merited insults of his conqueror, and the Roman name remained long a joke and a laugh for the barbarians. And this also was added to the severity of his punishment, that although he had an emperor for his son, he found no one to avenge his captivity and most abject and servile state. In fact, he was never even demanded back.

Afterward, when he had finished this shameful life under such great dishonor, he was flayed, and his skin, stripped from the flesh, was dyed with vermilion, and placed in the temple of the gods of the barbarians, that the remembrance of a triumph so signal might last forever. This spectacle would always be exhibited as a warning to Roman ambassadors. Seeing the spoils of their captive emperor in a Persian temple, they should not place too great confidence in their own strength.

Since God so punished the sacrilegious, is it not strange that anyone should afterward have dared to do, or even to devise, anything against the majesty of the one God, who governs and supports all things?

— ANF 7:301-303

THE FOURTH CENTURY

The Golden Age of Doctrine

In retrospect, we call the Nicene Era, the fourth Christian century, a "golden age."

We look back at a time of great teachers. It was then that St. Athanasius gave our Trinitarian faith its definitive expression. The same saint also created something of a sensation by writing a biography of St. Anthony of Egypt and inspiring thousands of men and women to flee the world and become hermits, monks, and nuns. In Cappadocia, the great bishop St. Basil directed rich development in monasticism, liturgy, theology, and charitable work. The fourth century was the time of the great Church historian Eusebius, and of the great catechetical bishops, St. Cyril of Jerusalem, St. Ambrose of Milan, and St. Gregory of Nyssa.

Two events precipitated this cultural flowering of Christianity. They were, we might say, some good news and some bad news. First came the long-awaited peace with the Roman Empire. The third century had ended with the persecution launched by the emperor Diocletian, perhaps the cruelest and bloodiest of all. Yet Christianity continued to grow, unabated, in spite of dungeon, fire, and sword. In fact, the Church seemed to grow most quickly when it was persecuted most ruthlessly. Tertullian, it seems, was right to say that "the blood of Christians is seed." In 311, the empire attempted yet another persecution, but the futility of the project was soon apparent. In 313, the new emperor, Constantine, whose mother was Christian, issued his Edict of Milan, which decreed universal toleration of Christianity.

Peace had come, but it would not last. In 318, Arius of Alexandria began to preach his heresy — that Jesus was not truly divine or co-eternal — and soon Arianism was sweeping the Church. With an alarming suddenness, Arius won over a great number of bishops, theologians, and imperial officials. As St. Jerome wrote, "The world awoke with a groan to find itself Arian."[66]

It was this controversy, which involved the core Christian doctrines of the Trinity and the Incarnation, that forced the fourth century to be a golden age. There was no alternative. The only way the Church could counter the eloquence and apparent reasonableness of Arius was with more eloquent, more reasonable, and most important, more holy men.

The Arian heresy would fuel further heresies, both spin-offs and overcorrections, for another three centuries or more. But, from the Council of Nicaea in 325 onward, the Church spoke clearly and consistently against the Christological errors.

Meanwhile, as Church and state embraced in concord, a new set of questions arose, regarding which things rightly belong to Caesar, and which to God and His vicars.

EUSEBIUS OF CAESAREA

Eusebius of Caesarea (263–340) is one of those historical oddities: a historian who made history. His most famous work, the *Church History*, shaped the way Christians would look at the past for centuries to come. More, Eusebius put forth a compelling vision of the future at a time of tremendous upheaval in both Church and state.

Eusebius received his early training in Caesarea, Palestine, from St. Pamphilus, a disciple of Origen and eventually a martyr. Eusebius himself was hunted down and jailed for his faith during one of the last gasps of Roman imperial persecution. In the same year that the emperor Constantine declared a lasting peace for Christians, the Church of Caesarea elected Eusebius as its bishop.

Having suffered for the faith, Eusebius saw Constantine's decree of toleration as a singular grace. It inspired in him a vision of an integrated Church and state, working together to bring about the kingdom of God on earth. To Eusebius, Constantine and the Roman Empire were nothing less than the chosen instruments of Providence.

Eusebius spoke of Constantine as "our divinely favored emperor," who directs "in imitation of God Himself, the world's affairs." Eusebius saw the emperor as an icon of God the Father and Christ the King. In an oration in praise of Constantine, he said this explicitly. The idea is implicit throughout his historical works, which emphasize events that prepared the way for the Christianization of the empire.

With his history, Eusebius managed to produce a voluminous and comprehensive record of the ancient Church. He preserved thousands of texts that would otherwise have been completely lost.

Yet, while the Church made peace with its longtime enemy outside, a new enemy arose within: the heresy of Arianism.

Arius, like Eusebius, was a historical oddity. A priest of the Church of Alexandria, he had been trained in the rival school of Antioch, which emphasized a literal reading of Scripture. Arius's literalism tended toward rationalism. He saw no way that the Divine Word could proceed from the Father yet still be co-eternal. So he proposed that Jesus was merely a creature, as was the Holy Spirit, though both were created to be semidivine, the greatest of God's creatures. Arius's heresy very quickly won an astonishingly large portion of the Church's intelligentsia, clergy, and bishops. Those who upheld the orthodox position were almost relegated to a faction in the Church. The situation threatened not only the newfound peace of the Church, but even the peace of the empire, a majority of whose population was, by this time, Christian.

Eusebius was heartsick to see the Church polarized this way. The emperor, for his part, was anxious to restore order before the controversy sparked a civil war. Constantine called a council at Nicaea (in what is now Turkey) to discern the correct teaching on the Trinity and the Incarnation. As a bishop, Eusebius would take an active part in the council's proceedings.

Eusebius saw good intentions on both sides, and he doubted that any one side could triumph peaceably over the other. Yet he desired peace. Rejecting both the explicitly "subordinationist" language of the Arian party and the explicitly "co-equal and co-eternal" language of St. Athanasius, he proposed common ground: a statement that was biblical, but sufficiently vague as to satisfy both parties.

The Council of Nicaea rejected the Eusebian compromise in favor of St. Athanasius's formulation: that Jesus was "one in being with the Father." Eusebius accepted the council's conclusions because the emperor Constantine had approved them.

Yet he was not satisfied, and he spent the following years assisting in the efforts to persecute St. Athanasius. In 335, he played a leading role in the Synod of Tyre, which excommunicated Athanasius. This time, the Father of Church History failed to read the signs of the times. History gives Eusebius mixed reviews.

IN PRAISE OF CONSTANTINE
Eusebius delivered a long tribute to Constantine on the thirtieth anniversary of the beginning of his reign. This is a brief excerpt.

Today is the festival of our great emperor: and we his children rejoice, feeling the inspiration of our sacred theme. He who presides over our solemnity is the Great Sovereign Himself; He, I mean, who is truly great.... I remember that our own victorious emperor renders praises to this Mighty Sovereign. I do well to follow [Constantine], knowing as I do that to Him alone we owe that imperial power under which we live. The pious Caesars, instructed by their Father's wisdom, acknowledge Him as the source of every blessing: the soldiery, the entire body of the people, both in the country and in the cities of the empire, with the governors of the several provinces, assembling together in accordance with the precept of their great Savior and Teacher, worship Him. In short, the whole family of mankind, of every nation, tribe, and tongue, both collectively and severally, however diverse their opinions on other subjects, are unanimous in this one confession; and, in obedience to the reason implanted in them, and the spontaneous and uninstructed impulse of their own minds, unite in calling on the One and only God.

This only-begotten Word of God reigns, from ages that had no beginning to infinite and endless ages, the partner of His Father's kingdom. And our emperor, ever beloved by Him, who derives the source of imperial authority from above, and is strong in the power of his sacred title, has controlled the empire of the world for a long period of years. Again, that Preserver of the universe orders these heavens and earth, and the celestial kingdom, consistently with His Father's will. Even so our emperor whom He loves, by bringing those whom he

rules on earth to the only-begotten Word and Savior, renders them fit
subjects of His kingdom....

— NPNF2 1:582-583

ON CHURCH HISTORY

*Eusebius's most valuable contribution to posterity is his Church history.
This passage serves as something of a mission statement for that great work.*

It is my purpose to write an account of the successions of the
holy Apostles, as well as of the times that have elapsed from the days
of our Savior to our own; and to relate the many important events
that are said to have occurred in the history of the Church; and to
mention those who have governed and presided over the Church in
the most prominent parishes, and those who in each generation have
proclaimed the divine word either orally or in writing. It is my purpose
also to give the names and number and times of those who, through
love of innovation, have run into the greatest errors and, proclaiming
themselves discoverers of knowledge falsely so-called (see 1 Tim 6:20),
have like fierce wolves unmercifully devastated the flock of Christ.

It is my intention, moreover, to recount the misfortunes that
immediately came upon the whole Jewish nation in consequence of
their plots against our Savior, and to record the ways and the times
in which the divine word has been attacked by the Gentiles, and to
describe the character of those who at various periods have contended
for it in the face of blood and of tortures, as well as the confessions that
have been made in our own days, and finally the gracious and kindly
consolation that our Savior has given them all. Since I propose to write
of all these things, I shall begin my work with the beginning of the
dispensation of our Savior and Lord Jesus Christ.

But at the outset I must crave for my work the indulgence of the
wise, for I confess that it is beyond my power to produce a perfect and
complete history, and since I am the first to enter upon the subject, I
am attempting to traverse a lonely and untrodden path. I pray that I
may have God as my guide and the power of the Lord as my aid, since
I am unable to find even the bare footsteps of those who have traveled
the way before me, except in brief fragments, in which some in one

way, others in another, have transmitted to us particular accounts of the times in which they lived. From afar they raise their voices like torches, and they cry out, as from some lofty and conspicuous watchtower, admonishing us where to walk and how to direct the course of our work steadily and safely.

Having gathered therefore from the matters mentioned here and there by them whatever we consider important for the present work, and having plucked like flowers from a meadow the appropriate passages from ancient writers, we shall endeavor to embody the whole in a historical narrative, content if we preserve the memory of the successions of the Apostles of our Savior; if not indeed of all, yet of the most renowned of them in those churches which are the most noted, and which even to the present time are held in honor.

This work seems to me of special importance because I know of no ecclesiastical writer who has devoted himself to this subject; and I hope that it will appear most useful to those who are fond of historical research.

— NPNF2 1:81-82

ST. ATHANASIUS

You can tell a lot about a Father by the enemies he took on. During much of his lifetime, St. Athanasius (297–373) was known throughout the world primarily as the opponent of the arch heretic Arius.

For this opposition, he suffered exile five times (for six years, he hid among the monks of the Egyptian desert), he was castigated by bishops and emperors, and he was a constant (though elusive) target for would-be assassins.

For St. Athanasius, the Arian heresy was an urgent, professional, and personal matter. Arius (256–336) was a senior priest of Alexandria, the same diocese as Athanasius. According to most accounts, Arius was a man of apparent piety and great outward asceticism. He had studied abroad, at the renowned school of Antioch, and displayed far more eloquence and intellectual subtlety than his bishop, Alexander.

Arius held Bishop Alexander in contempt. He probably also had little use for the allegorical teachings of the school of Alexandria, which, to a proud alumnus of Antioch, must have seemed like so much mystical claptrap. One day, while listening to Bishop Alexander expound on the Trinity, Arius could stand it no more. He stood up and denounced his bishop's teaching as heresy.

Arius had his own ideas about the Trinity, which he saw as far superior to his bishop's. Since 318 or so, he had been publicly teaching that Jesus was not divine, that Christ and the Holy Spirit were merely creatures. He saw this as the only way around such apparent follies as the claim that God is three and yet one, or that infinity and eternity — the fullness of divinity! — could be contained in a man from Palestine.

Arius was a rational man, and many of his brother priests mistook his rationalism for reason, and they accepted his Trinitarian doctrine over that of their bishop. The young priest Athanasius, himself a profound theologian, watched with horror as this happened. But he did not just watch. Around the same time Arius had begun preaching his heresy, Alexander had appointed Athanasius his secretary.

Arianism spread, far beyond Alexandria and Egypt, and at a rate that was alarming to many. In order to keep peace, the emperor Constantine summoned a council of all the bishops, to be convened at Nicaea in 325. There, Athanasius played a key role as adviser to his bishop, who had to deliver the opening deposition to the council on the case of Arius. At Nicaea, the Church adopted the language proposed by Athanasius: that Jesus was "consubstantial" with the Father, true God from true God, begotten, not made. The council fathers excommunicated Arius.

Orthodoxy had won the great battle, but the war was far from over. Though the Arians were suppressed, they remained to be convinced. Upon Alexander's death in 327, Athanasius was elected bishop of Alexandria. From that office, he faced continual opposition from persistent Arians — and some of these heretics had friends in high places. In 330, they prevailed upon Constantine to order Athanasius to readmit Arius, who was unrepentant, to communion. Athanasius refused, and so infuriated the Arians that they initiated a rumor campaign against him. So effective were they that Athanasius was called to stand trial for his alleged crimes before the emperor himself!

The hard times continued as Arian sympathizers arranged a council exclusively for the purpose of denouncing Athanasius — which it did — exiling him to Germany in 336. After Constantine's death, Arian fortunes rose and fell as emperors came and went. Thus, Athanasius found himself intermittently restored to Alexandria.

Ultimately, his case went before a synod presided over by the pope, who vindicated Athanasius. But all that was to little effect, as the east of the empire was ruled by an Arian. The emperor Constantius called puppet councils to condemn Athanasius, and then forced the pope to concur. Athanasius suffered further denunciations under the pagan revival of the emperor Julian and under later emperors who were Arian.

After long years of fight and flight, he was restored to his office in 366 (by an Arian emperor!), and he spent seven peaceful years in Alexandria before his death.

So closely identified with the fight against Arianism, St. Athanasius rarely receives the credit he deserves for promoting monasticism, a movement that was just emerging in the Church. His biography of St. Anthony of Egypt was something of a bestseller in the fourth-century Church, enticing many Christians to retreat to the desert or the forests.

In the Greek Church, St. Athanasius is called the "Father of Orthodoxy." The Catholic Church has named him one of the eight "Great Fathers."

WE WORSHIP THE WORD MADE FLESH

Bishop Adelphius of Onuphis was Athanasius's ally in the struggle against Arianism. This letter gave the bishop, who had once been exiled for the cause, both consolation and apologetical arguments.

We have read what Your Excellency has written to us, and genuinely approve your piety toward Christ. And above all we glorify God, Who has given you such grace as not only to have right opinions, but also, so far as that is possible, not to be ignorant of the devices of the devil. But we marvel at the perversity of the heretics, seeing that they have fallen into such a pit of impiety that they no longer retain even their senses, but have their understanding corrupted on all sides....

We do not worship a creature. Far be the thought. For such an error belongs to heathens and Arians. But we worship the Lord of Creation, Incarnate, the Word of God. For if the flesh also is in itself a part of the created world, yet it has become God's body. And we neither divide the body from the Word and worship it by itself, nor when we wish to worship the Word do we set Him far apart from the flesh. But knowing, as we said above, that "the Word was made flesh," we recognize Him also as God come in the flesh.

Testimony from Scripture

Who is so senseless as to say to the Lord: "Leave the Body that I may worship You"; or so impious as to join the senseless Jews in saying, on account of the Body, "Why do you, being a man, make yourself God?" (cf. Jn 10:33). But the leper was not one of this sort, for he worshiped God in the Body, and recognized that He was God, saying, "Lord, if you will, you can make me clean" (Mt 8:2). Neither by reason of the flesh did he think the Word of God a creature: nor because the Word was the maker of all creation did he despise the flesh which He had put on. But he worshiped the Creator of the universe as dwelling in a created temple, and he was cleansed.

These things happened, and no one doubted, as the Arians now venture to doubt, whether one is to believe the incarnate Word. Just looking at the man, they recognized that He was their maker, and when they heard a human voice, they did not, because it was human, say that the Word was a creature. On the contrary, they trembled, and recognized nothing less than that it was being uttered from a holy Temple. How then can the impious fail to fear lest "since they did not see fit to acknowledge God, God gave them up to a base mind and to improper conduct" (Rom 1:28)?

Creation does not worship a creature. Nor again did she, on account of His flesh, refuse to worship her Lord. But she beheld her maker in the Body, and "at the name of Jesus every knee" bowed and "should bow, in heaven and on earth and under the earth, and every tongue confess" — whether the Arians approve or not — "that Jesus Christ is Lord, to the glory of God the Father" (Phil 2:10-11).

Redeemer of the Flesh

For the flesh did not diminish the glory of the Word; far be the thought: on the contrary, it was glorified by Him. Nor, because the Son that was in the form of God took upon Him the form of a servant was He deprived of His Godhead. On the contrary, He has thus become the Deliverer of all flesh and of all creation. And if God sent His Son, brought forth from a woman, the fact causes us no shame, but, on the contrary, glory and great grace.

For He has become Man, that He might deify us in Himself! And He has been born of a woman, and begotten of a Virgin, in order to transfer to Himself our erring generation, and that we may become henceforth a holy race, and "partakers of the divine nature," as St. Peter wrote (2 Pet 1:4). "For God has done what the law, weakened by the flesh, could not do: sending his own Son in the likeness of sinful flesh and for sin, he condemned sin in the flesh" (Rom 8:3).

Seeing then that flesh was taken by the Word to deliver all men, raise all from the dead, and make redemption for sins, must not they appear ungrateful, and be worthy of all hatred, who make light of the flesh, as well as those who on account of it charge the Son of God with being a thing created or made?... For they who do not wish to worship the Word made flesh are ungrateful for His becoming man. And they who divide the Word from the flesh do not hold that one redemption from sin has taken place, or one destruction of death. But where at all will these impious men find the flesh that the Savior took, apart from Him? Yet they even venture to say, "We do not worship the Lord with the flesh, but we separate the Body, and worship Him alone." Why, the blessed Stephen saw in the heavens the Lord standing on [God's] right hand, while the angels said to the disciples, He "will come in the same way as you saw him go into heaven" (Acts 1:11); and the Lord himself says, addressing the Father, "I will ... that where I am you may be also" (Jn 14:3).

Anathema

Surely if the flesh is inseparable from the Word, does it not follow that these men must either lay aside their error, and for the future worship the Father in the name of our Lord Jesus Christ? Or, if they do not worship or serve the Word who came in the flesh, they must be cast out on all sides....

If they wish to live by their impieties, let them alone take their fill of them, and let them gnash their teeth like their father, the devil, because the faith of the Catholic Church knows that the Word of God is creator and maker of all things; and we know that while "in the beginning was the Word, and the Word was with God" (Jn 1:1), now that He has become also man for our salvation, we worship Him.

— *NPNF2 4:575-578*

On the Death of Arius

Athanasius wrote the following account in a letter to his fellow Egyptian bishop and onetime head of the school at Alexandria, St. Serapion of Thmuis.

You have asked me to make known ... the manner of the death of Arius.... I debated with myself for a long time, fearing lest anyone should suppose that I was exulting in the death of that man. Yet since a dispute about this heresy has arisen among you — raising the question whether Arius died after communicating with the Church — I felt the need to give an account of his death, thinking that the question would then be set to rest. By making this known, I should at the same time silence those who are fond of contention. For I believe that when the wonderful circumstances connected with his death become known, even those who questioned it before will no longer doubt that the Arian heresy is hateful in the sight of God.

I was not at Constantinople when he died, but Macarius the Presbyter was, and I heard the account of it from him. Arius had been invited by the emperor Constantine, through the interest of Eusebius and his fellows. [Editor's note: Athanasius speaks here of Eusebius of Nicomedia, not the famous historian from Caesarea.] When he entered the presence, the emperor asked him whether he held the faith of the

Catholic Church. And he declared upon oath that he held the right faith, and gave an account of his faith in writing, suppressing the points for which he had been cast out of the Church by the bishop Alexander, and speciously alleging expressions out of the Scriptures.

When he swore that he did not profess the opinions for which Alexander had excommunicated him, [the emperor] dismissed him, saying, "If your faith is right, you have done well to swear; but if your faith is impious, and you have sworn, may God judge you according to your oath."

When he emerged from the presence of the emperor, Eusebius and his fellows, with their accustomed violence, wanted to bring him into the Church. But Alexander, the bishop of Constantinople of blessed memory, resisted them, saying that the inventor of the heresy ought not to be admitted to communion. Then Eusebius and his fellows threatened, declaring, "As we have caused him to be invited by the emperor, in opposition to your wishes, so tomorrow, contrary to your desire, Arius shall have Communion with us in this church." It was the Sabbath when they said this.

Intrigues and Prayers

When Bishop Alexander heard this, he was greatly distressed, and entering into the church, he stretched forth his hands to God, and bewailed himself. And casting himself upon his face in the chancel, he prayed, lying upon the pavement. Macarius also was present, and prayed with him, and heard his words: he asked two things, saying, "If Arius is brought to Communion tomorrow, let me, Your servant, depart, and do not destroy the pious with the impious. But if You will spare Your Church (and I know that You will), look upon the words of Eusebius and his fellows, and do not give your inheritance to destruction and reproach. And remove Arius, lest if he enter into the Church, the heresy also may seem to enter with him, and henceforward impiety be accounted for piety."

When the bishop had thus prayed, he retired in great anxiety; and a wonderful and extraordinary circumstance took place. While Eusebius and his fellows threatened, the bishop prayed. But Arius, who had great confidence in Eusebius and his fellows, and talked very wildly, was urged by the necessities of nature and withdrew. Then, suddenly, in the language of Scripture, "falling headlong he burst asunder in the midst," and immediately expired as he lay, and was deprived at once of Communion and of his life....

For the Lord himself, judging between the threats of Eusebius and his fellows and the prayer of Alexander, condemned the Arian heresy, showing it to be unworthy of communion with the Church. He showed to all that, although it receive the support of the emperor and of all mankind, yet it was condemned by the Church herself.

— NPNF2 4:564-565

ST. APHRAHAT THE SAGE

St. Aphrahat gives us a glimpse of a lost world, a crucial stage in the development of the Church. In the work of this Persian monk-bishop, we see early Christianity, isolated from Roman and Greek influence — and very clearly in continuity with its Jewish roots.

We possess very few of the writings of Aphrahat, only twenty-three of his homilies, called *Demonstrations*. Most of these are defenses of the faith, but they are unusual — and even unique — among the ancient works of apologetics. Aphrahat aims most of his *Demonstrations* not at heretics who perverted Christian doctrine, nor at pagans who persecuted Christian people, but at Jews who rejected Christianity's development of the religion of Israel.

Aphrahat's world was far different from the world of the Greek-speaking Fathers. He wrote not in Greek or Latin, but in Syriac, a Semitic language related to the Aramaic spoken by Jesus. And his distinctiveness is not merely linguistic. He lived not in the Roman Empire, but just over the border in the Persian Empire, where Christians were ruthlessly persecuted long after Rome's decrees of toleration. Local tradition places Aphrahat at a monastery on the banks of the Tigris, near the city of Mosul in modern Iraq.

Christianity in Persia probably emerged from the well-established Jewish community there. Syriac Christianity bears many resemblances to Mesopotamian Judaism. It is likely that a fair number of Jews followed the new "Way" of Jesus as it spread eastward. It is clear, however, that many Jews did not. And so between the two groups there was some growing rivalry, tension, and competition for minds and hearts.

Jews were socially prominent in fourth-century Persia. They had lived and thrived there since the Babylonian exile almost nine centuries before. But the empire distinguished between Jews and Christians and chose to persecute the latter while tolerating the former. It seems that the Persians were encouraged in this by leaders of the Jewish community, who may have misrepresented Christian doctrine.

The Jews attacked certain aspects of Christianity that they regarded as breaks with Jewish law and tradition. Christians, they said, did not observe the ancient dietary laws or rest on the seventh day of the week. Christians did not circumcise their sons or celebrate Passover in the traditional way. Christian priests and monks observed celibacy rather than marrying, as was the custom for all pious Jewish men. Above all, Christians worshiped a Messiah whom these Jews declared illegitimate.

Aphrahat sought to remedy the situation by directly addressing Jewish arguments on Jewish terms. His sermons are primarily historical rather than theological, and he draws overwhelmingly from facts of history that the Jews held sacred and could not dispute.

He demonstrated, for example, that many heroes of the Old Testament — Moses, Joshua, Jeremiah, Elijah, and Elisha — were celibate, at least for part of their lives and ministry. He showed, too, how Jesus did not abolish but fulfilled the ancient law and prophecies.

We do not know when or how Aphrahat died. Christianity has never flourished in the lands of the former Persian Empire. But the Christian minority has always venerated this ancient monk, whom they call "Aphrahat the Sage."

In modern times, there has been a resurgence of interest in Aphrahat, thanks in part to the scholarship of Rabbi Jacob Neusner, who finds in the Persian sage a model —"remarkable and exemplary" — for Jewish-Christian dialogue. Aphrahat is, says Rabbi Neusner, "an enduring voice of civility and rationality amid the cacophony of mutual disesteem."[67]

On Persecution

A Persian Jew argued that the Christians' misfortune was a sign of God's disfavor toward them. Aphrahat answered this charge in his twenty-first Demonstration.

One day a man whom the Jews call wise questioned me, saying, "Jesus, your teacher, wrote for you that 'if you have faith as a grain of mustard seed, you will say to this mountain, "Move hence to yonder place," and it will move' (Mt 17:20). So it seems that there is, in all your people, not one wise man whose prayer is heard, and who asks God that your persecutions should cease from you. For it is clearly written for you in that passage, 'nothing will be impossible to you.'"

I saw that he was blaspheming and speaking against the Way, and my mind was disturbed. I understood that he would not acknowledge the interpretation of the words that he quoted to me. So I also questioned him on sayings from the law and from the prophets. I said to him: "Do you believe that even when you are dispersed God is with you?"

And he professed to me, "God is with us, because God said unto Israel: 'Yet for all that, when they are in the land of their enemies, I will not spurn them, neither will I abhor them so as to destroy them utterly and break my covenant with them' (Lev 26:44)."

I answered him, saying, "Very good is this that I have heard from you, that God is with you. Against your words, too, will I speak to you. For the prophet said to Israel, as from the mouth of God: 'When you pass through the waters I will be with you; and through the rivers, they shall not overwhelm you; when you walk through fire you shall not be burned, and the flame shall not consume you. For I am the Lord your God, the Holy One of Israel, your Savior' (Is 43:2-3). Thus there is not one righteous, good, and wise man out of all your people; for none could pass through the sea and live and not be drowned, or through the river without its overflowing him; or who could walk over fire and not be scorched and burned by the flame. If you offer me an explanation, I will not be persuaded, just as you are unmoved by my interpretation of the words about which you have questioned me." ...

Those who reproach us, saying, "You are persecuted and are not delivered," should be ashamed of themselves. Many times they, too, have been persecuted, even for many years before they were delivered. They were enslaved in Egypt two hundred and twenty-five years. And the Midianites made Israel serve in the days of Barak and Deborah. The Moabites ruled over them in the days of Ehud; the Ammonites in the days of Jephthah; the Philistines in the days of Samson, and also in the days of Eli and of Samuel the prophet; the Edomites in the days of Ahab; the Assyrians in the days of Hezekiah.

The king of Babylon uprooted them from their place and dispersed them; and after he had tried and persecuted them much, they did not improve, as He said to them: "In vain have I smitten your children, they took no correction" (Jer 2:30). And again He said: "I have hewn them by the prophets, I have slain them by the words of my mouth" (Hos 6:5). And to Jerusalem He said: By afflictions and plagues "be warned, O Jerusalem, lest I be alienated from you; lest I make you a desolation, an uninhabited land" (Jer 6:8). But they abandoned Him and worshiped idols, as Jeremiah said concerning them: "For cross to the coasts of Cyprus and see, or send to Kedar and examine with care; see if there has been such a thing. Has a nation changed its gods, even though they are no gods? But my people have changed their glory for that which does not profit. Be appalled, O heavens, at this, be shocked, be utterly desolate, says the LORD, for my people have committed two evils: they have forsaken me, the fountain of living waters, and hewed out cisterns for themselves, broken cisterns, that can hold no water" (Jer 2:10-13). The broken cisterns are the fear of images and idols. And He calls the heavens to astonishment, because they worshiped the hosts of the heavens. The heavens receive as a penalty that they shall be rolled up as a scroll, and all the host of them shall fall down.

All this discourse I have written to you, my beloved, because a Jew reproached the children of our people. But now I will instruct you, as best I can, about the persecuted, that they have received a great reward, while the persecutors have come to scorn and contempt....

Hear, my beloved, these names of martyrs, of confessors, and of the persecuted. Abel was murdered, and his blood cried out from the earth. Jacob was persecuted, and fled and became an exile. Joseph was persecuted, and sold and cast into a pit. Moses was persecuted, and fled to Midian. Joshua the son of Nun was persecuted, and made war. Jephthah and Samson and Gideon and Barak — they, too, were persecuted. Yet it is they of whom the blessed Apostle said: "Time would fail me to tell" their victories (Heb 11:32). David also was persecuted at the hands of Saul, and he fled in the mountains and in dens and caves. Samuel was persecuted, and mourned over Saul. Hezekiah was persecuted, and bound up in affliction. Elijah was persecuted, and wandered in the desert. Elisha was persecuted and became an exile; and Micaiah was persecuted, and cast into prison. Jeremiah was persecuted, and they cast him into the pit of mud. Daniel was persecuted, and cast into the pit of lions. Hananiah and his brethren were persecuted, and cast into the furnace of fire. Mordecai and Esther and the children of their people were persecuted at the hands of Haman. Judas Maccabee and his brothers were persecuted, and they too endured reproach. The seven brothers, sons of the blessed woman, endured torments by bitter scourgings, and were confessors and true martyrs. And Eleazar, old and advanced in years as he was, proved a noble example and made his confession and became a true martyr.

Great and excellent is the martyrdom of Jesus. He surpassed in affliction and in confession all who were before or after. And after Him was the faithful martyr Stephen, whom the Jews stoned. Simon Peter, too, and Paul were perfect martyrs. And James and John walked in the footsteps of their Master Christ. The other Apostles in far-flung places confessed and proved true martyrs.

And to our brothers and sisters in the West, in the days of Diocletian, there came great affliction and persecution to the whole Church of God throughout their region. The churches were overthrown and uprooted, and many confessors and martyrs professed the faith. But the Lord turned in mercy to them after they were persecuted.

In our days, too, these things happened to us on account of our sins — but also that what is written might be fulfilled, even as our Redeemer said: "This must take place" (Mt 24:6). The Apostle also said: "We are surrounded by so great a cloud of witnesses" (Heb 12:1). This is our honor, in which many give witness and are slain.

— NPNF2 13:392, 395, 401-402

―――――――――――ST. EPHREM OF SYRIA―――――――――――

In St. Ephrem we hear theology in a new key.

Ephrem was a profound theologian and a dazzling poet, who did not see these vocations as separate or contradictory. He sang his theological explorations. He chanted them in the Syriac language's rhythmic measures. He could move from metaphysics to praise in the briefest interval. He could soar from history to allegory without pausing for a rest.

Ephrem was born in Nisibis (now Nusaybin, Turkey) in the early years of the fourth century. His biographies tell conflicting stories. Some say he was raised in a pagan family, the son of a heathen priest; but the autobiographical passages in Ephrem's poems seem to imply a Christian upbringing.

He surely attended the catechetical schools and applied himself to a deep and wide study of the Scriptures. Foremost among his teachers was St. James of Nisibis, who attended the Council of Nicaea. Under James, Ephrem was ordained a deacon and appointed a teacher.

Ephrem wrote voluminously, in both poetry and prose. In prose, he favored a literal-historical treatment of the Scriptures. In poetry, he tended to allegory. He excelled in both methods.

Even during his lifetime, Ephrem became a celebrity throughout the Christian world. This was extremely unusual, since the Syriac Christian world was somewhat enclosed — isolated by language and by political boundaries, as most Syriac-speaking Christians lived within the Persian Empire.

Nisibis, however, was a border town, often battled for, often under siege. During Ephrem's early life, it was in Roman territory. Rome was, by then, tolerant of Christianity; Persia was not. So the border wars had tremendous consequences for East Syrian Christians. Three times in Ephrem's life, Nisibis fell under siege; once the Persians even dammed up the river to flood the perimeter of the city. History records that Ephrem, with his preaching and his songs, buoyed the weary spirits of the citizens.

In the year 363, the emperor Julian, an ex-Christian, was mortally wounded while in battle with the Persians. Julian's successor, Jovinian, sought to broker a treaty rather than continue the bloody fighting far from home. In the settlement, however, the city of Nisibis was conceded to Persia, and the Christians were expelled.

Ephrem spent the last ten years of his life in Edessa (modern-day Urfa, Turkey), where, according to some sources, he helped establish that city's theological school, which would rise to greatness in the following centuries. He died in 373. He is a Doctor of the Church.

A Song for Christmas

Ephrem's third Nativity Hymn explodes with the paradoxes of the Incarnation — Word made flesh, God become man. It is at once mystical and sensuous, and profoundly eucharistic.

> Glory to the Voice that became a Body,
> and to the Word of the Most High, which became Flesh!
> Hear Him also, O ears, and see Him, O eyes,
> and feel Him, O hands, and eat Him, O mouth!
> You limbs and senses, give praise to Him,
> who came and gave life to the whole body!
> Mary bore the silent baby,
> while in Him were hidden all tongues!
> Joseph bore Him, and in Him was hidden
> a nature more ancient than anything old!
> The Most High became like a little child,
> and in Him was hidden a treasure
> of wisdom sufficing for all!
> Though He was Most High, He sucked milk from Mary,
> and of His goodness all creatures suck!
> He is the Breast of Life, and the Breath of Life;
> the dead suck from His life and revive.
> Without the breath of the air no man lives,
> without the Might of the Son no man subsists.
> On His living breath that gives life to all,
> depend the spirits that are above
> and all that are beneath.
> When He sucked the milk of Mary,

He was suckling all with Life.
While He was lying upon His Mother's breast,
in His bosom were all creatures lying.
He was silent as a baby, and yet He was making
His creatures carry out His every command.
For without the Firstborn no man can approach
unto the Essence, to which He is equal.

For thirty years He was on the earth,
who was ordering all creatures,
and receiving the offerings of praise
from those above and those below.
He was wholly in the depths and wholly in the highest!
He was wholly with all things and wholly with each.
While His body was forming within the womb,
His power was fashioning all members!
While conceived, the Son was fashioned in the womb;
Yet He Himself was fashioning babes in the womb.
Yet not as His body was weak in the womb
was His power weak in the womb!
And not as His body was feeble on the cross
was His might also feeble on the cross....
While on the cross He gave life to the dead,
so while a Babe He was fashioning babes.
While He was slain, He opened the graves;
while He was in the womb, He opened wombs.

Come hear, my brothers,
of the Son of the hidden One,
who was revealed in His body,
while His power was concealed!...
It was by power from Him that Mary was able
to bear in her bosom who bears all things up!...
She gave Him milk from Himself who prepared it,
she gave Him food from Himself who made it!
He gave milk to Mary as God,

and He sucked it from her, as the Son of Man....
He the Lord of all gives all to us.
He who pays riches to all asks interest from all.
He gives to all things as wanting nothing,
and yet requires interest of all as if needy.
He gave us herds and flocks as Creator,
yet asked of us sacrifices as though in need.
He made the water wine as Maker,
and yet he drank of it as a poor man.
Of His own He mingled wine in the marriage feast,
His wine He mingled and gave to drink when He was a guest....
Of His own all that give have made their vows;
of His own treasures they placed upon His table.

— NPNF2 13:232-234

ST. BASIL THE GREAT

Holiness was the greatness in St. Basil the Great (329–379). He had significant intellectual gifts; yet he showed, beyond intelligence, a wisdom to search out the deep secrets of the mysteries of God. As bishop, he was an effective and efficient administrator; but, more, he was a just judge, a mild father. Confronted with an imperial demand for assent to heresy, St. Basil showed courage in refusing; but his courage was still greater in showing pure love, both for God and those in heresy.

St. Basil came from good Christian stock. Born at Caesarea in Cappadocia (in what is now Turkey), he was the grandson of a martyr. Both of his parents, Basil and Emmelia, are considered saints, as are his grandmother Macrina and three of his siblings, his sister Macrina and brothers Peter of Sebaste and Gregory of Nyssa (also a Father of the Church).

After receiving an excellent classical education from his father and grandmother, Basil pursued advanced studies in Caesarea, Constantinople, and Athens. At Athens, he studied alongside St. Gregory of Nazianzus, a childhood friend whose friendship Basil would treasure all his life. From Athens, Basil went to work teaching rhetoric in his hometown, where he underwent a profound conversion.

He recalled the experience in a letter: "Much time had I spent in vanity, and had wasted nearly all my youth acquiring the sort of wisdom made foolish by God. Then once, like a man roused from deep sleep, I turned my eyes to the marvelous light of the truth of the Gospel, and I perceived the uselessness of 'the wisdom of the princes of this world, that come to naught.' I wept many tears over my miserable life, and I prayed that I might receive guidance to admit me to the doctrines of true religion."

Turning to the Gospel, he read that the way to perfection is to sell all one's goods, give to the poor, and follow Christ. In this passage, Basil discerned his monastic vocation. He visited monasteries throughout Palestine, Syria, and Egypt, but could not find a home in any of them. He took up the hermit's life by the Iris River in Pontus (in what is today Turkey).

But he was not alone for long. Basil gained a reputation for holiness, wisdom, and the ability to teach. Many Christians came to Pontus seeking his counsel. Some stayed on as his disciples, and soon Basil found that he had founded a monastery. There he sought to imitate the community life of the early Church in Jerusalem. In short order, he composed a "Rule" of life for monastic communities, and then another, and he put them to use in the founding of many monasteries.

His friendship with Gregory of Nazianzus endured. Together they compiled an anthology of the writings of Origen. And when Gregory felt overwhelmed by the Arian heresy in his own diocese, he turned to Basil for advice and assistance.

Named bishop of Caesarea in 370, Basil again took up the work of a founder, this time establishing hospitals, poorhouses, and hostels. He taught and preached prodigiously, fighting the stubborn heresy of Arianism by constant persuasion. Thus, he was a thorn in the side of Arian officials of the empire, who desperately tried to make him recant. Basil sent even the emperor's emissaries home with the message that the bishop of Caesarea was not afraid of the "confiscation of goods"; he had already given up everything. Nor was he afraid of exile or "fire, sword, beasts, and instruments of torture." The emperors backed down and left Basil alone.

Basil saw the Church of his day torn apart by envy, rivalry, heresy, and political intrigue. He wrote and worked and pleaded for unity. From the accounts of his life, it seems that he worked himself to an early grave. But Basil's teaching laid the groundwork for the anti-Arian decisions of the Council of Constantinople, which convened in 381, two years after his death.

Basil is one of the Great Fathers of the Church, and he is numbered one of the three "Cappadocian Fathers," with his brother St. Gregory of Nyssa and his friend St. Gregory of Nazianzus.

ON HIS CONVERSION
In a letter to a friend, Basil described his sudden change from lukewarmness to repentance and fervor.

Much time had I spent in vanity, and had wasted nearly all my youth acquiring the sort of wisdom made foolish by God. Then once, like a man roused from deep sleep, I turned my eyes to the marvelous light of the truth of the Gospel, and I perceived the uselessness of the "wisdom ... of the rulers of this age, who are doomed to pass away" (1 Cor 2:6). I wept many tears over my miserable life and I prayed that I might receive guidance to admit me to the doctrines of true religion.

First of all, I thought to make some mending of my ways, long perverted as they were by my intimacy with wicked men. Then I read the Gospel, and I saw that a great means of reaching perfection was to sell one's goods, share them with the poor, giving up of all care for this life and refusing to allow the soul to be turned by any sympathy to things of earth.

I prayed that I might find one of the brethren who had chosen this way of life, that with him I might cross life's short and troubled strait. And I found many in Alexandria and in the rest of Egypt, and others in Palestine, Syria, and Mesopotamia.

I admired their continence in living, and their endurance in toil. I was amazed by their perseverance in prayer, and at their triumphing over sleep. Subdued by no natural necessity, they ever kept their souls' purpose high and free, in hunger, thirst, cold, nakedness, never yielding to the body. They were never willing to waste attention on it. As if living in a flesh that was not theirs, they showed in very deed what it means to sojourn for a while in this life, and what it means to have one's citizenship and home in heaven.

All this moved my admiration. I called these men's lives blessed, in that they indeed showed that they were "carrying in the body the death of Jesus" (2 Cor 4:10). And I prayed that I, too, might imitate them.

— *NPNF2 8:263*

A PLEA TO THE POPE
Basil looked around him and saw the Eastern churches in disarray. He believed the only remedy to be a personal visit from Pope St. Damasus, which he begged for in a letter to the pontiff.

To renew laws of ancient love, and once again to restore to vigorous life that heavenly and saving gift of Christ, which in course of time has withered away — the peace, I mean, of the Fathers — is a labor necessary and profitable to me. But it is pleasant, too, as I am sure it will seem to your Christ-loving disposition.

For what could be more delightful than to behold all, who are separated by distances so vast, bound together by the union effected by love into one harmony of members in Christ's body? Nearly all the East (I include under this name all the regions from Illyricum to Egypt) is being agitated, right honorable father, by a terrible storm and tempest. The old heresy, sown by Arius the enemy of the truth, has now boldly and unblushingly reappeared. Like some sour root, it is producing its deadly fruit and is prevailing. The reason is that in every district the champions of orthodoxy have been exiled from their churches by calumny and outrage, and the control of affairs has been handed over to men who are leading captive the souls of the simpler brethren. I have come to see the visit of your mercifulness as the only possible solution of our difficulties.

In the past, I have ever been consoled by your extraordinary affection; and for a short time my heart was cheered by the gratifying report that we shall be visited by you. But, as I was disappointed, I have been constrained to beg you by letter to be moved to help us, and to send some of those who are like-minded with us, either to conciliate the dissidents and bring the churches of God back into friendly union, or at all events, to make you see more plainly who are responsible for our unsettled state, that it may be clear to you, for future reference, with whom it befits you to be in communion. In this I am by no means making any novel request, but am only asking what has been customary in the case of men who, before our own day, were blessed and dear to God, and conspicuously in your own case.

For I well remember learning from the answers made by our fathers when asked, and from documents still preserved among us, that the illustrious and blessed Bishop Dionysius, conspicuous in your see as well for soundness of faith as for all other virtues, visited by letter my Church of Caesarea, and by letter exhorted our fathers, and sent men to ransom our brethren from captivity. But now our condition is yet more painful and gloomy and needs more careful treatment. We are lamenting no mere overthrow of earthly buildings, but the capture of churches. What we see before us is no mere bodily slavery, but a carrying away of souls into captivity, perpetrated day by day by the champions of heresy.

If you are not, even now, moved to console us, before long all will have fallen under the dominion of the heresy, and you will find none left to whom you may hold out your hand.

— *NPNF2 8:166-167*

On the Holy Spirit

Perhaps Basil's most famous doctrinal work is his teaching On the Holy Spirit, *from which the following is drawn.*

He is called Spirit, as "God is Spirit" (Jn 4:24), and "the breath of our nostrils, the LORD's anointed" (Lam 4:20). He is called holy, as the Father is holy, and the Son is holy, for to the creature holiness was brought in from without, but to the Spirit holiness is the fulfillment of nature, and it is for this reason that He is described not as being sanctified, but as sanctifying. He is called good, as the Father is good, and He who was begotten of the Good is good, and to the Spirit His goodness is essence. He is called upright, as "the LORD is upright" (Ps 92:15), in that He is Himself truth, and is Himself righteousness, having no divergence nor leaning to one side or to the other, on account of the immutability of His substance. He is called Paraclete, like the Only Begotten, as He Himself says, "I will pray the Father, and he will give you another Counselor" (Jn 14:16).

Thus names are borne by the Spirit in common with the Father and the Son, and He gets these titles from His natural and close relationship. From what other source could they be derived?

Again He is called royal, Spirit of truth, and Spirit of wisdom. "The spirit of God," it is said, "has made me" (Job 33:4), and God filled Bezalel with "the Spirit of God, with ability and intelligence, with knowledge and all craftsmanship" (Ex 31:3). Such names as these are supereminent and mighty, but they do not transcend His glory.

And His operations, what are they? For majesty ineffable, and for numbers innumerable. How shall we form a conception of what extends beyond the ages? What were His operations before that creation whereof we can conceive? How great the grace which He conferred on creation? What the power exercised by Him over the ages to come? He existed; He preexisted; He coexisted with the Father and the Son before the ages. It follows that, even if you can conceive of anything beyond the ages, you will find the Spirit yet further above and beyond.... Is it Christ's advent? The Spirit is forerunner. Is there the incarnate presence? The Spirit is inseparable. Working of miracles and gifts of healing are through the Holy Spirit. Demons were driven out by the Spirit of God. The devil was brought to naught by the presence of the Spirit. Remission of sins was by the gift of the Spirit, for "you were washed, you were sanctified ... in the name of the Lord Jesus Christ and in the Spirit of our God" (1 Cor 6:11).

There is close relationship with God through the Spirit, for "God has sent the Spirit of His Son into our hearts, crying, 'Abba! Father!'" (Gal 4:6). The resurrection from the dead is effected by the operation of the Spirit, for "when you send forth your spirit, they are created; and you renew the face of the [earth]" (Ps 104:30).

With these thoughts before us, are we to be afraid of going beyond due bounds in the extravagance of the honor we pay? Shall we not rather fear, lest, even though we seem to give Him the highest names which the thoughts of man can conceive or man's tongue utter, we let our thoughts about Him fall too low?

— *NPNF2 8:30-31*

ST. GREGORY OF NAZIANZUS

St. Gregory of Nazianzus (330–390) was the most reluctant of Fathers. An accomplished poet and preacher — the bishop of the imperial city and a world-class orator — he would rather have been elsewhere.

Gregory was born into an aristocratic family. His father was a bishop, also named Gregory, and something of an overbearing figure in the boy's life. (In the East, married clergy were customary. In the West, then as now, celibacy was the norm. A married Eastern priest, upon being chosen as bishop, would customarily begin living with his wife as "brother and sister.")

In boyhood, Gregory made the acquaintance of Basil, as both were studying at the rhetorical school in Caesarea of Pontus. They met again at Athens, where their friendship deepened through a shared love of literature. At Athens, Gregory was also a classmate of the future emperor Julian, who was then a Christian, but who would eventually lead a failed revival of paganism in the empire.

Shortly after he returned to Cappadocia, Gregory learned that Basil had retired to monastic seclusion by the Iris River. Soon, Gregory was among the men who joined Basil to live the contemplative life in community. There he lived a peaceful, joyful life, praying in solitude and collaborating with Basil.

His bliss was shattered, however, by his ailing father's summons to come home. Once home, Gregory discovered his father's designs for his life. The elder Gregory insisted on ordaining his son to the priesthood, quite against the younger Gregory's will. The bishop put the issue before the congregation, who heartily approved. And, in what the younger Gregory would later call an "act of tyranny," the bishop ordained his son.

Young Gregory did what came naturally then. He ran back to Pontus, to the little community by the river, to peaceful conversation with his best friend. But, ill at ease, he knew he must return. Now he was a priest, and he must minister. On returning, he was met by an indignant congregation, whom he tried to mollify by giving a speech explaining his reasons for fleeing.

Yet the temptation would not go away — not even when his friend Basil insisted, again against Gregory's instincts, that the latter should be made a bishop. Gregory reluctantly accepted, but bound by duties to his father, the young bishop was never able to enter his tiny see. On his father's death, Gregory once again withdrew to monastic seclusion.

Once again, however, he was called away, this time to aid the beleaguered orthodox minority in the Church of Constantinople. The city, its bishops, and parishes had long been captive to Arians. Gregory's lively preaching would set the city and its church on doctrinally solid ground once again, and just in time for the installation of an orthodox emperor, Theodosius, in 380.

Gregory was ill-suited for chancery politics, however, and disgusted by the machinations of his fellow bishops, he resigned after only two years in Constantinople. He returned to watch over the Church of Nazianzus for two years before announcing his retirement. This time it was definitive. The second of the Cappadocian Fathers withdrew to his family's estate to write and pray, till God took him home, about 390.

WHY I FLED

On returning to his church, the young priest Gregory attempted an explanation for his sudden disappearance. He took responsibility for his error, repenting, even as he acknowledged the good things that had lured him away to the cloistered contemplative life.

I have been defeated, and I own my defeat.... As to the cause of my original revolt and cowardice, in which I ran far away, and remained away from you for a time,... I will set forth the truth....

For to most men I did not at the time seem consistent with myself, or to be the man they had known, but to have undergone some breakdown, showing greater resistance and self-will than was right. The causes of this you have long been wanting to hear.

First, and most important, I was astounded at the unexpectedness of what had occurred, as people are terrified by sudden noises; and, losing the control of my reason, my self-respect, which had till then controlled me, gave way. In the next place, there came over me an eager longing for the blessings of quiet and seclusion, which I had preferred from the start ... and which, amid the greatest and most threatening dangers, I had promised to God, and which I had also experienced for so long.... I could not submit to be thrust into the midst of a life of turmoil by an arbitrary act of oppression, and to be torn away by force from the holy sanctuary of such a life as this.

For nothing seemed to me so desirable as to close the doors of my senses and escape from the flesh and the world — to recollect within myself, having no further connection than was absolutely necessary with human affairs — and to converse with myself and God, living superior to visible things, and ever preserving in myself the divine impressions pure and unmixed with the erring tokens of this lower world — to be, and to become constantly, more and more, a real unspotted mirror of God and divine things, as light is added to light, till what was still dark grew clearer, enjoying already by hope the blessings of the world to come, roaming about with the angels, even now being above the earth by having forsaken it, and stationed on high by the Spirit.

If any of you has been possessed by this longing, he knows what I mean and will sympathize with my feelings at that time.

— NPNF2 7:204-206

Soul and Body

Gregory left behind many poems. The following, translated by Elizabeth Barrett Browning,[68] describes a dialogue between the soul and the body. It touches on many of the struggles in Gregory's own life. His flesh would plead for comfort and for esthetic pleasures. But, counters Gregory's soul, "I cast earth's cares abroad, / That day when I turned to God."

What wilt thou possess or be?
O my soul, I ask of thee.

What of great or what of small,
Counted precious therewithal?
Be it only rare, and want it,
I am ready, soul, to grant it.
Wilt thou choose to have and hold
Lydian Gyges' charm of old,
So to rule us with a ring,
Turning round the jeweled thing,
Hidden by its face concealed,
And revealed by its revealed?
Or preferrest Midas' fate —
He who died in golden state,
All things being changed to gold?
Of a golden hunger dying,
Through a surfeit of "would-I"ing
Wilt have jewels brightly cold,
Or may fertile acres please?
Or the sheep of many a fold,
Camels, oxen, for the wold?
Nay! I will not give thee these!
These to take thou hast not will,
These to give I have not skill;
Since I cast earth's cares abroad,
That day when I turned to God....

Go, upon thy wing arise,
Pluméd by quick energies,
Mount in circles up the skies:
And I will bless thy wingéd passion,
Help with words thine exaltation,
And, like a bird of rapid feather,
Outlaunch thee, Soul, upon the ether.

But thou, O fleshly nature, say,
Thou with odors from the clay,
Since thy presence I must have

As a lady with a slave,
What wouldst thou possess or be,
That thy breath may stay with thee?
Nay, I owe thee nought beside,
Though thine hands be open wide.
Would a table suit thy wishes,
Fragrant with sweet oils and dishes
Wrought to subtle niceness? where
Stringéd music strokes the air ...
Wilt [thou] have measureless delights
Of gold-roofed palaces, and sights
From pictured or from sculptured art,
With motion near their life; and splendor
Of bas relief, with tracery tender,
And varied and contrasted hues?
Wilt thou have, as nobles use,
Broidered robes to flow about thee?
Jeweled finger? Need we doubt thee?
Gauds for which the wise will flout thee?
I most, who, of all beauty, know
It must be inward, to be so!

And thus I speak to mortals low,
Living for the hour, and o'er
Its shadow, seeing nothing more:
But for those of nobler bearing,
Who live more worthily of wearing
A portion of the heavenly nature —
To low estate of clayey creature,
See, I bring the beggar's mead,
Nutriment beyond the need!
O beholder of the Lord,
Prove on me the flaming sword!
Be mine husbandman, to nourish
Holy plants, that words may flourish
Of which mine enemy would spoil me,

Using pleasurehood to foil me!
Lead me closer to the tree
Of all life's eternity;
Which as I have pondered, is
The knowledge of God's greatnesses:
Light of One, and shine of Three,
Unto whom all things that be
Flow and tend!

In such a guise
Whoever on the earth is wise
Will speak unto himself: and who
Such inner converse would eschew —
We say perforce of that poor wight,
"He lived in vain!" and if aright,
It is not the worst word we might.

ST. GREGORY OF NYSSA

Of the Cappadocian Fathers, Gregory of Nazianzus usually appears as "the dreamer," Basil as "the doer," and Gregory of Nyssa (330–395) as "the thinker." He was, by most reckoning, the greatest speculative and systematic theologian of the three.

Like the other Gregory, he entered the work of the Church by fits and starts. Educated in early life by his brother Basil and sister Macrina, he was admitted at a young age to the order of lector in the Church. But he did not persevere, and instead he married and took a job teaching rhetoric. This work he found thoroughly depressing, and he lamented the apathy and ignorance of his students to his friend Gregory of Nazianzus. The Nazianzen persuaded his younger friend of the consolations of religious life. Thus, when his wife died young, Gregory of Nyssa entered his brother Basil's monastery at Pontus.

Basil first ordained Gregory a priest and later a bishop, appointing him to the see of Nyssa, in lower Armenia. Arians dominated the diocese and showed little liking for Gregory. This uncomfortable situation seems to have been aggravated by Gregory's incompetence as an administrator, a shortcoming for which his brother Basil upbraided him. Gregory's priests denounced his financial mismanagement, and he was deposed in 376. He returned in 378 and, from then on, distinguished himself in ecclesiastical work. He played a key role in the Council of Constantinople in 381, which confirmed the anti-Arian decrees of the Council of Nicaea.

But Gregory is more known for what he thought than for what he did. He wove the teachings of Origen and Plato into deep works of systematic and mystical theology. He wrote biblical commentaries, manuals for apologetics, and numerous pastoral letters. His biography of his sister Macrina is an important document for understanding the leadership and exemplary roles that women, especially virgins and widows, played in the early Church.

By the time of Gregory's death in 395, his doctrine was already revered. In the following decades, it was to have a profound influence on theology in the Eastern churches. The Second Council of Nicaea (680–681) called Gregory the "Father of Fathers."

WHY DO INFANTS DIE?

Gregory wrote this theological examination at the request of a friend.

You are anxious to know why it is that, while the life of one is lengthened into old age, another lives only long enough to breathe one gasp and die. If nothing in this world happens without God, and all is linked to the divine will, and if the Deity is skillful and prudent, then it follows necessarily that there is some plan in these things bearing the mark of His wisdom and His providential care. A blind unmeaning occurrence can never be the work of God; for it is the property of God, as the Scripture says, to make all things in wisdom (see Ps 104:24).

What wisdom, then, can we trace in the following? A human being enters on the scene of life. He draws in the air, beginning the process of living with a cry of pain. He pays the tribute of a tear to Nature, just tastes life's sorrows, before any of its sweets have been his, before his feelings have gained any strength. While he is still loose in all his joints, tender, pulpy, unset — in a word, before he is even human (if the gift of reason is man's peculiarity, and he has never had it in him) — such a human — with no advantage over the embryo in the womb except that he has seen the air — after so short a life, dies and goes to pieces again...,

What are we to think about him? How are we to feel about such deaths? Will a soul such as that behold its Judge? Will it stand with the rest before the tribunal? Will it undergo its trial for deeds done in life? Will it receive the just recompense by being purged, according to the Gospel utterances, in fire ...?

But in the case of infants prematurely dying there is nothing of that sort; but they pass to the blessed lot at once, if those who take this view of the matter speak truly....

Nothing happens without God; we know this from many sources. And everyone who realizes that God is Reason, Wisdom, Perfect Goodness, and Truth — and that He could not admit of anything that is not good and not consistent with His Truth — everyone who realizes this will admit that God's dispensations have no element of chance and confusion.... It befits us, then, to acknowledge that these things happen for the best....

— NPNF2 5:373-380

THE MYSTICAL DEATH
Gregory reveals the layers of meaning in the Rite of Baptism, in this passage adapted from his Great Catechism. *He compares our spiritual journey to the threading of a maze.*

The descent into the water, with the threefold immersion, involves a mystery. For the means of our salvation received its power not so much from the words Christ taught as from the deeds He did. Christ has accomplished an actual fellowship with man, and He has given life as a living fact. In taking on human flesh, He made human flesh divine. And in order that everything related to that flesh may be saved, it was necessary that something in the baptismal process should produce a kind of resemblance between those who follow and Him who leads the way.

It is, in fact, impossible for people to reach the same goal unless they travel by the same routes. People lost in the corridors of mazes can navigate the twists and turns and blind alleys, if they happen to find someone who has been through it all before. They can get to the end by following behind — which they could not do, if they did not follow their leader step by step. So I beg you to listen: Our human minds cannot thread the maze of this life unless we pursue that same path as He did. He was once in it, yet He got beyond the difficulties that hemmed Him in. By the maze I mean that prison of death that leaves no exit and encloses the miserable human race.

What, then, have we seen in the case of the pioneer of our salvation (see Heb 2:10, 12:2)? Three days of death and then life again. Now there must be some sort of plan to make us resemble Him in these things. What, then, is that plan? Everything that dies finds its proper and natural place in the earth in which it is laid and hidden. Now earth and water have much in common. Alone of the elements they have weight and gravitate downward; they live in each other; they confine each other.

In death the Author of life was subject to burial in the earth. So, in keeping with our common nature, we imitate that death in the next-closest element.

He, the Man from above, took death upon Himself. He was buried in the earth, and He returned back to life on the third day. So everyone who is joined to Him by virtue of His body may look forward to the same happy ending — I mean, he may arrive at life by having water, instead of earth, poured over him. Submerged in that element three times represents for him the three-days-delayed grace of the resurrection.

Nature does not allow us an exact and entire imitation, but it receives now as much as it can receive, while it keeps the rest for a later time. What, then, is the extent of our imitation? It consists in suppressing our sins in the sign of death that's given by water. Sin is not completely wiped away, but there is a kind of break in the continuity of evil. By our penance and by our imitation of death, we are freed from the innate tendency to evil; by penance we move ahead to a hatred of sin, and by the death we suppress evil. We imitate the transcendent power as far as our poor nature can, by having the water three times poured on us and rising again from the water. Thus we enact that saving burial and resurrection that took place on the third day.

Keep in mind: We have the power to be in the water and to rise out of it. He who has the universe at His disposal immersed Himself in death — as we immersed ourselves in the water — to return to His own blessedness. Each in proportion to the measure of his natural power achieved the results that were within reach. A human being may touch the water and yet be safe. The divine power, with infinitely greater ease, can handle death, and even be immersed in it, and yet not be changed or injured by it.

Notice, then, that we need to rehearse beforehand in the water the grace of our resurrection. We must come to learn that, as far as easiness goes, it's the same thing for us to be baptized with water and to rise again from death.

— NPNF2 5:502-503

On the Building of a Church
Ostensibly a progress report on the construction of a church, this letter to Bishop Amphilochus ends with that perennial pastoral coda: a witty plea for money.

I am well persuaded that by God's grace the business of the Church of the Martyrs is going well.... I will try to explain the whole structure by description. The form of the chapel is a cross, which has its figure completed throughout, as you would expect, by four structures. The junctions of the buildings intercept one another, as we see everywhere in the cruciform pattern. But within the cross there lies a circle, divided by eight angles (I call the octagonal figure a circle in view of its circumference), in such a way that the two pairs of sides of the octagon which are diametrically opposed to one another, unite, by means of arches, the central circle to the adjoining blocks of building; while the other four sides of the octagon, which lie between the quadrilateral buildings, will not themselves be carried to meet the buildings, but upon each of them will be described a semicircle like a shell, terminating in an arch above: so that the arches will be eight in all, and by their means the quadrilateral and semicircular buildings will be connected, side by side, with the central structure. In the blocks of masonry formed by the angles there will be an equal number of pillars, at once for ornament and for strength, and these again will carry arches built of equal size to correspond with those within. And above these eight arches, with the symmetry of an upper range of windows, the octagonal building will be raised to the height of four cubits: the part rising from it will be a cone shaped like a top, as the vaulting narrows the figure of the roof from its full width to a pointed wedge.... The height will be determined in proportion to the width. And the thickness of the wall, an interval of three feet from inside these spaces, which are measured internally, will run round the whole building....

I know that so far as skill and fairness in the matter of wages are concerned, the workmen in your neighborhood are better for our purpose than those who follow the trade here. The sculptor's work lies not only in the eight pillars, which must themselves be improved and beautified, but the work requires altar-like base-moldings, and capitals carved in the Corinthian style. The porch, too, will be of marble wrought with appropriate ornaments. The doors set upon these will be adorned with some such designs as are usually employed by way of embellishment at the projection of the cornice. Of all these, of course, we shall furnish the materials; the form to be impressed on the materials, art will bestow. Besides these there will be in the colonnade not less than forty pillars: these also will be of wrought stone.

Now if my account has explained the work in detail, I hope it may be possible for Your Holiness, on perceiving what is needed, to relieve us completely from anxiety so far as the workmen are concerned.... I know that we shall appear to most people to be wheeler-dealers, in being so particular about the contracts. But I beg you to pardon me; for Mammon — about whom I have so often said such hard things — has at last departed from me as far as he can go, disgusted, I suppose, at the nonsense that is constantly talked against him, and has fortified himself against me by an impassable gulf — poverty — so that neither can he come to me, nor can I pass to him.

— NPNF2 5:540-541

ST. ASTERIUS OF AMASEA

Though he was a bishop in Cappadocia and is listed among the Fathers, you'll rarely see Asterius of Amasea included on the short list of Cappadocian Fathers, with Basil and the two Gregorys. At this remove, we know so little about his life.

We possess a small number of his sermons, however, and they are stunning. Asterius seemed little concerned with the speculative theological debates that were roiling the Church in his lifetime. Instead he focused on very practical matters that concerned his congregation: how to keep a marriage together; how to overcome greed; how to live peacefully alongside one's neighbors, and in the presence of God. He handles the Scriptures, especially the Gospels, with loving familiarity.

Asterius lived at the same time as the three great Cappadocians. He worked as a lawyer before he was appointed bishop. One of his homilies, on the martyrdom of a local saint, includes a detailed description of a work of devotional art. It is quoted, not once but twice, by the Second Council of Nicaea (787) in its defense of the veneration of icons. That alone speaks in favor of Asterius's great authority in antiquity.

Against Divorce
Asterius preaches on Jesus' words to the Pharisees in Matthew's Gospel (19:3-9). This translation is adapted from that of Galusha Anderson and Edgar Goodspeed in Ancient Sermons for Modern Times *(New York: Pilgrim Press, 1904).*

These things were spoken to the Pharisees; but hear them now, you who do such things as these: you who change your wives as readily as your garments; who build bridal chambers as often and as easily as you build booths for feasts; who marry money and deal in women; who if provoked a little immediately write a bill of divorce; you who leave many widows while you are yet alive....

In marriage, O man, both soul and body are united, so that disposition is mingled with disposition, and flesh with flesh. How, then, are you going to sever the bond of marriage without suffering? How can you withdraw from this union easily and without pain, after taking your sister and wife not as a servant of a few days, but as a partner for life, a sister by reason of her formation and creation — for you were both made of the same element of earth and of the same substance — and wife because of the conjugal union, because of the law of marriage? What sort of a bond, then, are you about to break, for you are bound by both law and nature; and how will you set at naught the agreements which you made at marriage? What sort of compacts do you think I mean? Those made when the dowry had been agreed upon, when with your own hand you signed the roll, and set your seal to the contract? These are strong indeed, and possess stability enough, but I refer back to the utterance of Adam: "This is flesh of my flesh and bone of my bones. This shall be called my wife" (see Genesis 2:23). Not without reason is this utterance preserved in writing; for, uttered by the first man, it is the common covenant of men, made with the whole class of women, who are joined by law to their husbands. Do not be surprised if by what one has said, another is bound. For whatever happened in the beginning, in the case of those first created, has become the nature of their posterity.

If, then, the woman you have lightly divorced shall take the Book of Genesis and drag you unto the Judge, who is both Judge and witness, tell me, what will you say? How will you repudiate your own utterance, which you made in the name of God, which Moses, the servant of God, recorded, instead of some cheap notary? God gave Adam a wife without father and without mother; and for this reason, as a guardian He shielded the orphan. But now daughters strongly assert their mothers' rights against their unfeeling and undutiful husbands. So that from every point of view it is impossible for you to slight your wife with impunity, bound as you are by the ancient laws of God and the modern laws of men.

Let your wife's very helpfulness put you to shame. For she is a companion, a helper, a partner with whom to pass your life, and to bring children into the world, an aid in sickness, a comfort in distress, the guardian of the hearth, the custodian of the household goods, having the same sorrows, the same joys, sharing with you your wealth, if wealth be yours, or mitigating hard poverty, resourcefully and sturdily bearing up against its grievous consequences, and because of her marriage with you, enduring the toilsome rearing of children. And if perchance a change of fortune overtakes the husband, he overwhelmed thereby sinks into obscurity, and those who have been considered friends, measuring their friendship by the duration of his prosperity, desert him in his adversity, while the servants run away from both master and misfortunes. Only the wife is left, a partner of his distress, serving her husband amid manifold evils. She wipes away his tears, and heals his stripes if he be smitten. She follows him when he is led to prison; and if permitted to enter with him, she cheerfully shares his confinement. But if even this be forbidden she remains at the door of the prison, like a dog devoted to his master....

Now what can the man seeking divorce say to this? And what sort of specious defense of his own fickleness can he offer? "My wife's disposition," he says, "is mean and hateful, and her tongue is violent, and her tastes are not domestic, and her house is ill-managed." So be it. Granted. I am so far persuaded, and accept it, like the judges who are not very critical in hearing, but are readily carried away by the invectives of advocates. But tell me, when you first married her, didn't you know that you were being joined to a human being? And does anybody fail to see that to a human being sin attaches? For perfection is of God alone. And do you yourself, then, never sin? Do you not cause your wife pain by your conduct? Are you free from all fault? Do you preserve the ordinance of wedlock in purity? Oh, how many times, perhaps, your wife has endured your drunken violence! How many ready insults and shameful reproaches she has patiently suffered! And how many shortcomings of yours are kept secret, because your wife has not published them!

She has borne with you when you were angry without reason, and boiling with wrath; and the free woman, your equal in station, has remained silent like a slave from the market. When you failed through poverty or parsimony to furnish the necessities of life, though grieved, she did not reproach you. No, and furthermore, when you came home from a banquet, drunken and frenzied, she did not cast you off, hating you for your drunkenness, but with kindly forgiveness she received you, and though you resisted, she led you by the hand, and gently bathed your head, dizzied by the fumes of the wine, and guided you to the marriage bed, alone feeling sympathy, while the domestics were laughing and mocking at their master's drunken derangement.

Yet you stalk about the neighborhood heartlessly accusing and misrepresenting your wife, that you may awaken sympathy for yourself and secure approval of your prospective divorce. Hard is the heart of such men, savage and cruel, sprung, as the proverb says, from oak or rock. For wiping out the memory of all past kindnesses, they unfeelingly seek divorce. But who chops off a diseased limb, instead of healing it, and that, too, when no dangerous malady has attacked it, but when there is bright and certain prospect of restoration? A blister has risen on the hand; let us carefully attend to it. A boil has begun to annoy the foot; let us reduce the swelling with liniment. But if we decline the attendance of physicians and busy ourselves with amputation and the knife in the case of each of the disordered parts, before we have lived long we shall have pruned ourselves of all our limbs. But not so, sirs. Let there be some thought even of the limbs. Let the very services of your wives put you to shame. However much you are provoked, compare the pain of one childbirth with your grounds of complaint, and you will find your crowd of grievances outweighed.

ST. CYRIL OF JERUSALEM

Forty years a bishop, St. Cyril (315–386) spent almost half those years banished from his diocese. Such was the peril of living in the heat of the Arian controversy. St. Cyril was an orthodox bishop, but he had been ordained by an Arian, and so he often found himself under a cloud of suspicion.

At one point, indeed, he advocated a compromised wording in the creed, though he later retracted. Nevertheless, by entertaining the question, St. Cyril raised, in the minds of some fellow bishops, indelible questions about his orthodoxy. For this, he would often suffer the censure of some orthodox bishops.

Yet the Arians knew he was no Arian. And when the heretics gained control of the eastern empire, they had Cyril exiled, not once but three times.

During one of his stints at home, St. Cyril delivered a series of catechetical lectures for which he will forever be famous. Their precision and poetry have made them powerful instruction for Christians in all succeeding ages. Cyril emphasized the supernatural character of the sacraments his candidates were about to receive. "Already you stand on the frontier of mystery!" he told them, as the day of their initiation approached. These lectures are all the more remarkable because they were delivered extemporaneously, and what we have today are merely a stenographer's transcription.

By 379, however, so many bishops had raised suspicions about St. Cyril that the Council of Antioch appointed St. Gregory of Nyssa to travel to Jerusalem to investigate the situation. Gregory went and struck up what would be a lasting friendship with Bishop Cyril. St. Gregory ended his journey by pronouncing the Jerusalem diocese a moral and political mess, but its bishop orthodox.

St. Cyril and St. Gregory attended the Council of Constantinople in 381. There the Church definitively settled the Arian controversy. St. Cyril so effectively taught that council's faith that he has been declared a Doctor of the Church. He died in 386, having spent eight consecutive years in Jerusalem.

On Confession

Archbishop Cyril began his Catechetical Lectures *with a rousing call to repentance and peace.*

Now [Lent] is the season of confession. Confess what you have done in word or deed, by night or day. Confess in an acceptable time, and in the day of salvation receive the heavenly treasure.... Blot out from your mind all earthly care, for you are running for your soul. You are utterly forsaking the things of the world. Small are the things you are forsaking; great what the Lord is giving. Forsake things present, and put your trust in things to come.

Have you run so many circles of the years bustling vainly about the world, and have you not forty days to be free for prayer for your own soul's sake? "Be still, and know that I am God," says the Scripture (Ps 46:10). Excuse yourself from speaking many idle words. Neither backbite, nor lend a willing ear to backbiters, but rather be prompt to prayer. Show in ascetic exercise that your heart is strengthened. Cleanse your vessel, that you may receive grace more abundantly. For though remission of sins is given equally to all, the communion of the Holy Spirit is bestowed in proportion to each man's faith. If you have labored little, you receive little; but if you have worked much, the reward is great. You are running for yourself; see to your own interest.

If you have anything against any man, forgive it. You come here to receive forgiveness of sins, and you, too, must forgive him who has sinned against you. Or how will you say to the Lord, "Forgive me my many sins," if you have not yourself forgiven your fellow servant even his little sins.

Attend diligently the Church assemblies; not only now when diligent attendance is required of you by the clergy, but also after you have received the grace. For if, before you have received it, the practice is good, is it not also good after it is given? If before you are grafted in, it is a safe course to be watered and tended, is it not far better after the planting?

— NPNF2 7:7

On the Eucharist

The culmination of Cyril's teaching is the profound mystery of the Body and Blood of Jesus Christ.

Even of itself, the teaching of St. Paul is sufficient to give you a full assurance concerning those divine mysteries, of which you have been counted worthy, with which you have become of the same Body and Blood with Christ. For you have just heard him say distinctly, "That our Lord Jesus Christ on the night he was betrayed, took bread, and when he had given thanks he broke it, and gave it to his disciples, saying, 'Take, eat, this is my body.' And having taken the cup and given thanks, he said, 'Take, drink, this is my blood.'" [Note: Cyril here combines passages from 1 Cor 11 and Mt 26.] Since then He Himself declared and said of the Bread, "This is my body," who shall dare to doubt any longer? And since He has Himself affirmed and said, "This is my blood," who shall ever hesitate, saying, that it is not His Blood?

Once, in Cana of Galilee, He turned water into wine, akin to blood. Is it incredible that He should have turned wine into blood? When called to a bodily marriage, He miraculously wrought that wonderful work; yet, on the children of the bridechamber, shall He not much rather be acknowledged to have bestowed the fruition of His Body and Blood?

So with full assurance let us partake of the Body and Blood of Christ. For given to you in the figure of bread is His Body, and in the figure of wine His Blood; that you, by partaking of the Body and Blood of Christ, may be made of the same body and the same blood with Him. For thus we come to bear Christ in us, because His Body and Blood are distributed through our members; thus it is that, according to St. Peter, we became partakers of the divine nature (see 2 Pet 1:4)....

Consider, then, the Bread and Wine not as bare elements. They are, according to the Lord's declaration, the Body and Blood of Christ. For even though sense suggests this to you, let faith assure you. Judge not the matter from the taste, but from faith be fully assured without misgiving, that the Body and Blood of Christ have been given to you....

— *NPNF2 7:151-152*

On Reverence at Liturgy
A practical guide, from the Catechetical Lectures, *for receiving Holy Communion with attention and reverence.*

Trust not the judgment to your bodily palate, no, but to unfaltering faith. For those who taste are bidden to taste, not bread and wine, but the antitypical Body and Blood of Christ.

Do not approach, then, with your wrists extended or your fingers spread; but make your left hand a throne for the right, as for that which is to receive a king. And having hollowed your palm, receive the Body of Christ, saying over it, "Amen." Then, after having carefully blessed your eyes by the touch of the holy Body, consume it — carefully, lest you lose any portion. For whatever you lose is evidently a loss to you as it were from one of your own limbs. Tell me, if anyone gave you grains of gold, would not you hold them with all care, on your guard against losing any? Will you not keep watch more carefully, then, that not a crumb fall from you of what is more precious than gold and precious stones?

Then after you have consumed the Body of Christ, draw near also to the cup of His Blood; not stretching forth your hands, but bending, and saying with an air of worship and reverence, "Amen." Bless yourself by partaking also of the Blood of Christ. And while the moisture is still upon your lips, touch it with your hands, and bless your eyes and brow and the other organs of sense. Then wait for the prayer, and give thanks to God, who has counted you worthy of such great mysteries.

Hold fast these traditions undefiled, and keep yourselves free from offense. Do not separate yourselves from Communion; do not deprive yourselves, by the pollution of sins, of these holy and spiritual mysteries....

— NPNF2 7:153-157

ST. PACIAN OF BARCELONA

"Christian is my first name; Catholic is my surname."

Pacian would have none of the denominational factionalism that was dividing Christians of his land. As a fourth-century bishop of Barcino (modern Barcelona), he faced an incursion of Novatianism, the rigorist heresy that had originated in Rome a hundred years before.

Pacian noted that the true faith, unlike the heresies, bore the name of no human teacher. Novatianism was named for its third-century founder, Arianism for a priest of the fourth century. The true faith simply bore the name of Christ, Christian, because it had originated with Jesus. It was described as "Catholic" because it alone was truly universal (in Greek, *katholikos*), shared by the saints throughout the world since the time of the Apostles.

To counter Novatianism, Pacian explained the Catholic doctrine of penance and urged his congregations to make use of the sacrament of confession, which at that time was practiced publicly. It was, he said, an opportunity to grow in humility and experience mercy.

Most of what we know about Pacian comes from the small entry in Jerome's biographical dictionary, *On Illustrious Men*. In fact, Jerome dedicated his book to Pacian's son, Flavius Dexter, a civil servant of very high rank during the reigns of Theodosius I and Honorius. Jerome tells us that Pacian was "a man of chaste eloquence, and as distinguished by his life as by his speech." He died, said Jerome, in "extreme old age." Based on this information, historians place Pacian's lifetime around 310 to 391. His years as bishop may have begun as early as the 340s.

It's evident from his work that Pacian received an excellent education. He probably came from a noble family of some means. He was clearly well trained in rhetoric, and he knew classical literature. (When he complains that the Novatianists fault a Catholic bishop for quoting pagan poets, he is probably speaking from personal experience.)

Since he had a son, he was probably married early in life. Perhaps he was a widower at the time of his elevation to bishop. If not, then he and his wife would likely have gone to live in separate monastic or semi-monastic communities, giving their lives over to service of the Church.

On the Name Catholic

The following passage is adapted from Pacian's "Letter 1: On the Catholic Name," translated by C. H. Collyns in The Extant Works of S. Pacian *(London: Rivington, 1842).*

"But under the Apostles," you will say, "no one was called Catholic!" So be it. It may have been so. Allow even that. After the Apostles, however, heresies burst forth and were striving under various names to tear into pieces and divide the Dove and the Queen of God. Then did not the apostolic people require a name of their own, whereby to mark the unity of the people who were uncorrupted, lest the error of some should tear limb from limb the undefiled virgin of God? Was it not appropriate that the chief head should be distinguished by its own peculiar term?

Suppose, this very day, I entered a populous city. When I had found Marcionites, Apollinarians, Cataphrygians, Novatians, and others of the kind who call themselves Christians, by what name should I recognize the congregation of my own people, unless it were called Catholic? Come tell me, who gave so many names to the other peoples? Why have so many cities, so many nations, each their own description? The man who asks the meaning of the Catholic name will he be ignorant himself of the cause of his own name if I shall ask its origin? How was it delivered to me? Certainly that which has stood through so many ages was not borrowed from man. This name "Catholic" sounds not of Marcion, nor of Apelles, nor of Montanus, nor does it claim heretics as its authors....

And yet, my brother, do not be troubled. Christian is my first name; Catholic is my surname. The former gives me an identity, the latter distinguishes me. By the one I am approved; by the other I am marked.

Lastly we should give an account of the word Catholic, and draw it out from the Greek. "Catholic" means "everywhere one," or (as learned men think) "obedience in all," that is, in all the commands of God. Thus the Apostle says, "whether you are obedient in everything"(2 Corinthians 2:9).... Therefore he who is a Catholic is obedient. He who is obedient is a Christian. And thus the Catholic is a Christian. So our people, when named Catholic, are separated by this name from the heretical name.

ST. AMBROSE OF MILAN

Peace brought a new set of difficulties for the Church. When Constantine's Edict of Toleration ended three centuries of intermittent persecution, bishops gradually discovered that they had no clear model for living in a confessionally Christian empire. The new situation raised serious and urgent questions: What role should a Christian state play in enforcing Church discipline? What authority did the emperor have in judging doctrinal disputes, especially when they threatened the civil order?

Eusebius of Caesarea represented one view of Church-state relations: one that ever more closely identified the throne with the altar. The Christian king, according to this view, was God's instrument for bringing about heaven's kingdom on earth. Eusebius's became the dominant model in the East, as we have seen in the profiles of St. Athanasius, St. Cyril of Jerusalem, and Eusebius himself.

St. Ambrose (340–397) could be said to embody the Western Church's attitude toward the state. Making a strict distinction between what is Caesar's and what is God's, St. Ambrose insisted upon the Church's autonomy in sacred matters. He wrote to the emperor Valentinian: "When have you heard, most gracious emperor, that laymen gave judgment concerning a bishop in a matter of faith? Are we so prostrate through the flattery of some as to be unmindful of the rights of the priesthood, and do I think that I can entrust to others what God has given me?"

Again, he was clear about the distinction, saying that he willingly obeyed Caesar in matters in which Caesar legitimately had authority. "If a bishop is to be taught by a layman, what will follow? Let the layman argue, and the bishop listen; let the bishop learn of the layman. But undoubtedly, whether we go through the series of the holy Scriptures, or the times of old, who is there who can deny that, in a matter of faith — in a matter, I say, of faith — bishops are accustomed to judge of Christian emperors, not emperors of bishops."

In the cases of St. Cyril and St. Athanasius, the Eastern emperors claimed the right to appoint and remove bishops, and the bishops tacitly concurred. According to St. Ambrose, it would not be that way in the West. The difference between Eusebius and Ambrose illustrates the widening cultural differences between the Eastern and Western halves of the empire, and the Eastern and Western halves of the Church.

For service of the Church, the young Ambrose had renounced a promising career in government. Brilliant, wealthy, and from an aristocratic family, in his early thirties he was appointed governor of his province by the emperor. This was in the heat of the Arian controversy, and the governor found himself pulled ever more into the midst of it. When the bishop of Milan died in 374, the dispute threatened to rage out of control. Fearing riots, Ambrose, who was a believer but as yet unbaptized, went to the cathedral to calm the crowds.

In a remarkable turn of events, he was unanimously elected bishop, winning the votes of both the Arians and the Catholics. Ambrose, sensibly, refused the honor. The emperor, Valentinian I, however, confirmed the appointment, forcing Ambrose to accede.

Ambrose gave away all his possessions, including his sizable family patrimony, keeping back just enough to support his sister, a nun. Then he applied himself to the study of theology and Scripture with the same rigor with which he had studied law. And with the same result: he became a bishop's bishop.

An intellectual, he could move the movers and shakers of Latin culture. It was he who finally persuaded the stubborn Augustine to proceed to Baptism.

An aristocrat, Ambrose operated with ease in influential circles. He did not hesitate to speak his mind to emperors. After Theodosius ordered the massacre of seven thousand people in Thessalonica, Ambrose refused him the sacraments, demanding of the emperor a severe and humiliating public penance. Theodosius complied.

Another challenge presented itself when the emperor Valentinian's mother, who was Arian, moved to Milan and asked her son to give her control of several churches. The emperor complied, issuing the order. But Ambrose incited the people to fill the churches and occupy them, singing, until the emperor saw the error of his ways. Ambrose, of course, prevailed.

Among his other concerns was a resurgent official paganism, which he successfully advised the emperors to quash.

St. Ambrose was a teaching bishop, himself instructing catechumens and candidates in the mysteries of the Christian religion. He gave regular, informal conferences to the priests of his diocese, leading them in the cultivation of wisdom and the virtues. Ambrose was the first Westerner to encourage congregational hymn-singing in Church, writing simple hymns himself, and he adapted Eastern chant for use in Latin churches.

For good reason, he is known as a Doctor of the Church and one of the eight Great Fathers.

TO THE EMPEROR VALENTINIAN
Ambrose composed the following letter to decline the emperor's invitation to a Church council that, Ambrose believed, an emperor had no authority

to convene. This Church-state wrestling for authority and power would continue for many centuries.

Dalmatius, the tribune and notary, summoned me by your orders.... He added that there was to be a discussion in the consistory, and that your judgment would give the decision.

To this I make, I think, a suitable answer. No one ought to consider me rebellious when I affirm what your father (of august memory) not only replied by word of mouth, but also sanctioned by his laws, that, in a matter of faith, or any ecclesiastical ordinance, the man should judge who was best suited by office, and not disqualified by equity. These are the words of his rescript.

That is, it was his desire that priests should judge concerning priests. Moreover, if a bishop were accused of other matters, and a question of character was to be investigated, it was his will that this should be reserved for the judgment of bishops.

Who, then, has answered Your Clemency rebelliously? He who desires that you should be like your father, or he who wishes you to be unlike him? Unless, perhaps, the judgment of so great an emperor seems to anyone to be of small account, whose faith has been proved by the constancy of his profession, and his wisdom declared by the continual improvement of the state.

When have you heard, most gracious emperor, that laymen gave judgment concerning a bishop in a matter of faith? Are we so prostrate through the flattery of some as to be unmindful of the rights of the priesthood, and do I think that I can entrust to others what God has given me? If a bishop is to be taught by a layman, what will follow? Let the layman argue, and the bishop listen; let the bishop learn of the layman. But undoubtedly, whether we go through the series of the holy Scriptures, or the times of old, who is there who can deny that, in a matter of faith — in a matter, I say, of faith — bishops are accustomed to judge of Christian emperors, not emperors of bishops.

You will, by the favor of God, attain to a riper age, and then you will judge what kind of bishop he is who subjects the rights of the priesthood to laymen. Your father, by the favor of God a man of riper age, used to say: "It is not my business to judge between bishops." Your

Clemency now says: "I ought to judge." And he, though baptized in Christ, thought himself unequal to the burden of such a judgment. Does Your Clemency, who have yet to earn for yourself the Sacrament of Baptism, arrogate to yourself a judgment concerning the faith, though ignorant of the sacrament of that faith?...

And how, O Emperor, are we to settle a matter on which you have already declared your judgment, and have even promulgated laws, so that it is not open to anyone to judge otherwise?...

Ambrose is not of sufficient importance to degrade the priesthood on his own account. The life of one is not of so much value as the dignity of all priests....

If anything has to be discussed I have learned to discuss it in Church, as those before me did. If a conference is to be held concerning the faith, there ought to be a gathering of bishops, as was done under Constantine, the prince of august memory, who did not promulgate any laws beforehand, but left the decision to the bishops....

I would have come, O Emperor, to your consistory, and have made these remarks in your presence, if either the bishops or the people had allowed me, but they said that matters concerning the faith ought to be treated in the Church, in presence of the people.

— NPNF2 10:427-428

To the Catechumens
With Cyril of Jerusalem in the East, Ambrose ranks as the great catechetical instructor of the Patristic Era. The following excerpt comes from his series On the Mysteries, *delivered to Christians preparing for Baptism. "Mystery" is a synonym for "sacrament."*

Perhaps you will say, "I see something else; how is it that you assert that I receive the Body of Christ?" And this is the point which remains for us to prove. And what evidence shall we make use of? Let us prove that this is not what nature made, but what the blessing consecrated, and the power of blessing is greater than that of nature, because by blessing, nature itself is changed.

Moses was holding a rod; he cast it down, and it became a serpent (see Ex 4:3-4). Again, he took hold of the tail of the serpent, and it returned to the nature of a rod. You see that, by virtue of the prophetic office, there were two changes, of the nature of the serpent and of the rod. The streams of Egypt were running with a pure flow of water; and suddenly, from the veins of the sources, blood began to burst forth, and none could drink of the river. Again, at the prophet's prayer, the blood ceased, and the nature of water returned (see Ex 7:20ff). The people of the Hebrews were shut in on every side, hemmed in on the one hand by the Egyptians, on the other by the sea; Moses lifted up his rod, the water divided and hardened like walls, and a way for the feet appeared between the waves (see Ex 14:21ff). Jordan being turned back, returned, contrary to nature, to the source of its stream (see Jos 3:16).

Grace Greater Than Nature

Is it not clear that the nature of the waves of the sea and of the river was changed? The people of the fathers thirsted, Moses touched the rock, and water flowed out of the rock. Did not grace work a result contrary to nature, so that the rock poured forth water, which by nature it did not contain? Marah was a most bitter stream, so that the thirsting people could not drink. Moses cast wood into the water, and the water lost its bitterness, which grace suddenly tempered....

We observe, then, that grace has more power than nature, and yet so far we have only spoken of the grace of a prophet's blessing. But if the blessing of man had such power as to change nature, what are we to say of that divine consecration where the very words of the Lord and Savior operate? For the sacrament that you receive is made what it is by the word of Christ. But if the word of Elijah had such power as to bring down fire from heaven, shall not the word of Christ have power to change the nature of the elements? You read concerning the making of the whole world: "He commanded and they were created" (Ps 148:5). Shall not the word of Christ, which was able to make out of nothing that which was not, be able to change things which already are into what they were not? For it is not less to give a new nature to things than to change them.

But why make use of arguments? Let us use the examples He gives, and by the example of the Incarnation prove the truth of the mystery. Did the course of nature proceed as usual when the Lord Jesus was born of Mary? If we look to the usual course, a woman ordinarily conceives after connection with a man. And this Body which we make is that which was born of the Virgin. Why do you seek the order of nature in the Body of Christ, seeing that the Lord Jesus Himself was born of a virgin, not according to nature? It is the true Flesh of Christ that was crucified and buried. This is, then, truly the Sacrament of His Body.

The Lord Jesus Himself proclaims: "This is my body" (Mt 26:26). Before the blessing of the heavenly words, another nature is spoken of; after the consecration, the Body is signified. He Himself speaks of His Blood. Before the consecration, it has another name; after, it is called Blood. And you say: "Amen," that is, "It is true." Let the heart within confess what the mouth utters; let the soul feel what the voice speaks.

— *NPNF2 10:324-325*

On True Fortitude

Ambrose regularly met with the clergy of Milan and gave them informal talks on the virtues or growth in prayer. Here he connects fortitude with self-mastery and strength of mind and will.

The glory of fortitude does not rest only on the strength of one's body or of one's arms, but rather on the courage of the mind. Nor is the law of courage exercised in causing, but in driving away all harm. He who does not keep harm off a friend, if he can, is as much in fault as he who causes it. This is why holy Moses gave this as a first proof of his fortitude in war. For when he saw a Hebrew receiving hard treatment at the hands of an Egyptian, he defended him, and laid low the Egyptian and hid him in the sand. Solomon also says: "Rescue those who are being taken away to death" (Prov 24:11).

It is perfectly clear, then, where Cicero, Panaetius, or even Aristotle, got these ideas. For though living before these men, Job had said: "I delivered the poor who cried, and the fatherless who had none to help him. The blessing of him who was about to perish came upon me" (Job 29:12-13). Was not he most brave in that he bore so nobly the attacks of the devil, and overcame him with the powers of his mind? Nor have we cause to doubt the fortitude of him to whom the Lord said: "Gird up your loins like a man. Put on loftiness and power. Humble everyone who does wrong" (see Job 40:7-12). The Apostle also says that we "have strong consolation" (cf. Heb 6:18). He, then, is brave who finds consolation in any grief.

Self-Mastery

And in truth, rightly is that called fortitude when a man conquers himself, restrains his anger, yields and gives way to no allurements, is not put out by misfortunes, nor gets elated by good success, and does not get carried away by every varying change as by some chance wind. But what is more noble and splendid than to train the mind, keep down the flesh, and reduce it to subjection, so that it may obey commands, listen to reason, and in undergoing labors readily carry out the intention and wish of the mind?

This, then, is the first notion of fortitude. For fortitude of the mind can be regarded in two ways. First, as it counts all externals as very unimportant, and looks on them as rather superfluous and to be despised than to be sought after. Secondly, as it strives after those things which are the highest, and all things in which one can see anything moral (or as the Greeks call it, *prepon*) with all the powers of the mind. For what can be more noble than to train your mind so as not to place a high value on riches and pleasures and honors, nor to waste all your care on these? When your mind is thus disposed, you must consider how all that is virtuous and seemly must be placed before everything else; and you must so fix your mind upon that, that if anything happens that may break your spirit, whether loss of property, or the reception of fewer honors, or the disparagement of unbelievers, you may not feel it, as if you were above such things — so that even dangers that menace your safety, if undertaken at the call of justice, may not trouble you.

Fighting for God

This is the true fortitude that Christ's warrior has, who receives not the crown unless he strives lawfully. Or does that call to fortitude seem to you but a poor one: "Suffering produces endurance, and endurance produces character, and character produces hope" (Rom 5:3-4)? See how many a contest there is, yet only one crown! That call none gives, but he who was strengthened in Christ Jesus, and whose flesh had no rest. Affliction on all sides, fighting without and fears within. And though in dangers, in countless labors, in prisons, in deaths, he was not broken in spirit, but fought so as to become more powerful through his infirmities.

Think, then, how he teaches those who enter upon their duties in the Church, that they ought to have contempt for all earthly things: "If with Christ you died to the elemental spirits of the universe, why do you live as if you still belonged to the world? Why do you submit to regulations, 'Do not handle, Do not taste, Do not touch' (referring to things which all perish as they are used)" (Col 2:20-22). And further: "If then you have been raised with Christ, seek the things that are above, where Christ is, seated at the right hand of God. Set your minds on things that are above, not on things that are on earth" (Col 3:1-2). And again: "Put to death therefore what is earthly in you" (Col 3:5). This, indeed, is meant for all the faithful. But you, especially, my son, he urges to despise riches and to avoid profane and old wives' tales, allowing nothing but this: "Train yourself in godliness; for while bodily training is of some value, godliness is of value in every way" (1 Tim 4:7-8).

Let, then, godliness exercise you unto justice, continence, gentleness, that you may avoid childish acts, and that rooted and grounded in grace you may fight the good fight of faith. Do not entangle yourself in the affairs of this life, for you are fighting for God.

— NPNF2 10:30-31

THE HYMNS OF THE LITTLE HOURS

These are among the earliest congregational hymns sung in the Western Church. Each hymn marks a different time of day. The "First Hour" roughly corresponds to sunrise; the "Sixth Hour" is around noon; and so on. Venerable John Henry Newman made these translations for Tracts for the Times, *number 75 (1836).*

At the First Hour
> The star of morn to night succeeds;
>> We therefore meekly pray,
> May God in all our words and deeds,
>> Keep us from harm this day;
> May He in love restrain us still
> From tones of strife and words of ill,
> And wrap around and close our eyes
>> To earth's absorbing vanities.
> May wrath and thoughts that gender shame
> Ne'er in our breasts abide;
> And cheerful abstinences tame
>> Of wanton flesh the pride:
> So, when the weary day is o'er,
>> And night and stillness come once more,
> Strong in self-conquering purity,
>> We may proclaim, with choirs on high.

At the Third Hour
> Come, Holy Ghost, who, ever one,
>> Reignest with Father and with Son,
> It is the hour, our souls possess
>> With Thy full flood of holiness.
> Let flesh and heart, and lips and mind,
>> Sound forth our witness to mankind;
> And love light up our mortal frame
>> Till others catch the living flame.
> Now to the Father, to the Son,
>> And to the Spirit, three in one,
> Be praise and thanks and glory given,
>> By men on earth, by saints in heaven.

At the Sixth Hour
> O God, who cannot change nor fail,
>> Guiding the hours as they roll by;

Brightening with beams the morning pale,
   And burning in the midday sky.

Quench Thou the fires of hate and strife,
   The wasting fever of the heart;
From perils guard our feeble life,
   And to our souls Thy peace impart.

At the Ninth Hour
O God, unchangeable and true,
   Of all the Light and Power,
Dispensing light in silence through
   Every successive hour;

Lord, brighten our declining day,
   That it may never wane,
Till death, when all things round decay,
   Brings back the morn again.

Upon Retiring
Now that the daylight dies away,
   By all Thy grace and love,
Thee, Maker of the world, we pray
   To watch our bed above.

Let dreams depart and phantoms fly,
   The offspring of the night,
Keep us, like shrines, beneath Thine eye,
   Pure in our foe's despite.

This grace on Thy redeemed confer,
   Father, co-equal Son,
And Holy Ghost, the Comforter,
   Eternal, three in one.

THE LATER FATHERS

The Church and the Changing World

Though it marks the last of the Fathers, the Post-Nicene Era can hardly be called a "waning" or "twilight." This period includes one of the four Great Fathers from the East and three of the four Great Fathers of the West, including St. Augustine, who is arguably the greatest of the Fathers. Indeed, with the very last of the Fathers, St. John of Damascus, Providence closed the era with a blaze of glory. As monk, apologist, theologian, and spiritual and intellectual warrior, St. John brought together the skills and virtues of the generations of Fathers who had gone before him.

Yet those years, from the fifth century through the eighth, were waning days of an old world order. As St. Augustine lay dying, the barbarians were at the gate of his city. Only with difficulty did Pope St. Leo turn Attila the Hun away from Rome; and he found it impossible to deter later invasions. Weakened by dissension in its military, by rebellion in its provinces, and by the sheer unwieldiness of its size, the Roman Empire gradually crumbled. The great work of the later Fathers was the continued evangelization of the "barbarian" peoples, the preservation of civil and moral order, and the salvaging of Christian and classical learning.

From 395 onward, the empire was split into two nominally united halves, East and West, each with its own emperor. It was an uneasy alliance, sadly reflected in the relations between the Eastern and Western churches. Disputes arose in these latter centuries, mostly over issues of authority, but also over doctrinal matters. East and West disagreed, for example, on whether the Holy Spirit proceeds "from the Father" (as professed in the East) or "from the Father and the Son" (as professed in the West). These disputes would culminate, tragically, in the Great Schism of 1054, centuries after the close of the Patristic Era.

The Late Patristic Era also witnessed the rise of Islam, the religion of Mohammed, which soon swept away several of the Christian lands of the Near East. Islam's un-nuanced monotheism, some Fathers claimed, was an aftereffect of the Arian heresy.

────────────ST. EPIPHANIUS OF SALAMIS────────────

Epiphanius was born in the Gaza region of Palestine, just as Christianity was enjoying its first years of official toleration. His family was Christian, and his parents provided him with excellent cultural and religious education. When he was very young, he discerned a calling to live as a monk, and so he traveled to visit the famous recluses of the Egyptian desert. There he received basic formation in the ascetical life and had memorable encounters with heretical Christians who followed the Gnostic teachings of Valentinus.

Returning home to Palestine, he founded a monastic community in a place called Ad. He was ordained to the priesthood there, and he served as superior for a growing, thriving community of monks. He seems never to have slowed in his studies. His curiosity led him to explorations in the natural sciences, history, and geography. He placed all of it at the service of his biblical scholarship. St. Jerome, who knew the man well, called Epiphanius "Five-Tongued," because he spoke so many languages fluently: Greek, Latin, Coptic, Syriac, and Hebrew.

He led his monastic community for thirty years before receiving the summons to serve as bishop on the island of Constantia (formerly known as Salamis; modern Cyprus). The church there was large and influential, having been established by the Apostles (see Acts 11:19-20, 15:39, 21:3 and 21:16).

Epiphanius was a teaching bishop. To help Christians maintain their composure in times of doctrinal dispute and political upheaval, he wrote his *Ancoratus* (on the "anchored" life). His most famous work is the *Panarion*, or "Medicine Chest," which is a catalog of eighty heresies with sure "cures" for each, in the form of doctrinal responses. He includes passages from the heretics' own writings, and in some cases these are the only scraps from these authors that have survived to modern times.

He also drew from his long life in the Holy Land to make the Bible come alive for scholars and ordinary Christians. He wrote a handbook of weights and measures, explaining the various units found in the Bible — dry and fluid measurements, monetary values, distances, and so on. He explained the history of the Old Testament canon and the various translations of Scripture. Though *On Weights and Measures* survives only in the bishop's rough notes, the book remains an important reference for the study of the ancient world.

Epiphanius also wrote an extended allegorical interpretation of the twelve different gems that adorned the breastplate of the Old Testament high priest. In that work, he moves easily from the data of geological research to their application as metaphors for the Christian ascetical and moral life.

Whatever writing he did, he did it in service to his office, and it was only one small part of his ministry. He labored for Church unity, traveling in all directions to attend synods on doctrinal and disciplinary matters. He strove to heal the distant Church in Antioch, which had long been divided into several factions, each with its own shepherd. The Antiochenes had spread their dissension abroad by getting foreign bishops to take sides. Epiphanius worked with the pope to resolve the dispute for good.

But his great passion was the fight against errant doctrine — heresy. And no one did he oppose more passionately than he opposed Origen. As bishop, he became standard-bearer for the anti-Origenist movement, whose intellectual roots reached back to the time of Methodius. By now, Origen was long dead, but Epiphanius blamed the Egyptian's influence for many of the heresies that had arisen in the past century, especially Arianism. The bishop built up a network of prestigious intellectual allies, whom he encouraged to oppose Origenistic teaching wherever they found it — with or without the help or approval of their local bishops.

It was this passion that drew him into the disciplinary actions brought against St. John Chrysostom. John's nemesis, Theophilus, the bishop of Alexandria, led Epiphanius to believe that John was an

Origenist and was making the imperial capital a haven for heretics. Epiphanius, however, on arriving in Constantinople, saw through the ruse and knew that he was being used — that the current controversy had nothing to do with Origenism — and so he began the return trip to his island.

He died on the way home, in 403.

Against Origen

Epiphanius had a longstanding feud with Jerusalem's bishop, John. The latter had some sympathies for Origen and had been less than congenial to Epiphanius's allies, such as Jerome. In a letter to John, Epiphanius makes his case against Origen's doctrines.

I speak plainly. To use the language of Scripture, I do not spare to pluck out my own eye if it cause me to offend, nor to cut off my hand and my foot if they cause me to do so (see Mt 18:8-9). And you must be treated in the same way whether you are my eyes, or my hands, or my feet. For what Catholic, what Christian who adorns his faith with good works, can hear with calmness Origen's teaching and counsel, or believe in his extraordinary preaching? The Son, he tells us, cannot see the Father, and the Holy Spirit cannot see the Son. These words occur in his book *On First Principles*; thus we read, and thus Origen has spoken: "For as it is unsuitable to say that the Son can see the Father, it is consequently unsuitable to suppose that the Spirit can see the Son" (First Principles 1.1, 2.4).

Can anyone, moreover, brook Origen's assertion that men's souls were once angels in heaven, and that having sinned in the upper world, they have been cast down into this, and have been confined in bodies as in barrows or tombs, to pay the penalty for their former sins; and that the bodies of believers are not temples of Christ, but prisons of the condemned? Again, he tampers with the true meaning of the narrative by a false use of allegory, multiplying words without limit; and he undermines the faith of the simple by the most varied arguments. Now he maintains that … the soul is shut up within the body in the same way as the corpses of the dead are shut up in tombs and barrows. If this doctrine is true, what becomes of our faith? Where is the preaching of the resurrection? Where is the teaching of the Apostles, which lasts on to this day in the churches of Christ? Where is the blessing to Adam, and to his seed, and to Noah and his sons? Be fruitful, and multiply, and replenish the earth (see Gen 1:28 and 9:7).

According to Origen, these words must be a curse and not a blessing; for he turns angels into human souls, compelling them to leave the place of highest rank and to come down lower, as though God were unable through the action of his blessing to grant souls to the human race, had the angels not sinned, and as though for every birth on earth there must be a fall in heaven. We are to give up, then, the teaching of Apostles and Prophets, of the law, and of our Lord and Savior himself, in spite of his language loud as thunder in the gospel.

Origen, on the other hand, commands and urges — not to say binds — his disciples not to pray to ascend into heaven, lest sinning once more worse than they had sinned on earth they should be hurled down into the world again. Such foolish and insane notions he generally confirms by distorting the sense of the Scriptures and making them mean what they do not mean at all. He quotes this passage from the Psalms: "Before I was afflicted I went astray" (Ps 119:67); and this, "Return, O my soul, to your rest" (Ps 116:7); this also, "Bring me out of prison" (Psalm 142:7).... There can be no doubt that the meaning of the divine Scripture is different from the interpretation by which he unfairly wrests it to the support of his own heresy.

This way of acting is common to the Manichæans, the Gnostics, the Ebionites, the Marcionites, and the votaries of the other eighty heresies, all of whom draw their proofs from the pure well of the Scriptures, not, however, interpreting it in the sense in which it is written, but trying to make the simple language of the Church's writers accord with their own wishes.... Who, then, will put up with the follies of Origen?

— NPNF2 6:85-86

ST. JOHN CHRYSOSTOM

John of Antioch (347–407), patriarch of Constantinople, was Midas in the pulpit. We know this not only from his homilies, of which hundreds have been preserved, but even from the nickname he earned — Chrysostom, which means "Golden-Tongued."

While the school at Alexandria reached its zenith in the allegorical studies of Clement and Origen, the rival school of Antioch may have peaked in the practical preaching of St. John Chrysostom. St. John was surely brilliant, but he was no ethereal academic. For him, the power in Scripture was a power to transform the minute particulars of everyday work, family, and society. The method he learned at Antioch for searching out the concrete historical situations in Jesus' life he used equally well in analyzing the concrete existential circumstances of his congregations. St. John's homilies hit home. They spoke of the marketplace, the marriage bed, the sports arena, of cooking, investments, and cosmetics. And they were practical. He not only described what he saw, but he also prescribed a moral and ascetical course of action.

Yet preaching was, perhaps, the last thing he wanted to do. The only son of a pious widow, John studied law and rhetoric in Antioch. Early on, he was attracted to the solitary contemplative life. His mother, however, begged him not to make her "a widow again" by fleeing to the desert. For a time, he respected her wishes by living, as much as possible, a life of silence and fasting at home. But by 374, he had clearly discerned the call to live as a solitary. He retired first as a monk and then as a hermit. But years of fasting and sleeplessness proved the limits of his bodily endurance. In ill health, John returned to Antioch, where he was ordained a deacon in 381 and a priest in 386.

In the city, John won renown for his preaching and soon found himself assigned to the most prestigious pulpit. His fame spread far beyond Syria. And in 398, he received word that he had been named patriarch of Constantinople. He tried to refuse the position, but the emperor sent for him with an armed escort. John could not refuse.

In the imperial city, he found a demoralized clergy, many living in sin, fornicating and carousing. John set about the reform of the clergy, renewing the enforcement of priestly disciplines, and defrocking priests who proved unrepentant. His course of renewal pleased many in Constantinople who had been disgusted by the state of their church, but it earned him enemies as well. The foe who mattered most was the empress Eudoxia, whom John had specifically targeted in his masterful homilies on vanity. John also discovered an enemy in the influential archbishop of Alexandria, Theophilus, who roused other bishops to band together and have John deposed and exiled.

Theophilus's maneuverings worked. John was sent away in 403. But the people of Constantinople nearly revolted, and so the empress herself had him recalled to his see. But shortly after returning, John dared to preach against the public games and celebrations when the city erected a silver statue of Eudoxia. In 404, he was exiled to Armenia. He appealed to the pope, who supported him but was unable to prevail upon the emperor.

In Armenia, St. John continued to win fame for his preaching and counsel, further infuriating his enemies. They asked the emperor to banish him to a more severe wilderness on the Black Sea, which the emperor did. On the way there, John was forced to march long distances in driving rain and oppressive heat. Never in good health, he was, at age sixty, little able to withstand this torture. He died en route in 407.

The pope and the Western Church broke off communion with the sees that had persecuted John, and restored this communion only when the latter had repented. When John's body was returned to Constantinople, Eudoxia's son, the emperor Theodosius II, went out to greet his coffin and begged forgiveness for his mother.

At the Council of Chalcedon in 451, St. John Chrysostom was named a Doctor of the Church. He is a Great Father of the Church. Pope St. Pius X, in the twentieth century, named him patron of preachers.

On Riches

The wages of sin might seem high, but St. John warns his congregations away from such temptations in one of his homilies on 1 Corinthians.

When you see an enemy of God wealthy, with armed attendants and many flatterers, do not be downcast, but lament, weep, call upon God, that He may enroll him among His friends. And the more he prospers being God's enemy, the more you should mourn for him. For we ought always to weep for sinners, but especially when they enjoy wealth and good times, even as one should pity the sick when they eat and drink to excess.

But some who hear these words are made so unhappy that they sigh bitterly and say, "Tears are due to me. I have nothing." You said it well — "I have nothing" — not because you lack what another has, but because you think that things will make you happy. For this you are worthy of infinite lamentations. It is as if a healthy person should call "happy" a man who is sick and lying on a soft couch. The latter is not nearly so wretched and miserable as he, because he has no sense of his own advantages. Such is the result in these men's case as well, and thus our whole life is confounded and disordered. For these sayings have undone many, and betrayed them to the devil, and made them more pitiable than those who are wasted with famine.

— NPNF1 12:240-241

ON LUXURY

St. John Chrysostom saw clearly how a mania for investment could make someone inhuman. In this passage, from his series of homilies on 1 Corinthians, he cites the case of a merchant who prays for famine so that his goods may be more valuable.

Do you see how gold does not allow men to be men, but wild beasts and fiends? For what can be more pitiful than this rich man whose daily prayer is that there may be famine so that he may have a little gold? And his passion is now come round to contradict itself. He is not even happy with his abundant store of the fruits of the earth, but on this very account he is sad because his possessions are not infinite! Although one who has much ought to be joyful, this man is dejected. Do you see?

As I said, the rich do not reap as much pleasure from what is present as they endure sorrow for what has not yet been added. For he who has had numberless quantities of wheat grieved and lamented more than he who suffered hunger. And while the one, on merely having his necessary food, was crowning himself and leaping for joy and giving thanks to God, the other who had so much was fretting and thought he was undone.

It is not luxury that causes our pleasure, but a self-controlling mind, since without this — even though one should obtain and have everything — he will feel as if deprived of everything and will mourn, like the man of whom we are now speaking. Even if he had sold all he had for as large a sum as he wished, again would he have grieved that it was not for more. And if he could have had more, he would again have sought another advance. And if he had disposed of the bushel for a dollar more, he would even then have been distracted for sorrow, that the half-bushel could not be sold for as much. And if the price were not set so high at first, do not wonder. Drunkards, too, are not inflamed at first; but when they have loaded themselves with wine, then they kindle the flame into greater fierceness. So these men, by how much more they have grasped, find themselves in greater poverty, and they who gain more than others are the very persons to be the most in want.

I say these things not only to this man, but also to each one of those who are so diseased — those, I say, who raise the price of their wares and make a traffic off the poverty of their neighbors. For no one anywhere takes humanity into account, but everywhere covetous desire brings out many at the time of sale. Oil and wine are sold by one more quickly, by another more slowly, but neither out of regard to others. Rather, the one seeks gain, the other to avoid loss by the spoiling of his produce. Thus, because most men — not making much account of the law of God — shut up and keep all indoors, God by other means leads them to humanity. That they may do something kind, God has infused into them the fear of greater loss, not allowing the fruits of the earth to keep any long time, in order that out of mere dread of the damage from their spoiling they may expose for sale to the needy, even against their will, such things as they wickedly bury at home and keep.

But after all this, some are so insatiable that even now they are not corrected. Many, for example, have gone so far as to empty whole casks, not giving even a cupful to the poor man, nor a piece of money to the needy. But after the wine has become vinegar, they dash it all upon the ground and destroy their casks together with the fruit. Others who would not give a part of a single cake to the hungry have thrown whole granaries into some river. And because they listened not to God, who bade them give to the needy, at the bidding of the moth, even unwillingly they emptied out all they had in their houses, in utter destruction and waste, drawing down upon their own heads together with this loss much scorn and many a curse.

Such is the course of their affairs here. But of the hereafter, what shall we say? As these men in this world cast their moth-eaten grain, become useless, into rivers, even so the doers of such things — on this very account become useless — God casts into the river of fire. Because as the grain by the moth and worm, so are the souls devoured by cruelty and inhumanity. And the reason of these things is their being nailed to things present and gaping after this life only.

— *NPNF1 12:241*

HUSBANDS, LOVE YOUR WIVES
St. John's homilies on the Letter to the Ephesians focused especially on Christian marriage.

A certain wise man ... set this down in the rank of a blessing, "A wife agreeing with her husband" (cf. Sir 25:1). Elsewhere again he sets it down among blessings that a woman should dwell in harmony with her husband (cf. Sir 40:23). And indeed from the beginning, God appears to have made special provision for this union; and discoursing of the twain as one, He said thus, "Male and female he created them" (Gen 1:27)....

Indeed, this love is more despotic than any despotism: for others indeed may be strong, but this passion is not only strong, but unfading. For there is a certain love deeply seated in our nature, which imperceptibly knits together these bodies of ours. Thus even from the very beginning woman sprang from man, and afterwards from man and woman sprang both man and woman. Do you see the close bond and connection?...

This produces great evils and great benefits, both to families and to states. For nothing so welds our life together as the love of man and wife. For this, many will lay aside even their arms; for this they will give up life itself....

[Paul] proceeds with arguments and says that "the husband is the head of the wife as Christ is the head of the church, his body, and is himself its Savior. As the church is subject to Christ, so let wives also be subject in everything to their husbands" (Eph 5:23-24)....

You have seen the measure of obedience; now hear the measure of love. Would you have a wife obedient to you, as the Church is to Christ? Then take the same provident care for her, as Christ takes for the Church. Even if it shall be needful for you to give your life for her, and to be cut into pieces ten thousand times, and to endure and undergo any suffering whatsoever — do not refuse. Though you should undergo all this, yet you will not even then have done anything like Christ. For you are doing it for one to whom you are already knit; but He for one who turned her back on Him and hated Him.

In the same way ... though you see her looking down upon you, and disdaining and scorning you, yet by your great thoughtfulness for her, by affection, by kindness, you will be able to lay her at your feet. For there is nothing more powerful to sway than these bonds, and especially for husband and wife. One can, perhaps, bind a servant down by fear.... But the partner of one's life, the mother of one's children, the foundation of one's every joy, one ought never to chain down by fear and menaces, but with love and good temper. For what sort of union is that, where the wife trembles at her husband? And what sort of pleasure will the husband himself enjoy, if he dwells with his wife as with a slave, and not as with a freewoman? Though you should suffer anything because of her, do not upbraid her; for neither did Christ do this....

Praise her, but not for her beauty. Praise and hatred and love based on physical beauty belong to unchaste souls. Seek instead for beauty of soul. Imitate the Bridegroom of the Church. Outward beauty is full of conceit and great license, and throws men into jealousy, and itself often makes you suspect monstrous things. But has it any pleasure? For the first or second month, perhaps, or at most for the year, but then no longer. Familiarity wastes away the admiration. Meanwhile the evils which arose from the beauty still abide, the pride, the folly, the contemptuousness. But in one who is not this way, there is nothing of this kind. Since the love began on just grounds, it remains ardent; its object is beauty of soul, and not of body.

Tell me what is better than heaven? What is better than the stars? Tell me of what body you will, yet is there none so fair. Tell me of what eyes you will, yet are there none so sparkling. When these were created, the very angels gazed with wonder, and we gaze with wonder now — yet not in the same degree as at first. Such is familiarity; things do not strike us in the same degree. How much more in the case of a wife! And if disease comes, too, all is at once fled.

Let us seek in a wife affection, modesty, gentleness; these are the characteristics of beauty. But let us not seek loveliness of person, or upbraid her upon these things, over which she has no power. Rather, let us not upbraid at all (it is rudeness), neither let us be impatient or sullen. Do you not see how many, after living with beautiful wives, have ended their lives pitiably, and how many, who have lived with those of no great beauty, have run on to extreme old age with great enjoyment. Let us wipe off the "spot" that is within, let us smooth the "wrinkles" that are within, let us do away the "blemishes" that are on the soul. Such is the beauty God requires. Let us make her fair in God's sight, not in our own....

Show her that you set a high value on her company, and that you would rather be at home by her side than in the marketplace. And honor her before all your friends, and above the children who are born of her, and love these very children for her sake. If she does any good act, praise and admire it; if any foolish one, such as girls may chance to do, advise her and remind her....

Let your prayers be common. Let each go to church; and, once back home, let the husband ask his wife, and she ask her husband, what was said and read there. If any poverty should overtake you, cite the case of those holy men, Paul and Peter, who were more honored than any kings or rich men; and yet how they spent their lives in hunger and in thirst. Teach her that there is nothing in life that is to be feared but offending God. If any marries this way, with these views, he will be hardly inferior to monks; married, but little below the unmarried.

—NPNF1 13:143-152

To Parents
The homilies on Ephesians move, naturally, from marriage to child rearing.

Do you wish your son to be obedient? From the first, "but bring them up in the discipline and instruction of the Lord" (Eph 6:4). Never deem it unnecessary that he should listen diligently to the divine Scriptures. For there the first thing he hears will be this: "Honor your father and your mother" (Ex 20:12), so you will win your reward.

Never say that the reading of Scripture is the business of monks. Am I making a monk of him? No. There is no need for him to become a monk. Why be so afraid of a thing so replete with so much advantage? Make him a Christian. For it is altogether necessary for laymen to be acquainted with the lessons derived from this source — but especially for children. For theirs is an age full of folly; and to this folly are added the bad examples derived from the pagan myths, where they are made acquainted with heroes so admired, who are slaves of their passions, and cowards with regard to death — as, for example, Achilles, when he relents, when he dies for his concubine, when another gets drunk, and many other things of the sort.

He requires therefore the remedies against these things. Is it not absurd to send children out to jobs, and to school, and to do all you can for these objects, and yet, not to "bring them up in the discipline and instruction of the Lord"?

"Bring them up in the discipline and instruction of the Lord"; do not conspire to make him a politician, but train him instead to be a philosopher. In the lack of the one, there will be no harm whatever; in the absence of the other, all the rhetoric in the world will be of no advantage. Discipline is needed, not talking; character, not cleverness; deeds, not words. These gain a man the kingdom. These confer what are benefits indeed. Whet not his tongue, but cleanse his soul. I do not say this to prevent your teaching him these things, but to prevent your attending to them exclusively. Do not imagine that the monk alone stands in need of these lessons from Scripture. Of all others, the children just about to enter into the world specially need them.

— *NPNF1 13:154*

ST. JOHN CASSIAN

At a young age, John Cassian was a prodigy in matters intellectual and spiritual. Well educated, he was in his teens when he and a friend, Germanus, decided to leave their native Scythia (modern Romania and Bulgaria) and learn, firsthand, about the monasteries in the East.

It was around 380 when they traveled to Bethlehem in Palestine. There they learned the basics of the ascetical life before setting off to the major league: the communities of the Egyptian wilderness. By this time, the desert had indeed become a city. The reputation of the great founders, St. Anthony and St. Pachomius, had gone out into the world. Athanasius's *Life of Anthony* was a best seller, already translated into Latin. Cassian and Germanus were not the only spiritual seekers who made their way to Egypt.

There the young men encountered different types of communities and masters, who represented a variety of approaches to prayer and ascetical struggle. They spent time with many of the Desert Fathers, probing them on practical matters.

It was in Egypt, in the last years of the fourth century, that Cassian found himself caught up in Origenist controversies that then roiled the monasteries, pitting simple monks against the wily Alexandrian bishop, Theophilus. With hundreds of fellow monks, John traveled to Constantinople to plead their case before the emperor. While in the imperial capital, they sought refuge with the bishop, John Chrysostom.

Cassian made a positive impression on John, who ordained him a deacon.

Chrysostom's fortunes soon soured, however, and he was himself exiled from Constantinople. Cassian went to Rome, on behalf of the clergy of Constantinople, to present Chrysostom's case before the pope. Chrysostom would die in exile.

But Providence had another purpose for Cassian's journey. His vast knowledge of Egyptian monasteries made him a celebrity in Rome. Opportunities for such travel were rare, and Christians found the stories of Egypt's saints fascinating. Eventually, Cassian was invited to Gaul to establish a monastery there after the Egyptian models.

In Gaul, his local bishop — as well as important clergy in the papal court (including the future Pope Leo the Great) — prevailed upon him to set down his memories of Egypt in books titled *The Institutes* and *The Conferences*. In these he presented the basic customs and social order of the Egyptian communities. He also recounted his conversations with individual Desert Fathers on a great range of subjects, from persevering in prayer to overcoming specific sins and temptations.

Cassian's books became foundational works of ascetical literature, and they are still consulted widely today. He gave a lasting form to many of the basic categories of Western spirituality, for example: the three ages of the interior life (purgation, illumination, and union), the four types of prayer (adoration, contrition, thanksgiving, supplication), and the deadly sins (he counts eight, the seven known from Aquinas, plus sadness).

His writings were immediately influential in the development of monasticism. They were even translated into Greek, and so they brought the words of the Egyptian Fathers back to Egypt. In Italy, St. Benedict was dependent on Cassian as he founded his own great order.

Cassian died in 435 and was immediately revered as a saint. Because he placed such a strong emphasis on individual effort, some people later accused him of the heresy of Semi-Pelagianism. But the Council of Orange (529), which officially condemned that heresy, spoke of John Cassian as a saint.

THE ATHLETE OF CHRIST
The struggle does not end, so long as we are on earth. So explains Cassian in his Institutes *5.19.*

The athlete of Christ, as long as he is in the body, is never in want of a victory to be gained in struggle. As he grows by triumphant successes, however, so does a severer kind of struggle confront him. For when the flesh is subdued and conquered, what swarms of foes, what hosts of enemies are incited by his triumphs and rise up against the victorious soldier of Christ! He should fear lest in the ease of peace the soldier of Christ might relax his efforts and begin to forget the glorious struggles of his contests — and so be rendered slack through the idleness caused by freedom from danger, and so be cheated of the reward of his prizes and the recompense of his triumphs.

If we want to rise with ever-growing virtue to these stages of triumph we too ought to enlist for battle and begin by saying with the Apostle: "I do not box as one beating the air; but I pommel my body and subdue it" (1 Cor 9:26-27). Thus, when this conflict is ended we may once more be able to say with him: "we are not contending against flesh and blood, but against the principalities, against the powers, against the world rulers of this present darkness, against the spiritual hosts of wickedness in the heavenly places" (Eph 6:12). Otherwise, we cannot possibly join battle with them nor deserve to make trial of spiritual combats if we are baffled in a fleshly contest, and smitten down in a struggle with the belly. Deservedly will it be said of us by the Apostle in the language of blame: "No temptation has overtaken you that is not common to man" (1 Cor 10:13).

—NPNF2 11:240-241

BEGIN WITH AN END IN MIND
At the start of his book of Conferences, *Cassian describes his stay in Skete and "what we proposed to Abbot Moses."*

In the desert of Skete are the most excellent monastic fathers, and all perfection flourishes. And there I was with the holy father Germanus. Since the earliest days of spiritual service he had been my closest companion, first in the monastery and then in the desert. To show the harmony of our friendship and aims, everybody would say that a single heart and soul existed in our two bodies.

In my eagerness for basic instruction I sought out Abbot Moses, who was eminent amid those splendid flowers, not only in practical but also in contemplative virtue. Together we implored him to give us a discourse for our edification. We begged him with tears, for we knew full well his determination never to consent to open the gate of perfection, except to those who desired it with all faithfulness, and sought it with all sorrow of heart. He feared after all that he might show it at random to those who cared nothing for it, or who only desired it in a half hearted way — that he might open for unworthy persons what ought only to be discovered by those seeking perfection, and that they would receive it with scorn. Thus, he might appear to lay himself open either to the charge of bragging, or to the sin of betraying his trust.

At last, being overcome by our prayers, he thus began.

"All the arts and sciences," said he, "have some goal or mark, an end or aim of their own, on which the diligent pursuer of each art has his eye, and so endures all sorts of toils and dangers and losses, cheerfully and with equanimity. The farmer, for example, shuns neither the scorching heat of the sun, nor the frost and cold, and so he works the earth untiringly, and again and again subjects the clods of his field to his plow, while he keeps before him his goal: that is, by diligent labor to break it up small like fine sand, and to clear it of all briers, and free it from all weeds, as he believes that in no other way can he gain his ultimate end, which is to secure a good harvest, and a large crop. On that he can either live free from care, or can increase his possessions. Again, when his barn is well stocked he is quite ready to empty it, and with incessant labor to commit the seed to the crumbling furrow, thinking nothing of the present lessening of his stores in view of the future harvest.

"Those men, too, who are engaged in selling, have no dread of the uncertainties and chances of the ocean, and fear no risks. An eager hope urges them forward to their goal of profit.

"And those who are inflamed with the ambition of military life, while they look forward to their aim of honors and power, take no notice of danger and destruction in their wanderings. Nor are they crushed by present losses and wars. They are eager to obtain the end of some honor held out to them.

"And our profession too has its own goal and end, for which we undergo all sorts of toils not merely without weariness, but actually with delight. On account of that goal, the want of food in fasting is no trial to us, the weariness of our vigils becomes a delight; reading and constant meditation on the Scriptures does not pall upon us; nor do we find terrors in incessant toil, self-denial, the privation of all things, and the horrors of this vast desert.

"Surely this is why you yourselves renounced the love of family, and scorned your homeland and the delights of this world, and passed through so many countries. You did it so that you might come to us, plain and simple folk as we are, living in this wretched state in the desert.

"So," said he, "answer and tell me what is the goal and end that incite you to endure all these things so cheerfully."

And when he insisted on drawing an opinion from us on this question, we replied that we endured all this for the sake of the kingdom of heaven.

—NPNF2 11:295-296

THEODORE OF MOPSUESTIA

Theodore of Mopsuestia is one of those Fathers whose legacy is complicated. As Origen (though long dead) came to be tagged as a forerunner of the Arian heresy, so Theodore (dead but a short time) took the hit for the errors of Nestorius.

Nestorius had, in fact, been Theodore's student. But Theodore had many students. He was, after all, the most renowned exegete of the Antiochene school alive in the early fifth century. His writings earned him the title by which he is known in the Christian Orient: The Interpreter.

Theodore was born around 350 into a prominent family of civil servants in Antioch. He was a companion of John Chrysostom in the classes of Libanius the rhetorician. With John and another friend, Theodore left to pursue a monastic life of prayer and study. Not long into their venture, however, Theodore began to waver. He had fallen hard for a young woman named Hermione, and he made the decision to forsake religious life, go back to Antioch, pursue the practice of law, and get married.

Chrysostom rose to the circumstance and composed his two "Letters to Theodore upon His Fall." The letters apparently accomplished their purpose, because Theodore resumed his monastic life, was ordained to the priesthood, and eventually was named bishop of Mopsuestia, a town about a dozen miles from Antioch.

As bishop he continued his researches, and his congregations were the beneficiaries. He attracted many students who wished to learn from a man known for his scholarship as well as his sanctity. He was a prolific author, producing commentaries for many books of the Bible, catechetical works on the creed and the sacraments, and practical works on Christian life and prayer.

He wrote with precision, clarity, and simplicity. He strove to anticipate possible misunderstandings and cut them off. Of Jesus' Real Presence in the Eucharist Theodore wrote: "when He gave the bread He did not say 'This is the symbol of My body,' but rather 'This is My body'; likewise when He gave the cup he did not say: 'This is the symbol of My blood,' but rather 'This is My blood.'"[69] He also noted that, in receiving the Eucharist, Christians take "a small portion, but we believe that in that small portion we receive all of Him."

Theodore was a loyal friend. He remained in touch with John Chrysostom to the end of John's life and was supportive during his exile.

But Nestorius was indeed Theodore's student, however briefly, and Nestorius did turn out to be a heretic, and all the while was pleased to call the great Theodore his master. And so, as the opposition to Nestorius escalated into an opposition to Antioch in general, Theodore (though dead by then) presented a rather large target. Quotations from his works were wrenched out of context and published in broadsides that made him appear to be an almost demonic teacher of error. Some passages were altered to mean the opposite of Theodore's intention. Others may have been entirely fabricated. Based on such falsified evidence, the Second Council of Constantinople (in 553) condemned both Theodore and his writings. In the last century, however, as more of his writings have come to light, Theodore has been somewhat vindicated. After careful study, no less an authority than Father Quasten concluded that "nobody contributed more to the progress of Christology in the generation of theologians between 381 and 431 than Theodore of Mopsuestia."[70]

Father Jurgens proposed that he was "more deserving of tribute than condemnation."[71] In his treatise On the Incarnation Theodore clearly distinguishes two natures while insisting that Christ is one person. It seems that he was not, as his enemies called him, "Nestorius before Nestorius."

If he can be faulted for anything, many experts agree, it is an extreme aversion to allegory, and that is indeed the characteristic most associated with Antiochene biblical interpretation. In some of his works Theodore presents himself almost as Antioch's caricature, foregoing a Christological interpretation even of the messianic prophecies in the Old Testament.

Because of the conciliar condemnation, Theodore's works were suppressed, and many have been lost for centuries. Some have been recently discovered in Syriac editions and have been translated to edify new generations.

The Meaning of "Consubstantial"
Theodore's catechetical lectures begin with his Commentary on the Nicene Creed. *He explains and defends Nicaea's christology against Arian misunderstanding. This small portion focuses only on the Greek word homoousion (consubstantial). The translation is from A. Mingana,* Commentary of Theodore of Mopsuestia on the Nicene Creed *(Cambridge: Heffer, 1932).*

Our blessed Fathers added that the Son was "consubstantial" with His Father, a word that confirms the children of faith and rebukes the unbelievers. Although this word is not explicitly written in Holy Scripture, its meaning is found there. They explained here by means of a clear word the meaning of that which they had previously stated, because the phrase "Consubstantial with the Father" is not different from that of "True God of true God." They did not wish to insinuate by this sentence "Consubstantial with the Father" any other thing than that the being who — as previously stated by them, was God and born of His Father before all ages and not made — is God.

Indeed, if He is born of Him before all ages and is not made, and if He is not a creature but a true Son of His Father, it is evident that He is from Him and not from outside Him, and that He is born of the nature of the Father and consubstantial with Him; and if He is true God of true God, it is evident that He is consubstantial with Him, because anyone who is truly God in nature is consubstantial with one who is truly God in nature.

The meaning of "consubstantial with His Father" is clearly found in the Bible. When it says: "In the beginning ... He was with God and He was God" (see John 1:1), it shows by means of these two phrases that He is God in nature and that He is consubstantial with God. This is also the meaning of the sentence: "I and the Father are one" (Jn 10:30). If the Son is one with His Father in power and in nature, He is consubstantial with Him. By His statement "My sheep hear my voice, and I know them, and they follow me; and I give them eternal life, and they shall never perish, and no one shall snatch them out of my hand" (Jn 10:27-28), He bore witness to His omnipotence and to the fact that no man can prevail against Him. And because this sentence conveyed higher things than the simple man who was seen in him, He added, "My Father, who has given them to me, is greater than all, and no one is able to snatch them out of the Father's hand." ...

He made clear in this what He had implicitly insinuated in the meaning of the preceding words He had uttered. It is as if He had said, "My power is identical with that of My Father and higher than all like His power, and no man can prevail against Me even as no man can prevail against My Father, because My Father and I are one, and have one power and one dominion that is higher than all." This is the reason why the Jews called Him a blasphemer. Indeed they did not know the divine nature that was dwelling in Him, but knew only that which was visible in Him, and wished to stone Him like a man making use of blasphemous words.

To the same effect is the sentence "He who has seen me has seen the Father" (Jn 14:9) and "I am in the Father and the Father in me" (Jn 14:10-11). If the Father is seen in the Son it is evident that both share one nature, and each of Them is seen and known in the other. In this way their mutual equality shows also the unity of their nature, and the consubstantiality of the Son with the Father.

ST. CYRIL OF ALEXANDRIA

St. Cyril of Alexandria was a successor to St. Athanasius in more ways than one. He succeeded Athanasius as patriarch of the great Egyptian city; but he also succeeded him as defender of the faith — teaching with clarity, rousing a council of the Church, and defying even the emperor.

He had a privileged Christian upbringing. He was born in Alexandria around 375, the nephew of a prominent priest named Theophilus. Cyril received a thoroughgoing Christian education, and he maintained correspondence with his teachers throughout his life. Ordained to the priesthood, Cyril served as assistant to his uncle Theophilus, who had by then been elevated to patriarch of Alexandria. In history, Theophilus is notorious as the dogged prosecutor of St. John Chrysostom. Cyril accompanied his uncle to the infamous Synod of the Oak (403), which deposed St. John. Theophilus died in 412, but the Alexandrian clergy chose to keep the patriarchate in his family. They chose Cyril, who was then a relatively young man, in his thirties.

In 428, a man named Nestorius was elevated to be patriarch of Constantinople. Nestorius was an Antiochene scholar. Something of a rationalist, he had a penchant for semantic fussiness; he was fond of the phrase "strictly speaking." He could not, strictly speaking, accept certain traditional formulas the Church had passed on from the earlier Fathers. He rejected, for example, the title "Mother of God" applied to Mary — since, strictly speaking, she did not precede God in time, as an ordinary mother precedes an ordinary child. Nestorius favored safer terms, like "Mother of Christ," opining that Mary gave birth only to Christ's human nature.

Nestorius's doctrine did not play well to the congregations, who nurtured a deep, traditional Marian devotion. Nor did it ring true for his fellow patriarch, Cyril of Alexandria.

On the subject of the Mother of God, Cyril responded that a mother does not give birth to a nature, but to a person. Nestorius seemed to be dividing Christ into two different persons united as one. He tried to draw Nestorius out, asking him to clarify what he meant. But perhaps because of the recent hostilities between Constantinople and Alexandria — or maybe because of the long standing rivalry between Antioch and Alexandria — Nestorius just got defensive and dug in. His arrogant intellectualism drove him from mere idiosyncrasy into explicit heresy.

Cyril prevailed over Nestorius at the Council of Ephesus in 431 — a council that Nestorius himself had asked the emperor to summon. There the bishops overwhelmingly acclaimed the doctrine long hallowed by the worship of the Church: that Christ the God-man is a single subject, and so Mary could be called "Mother of God." The title "Mother of God" (in Greek *Theotokos*, literally "God-bearer") was more than an isolated Marian dogma. It preserved the integrity of the incarnation of the eternal Word. Cyril held the day because of his sustained, consistent, and subtle theological argument. Theological truth won the war, but the victory belonged to more than the theologians. Throngs of common people celebrated the council's decision by carrying the bishops aloft in a torchlit procession and singing hymns throughout the night.

Cyril was an inexhaustible teacher and writer. Over the course of his long tenure as patriarch, he wrote theological studies, commentaries on many of the books of the Bible, and countless letters.

In past centuries, it was a commonplace for historians to dismiss Cyril as an irascible, bigoted, and politically motivated wheeler-dealer. But recent studies — especially those by Robert Louis Wilken and John Anthony McGuckin — have vindicated his reputation, as a churchman and a saint.

St. Cyril died in 444, and with his death the glory of Alexandrian theology began to wane. He is venerated as a Doctor of the Church.

REACHING OUT TO NESTORIUS
The Council of Ephesus adopted Cyril's Second Letter to Nestorius, in its entirety, as a statement of the Church's dogmatic teaching. The letter spells out some important ideas, just then emerging. It explains the "hypostatic union" — that Jesus Christ is a single subject, single person, single "self," in whom divine and human natures are united. Another key concept spelled out here (though not named) is the "communication of idioms" — the idea that any statement made of either of Christ's natures can be made of

Christ; for example, when we describe the passion of Christ, we may say that "God suffered and died," even though divinity cannot suffer or undergo any change.

Cyril sends greeting in the Lord to the most religious and reverend fellow-minister Nestorius.

I understand that there are some who are talking rashly of the reputation in which I hold Your Reverence, and that this is frequently the case when meetings of people in authority give them an opportunity. I think they hope in this way to delight your ears, and so they spread abroad uncontrolled expressions. They are people who have suffered no wrong, but have been exposed by me for their own profit, one because he oppressed the blind and the poor, a second because he drew a sword on his mother, a third because he stole someone else's money in collusion with a maidservant and since then has lived with such a reputation as one would hardly wish for one's worst enemy. For the rest I do not intend to spend more words on this subject in order not to vaunt my own mediocrity above my teacher and master or above the Fathers. For however one may try to live, it is impossible to escape the malice of evil people, whose mouths are full of cursing and bitterness and who will have to defend themselves before the judge of all.

But I turn to a subject more fitting to myself and remind you as a brother in Christ always to be very careful about what you say to the people in matters of teaching and of your thought on the faith. You should bear in mind that to scandalize even one of these little ones who believe in Christ lays you open to unendurable wrath. If the number of those who are distressed is very large, then surely we should use every skill and care to remove scandals and to expound the healthy word of faith to those who seek the truth. The most effective way to achieve this end will be zealously to occupy ourselves with the words of the holy Fathers, to esteem their words, to examine our words to see if we are holding to their faith as it is written, to conform our thoughts to their correct and irreproachable teaching.

Measuring Up to Nicaea

The holy and great synod (the Council of Nicaea), therefore, stated that

(1) the only-begotten Son, begotten of God the Father according to nature, true God from true God, the light from the light, the one through whom the Father made all things, came down, became incarnate, became man,

(2) suffered, rose on the third day, and ascended to heaven.

We, too, ought to follow these words and these teachings and consider what is meant by saying that the Word from God took flesh and became man. For we do not say that the nature of the Word was changed and became flesh, nor that He was turned into a whole man made of body and soul. Rather do we claim that the Word in an unspeakable, inconceivable manner united to Himself hypostatically flesh enlivened by a rational soul, and so became man and was called Son of Man, not by God's will alone or good pleasure, nor by the assumption of a person alone. Rather did two different natures come together to form a unity, and from both arose one Christ, one Son. It was not as though the distinctness of the natures was destroyed by the union, but divinity and humanity together made perfect for us one Lord and one Christ, together marvelously and mysteriously combining to form a unity. So He who existed and was begotten of the Father before all ages is also said to have been begotten according to the flesh of a woman, without the divine nature either beginning to exist in the holy Virgin, or needing of itself a second begetting after that from His Father. (For it is absurd and stupid to speak of the one who existed before every age, and who is co-eternal with the Father, needing a second beginning so as to exist.) The Word is said to have been begotten according to the flesh, because for us and for our salvation He united what was human to Himself hypostatically and came forth from a woman. For He was not first begotten of the holy Virgin, a man like us, and then the Word descended upon Him; but from the very womb of His mother He was so united and then underwent begetting according to the flesh, making His own the begetting of His own flesh.

In a similar way we say that He suffered and rose again, not that the Word of God suffered blows or piercing with nails or any other wounds in His own nature (for the divine, being without a body, is incapable of suffering), but because the body which became His own suffered these things, He is said to have suffered them for us. For He was without suffering, while His body suffered. Something similar is true of His dying. For by nature the Word of God is of itself immortal and incorruptible and life and life-giving, but since on the other hand His own body by God's grace, as the Apostle says, tasted death for all, the Word is said to have suffered death for us, not as if He Himself had experienced death as far as His own nature was concerned (it would be sheer lunacy to say or think that), but because, as I have just said, His flesh tasted death. So too, when His flesh was raised to life, we refer to this again as His resurrection, not as though He had fallen into corruption — God forbid — but because His body had been raised again.

A Confession of Faith

So we shall confess one Christ and one Lord. We do not adore the man along with the Word, so as to avoid any appearance of division by using the word "with." But we adore Him as one and the same, because the body is not other than the Word, and takes its seat with Him beside the Father, again not as though there were two sons seated together but only one, united with His own flesh. If, however, we reject the hypostatic union as being either impossible or too unlovely for the Word, we fall into the fallacy of speaking of two sons. We shall have to distinguish and speak both of the man as honored with the title of son, and of the Word of God as by nature possessing the name and reality of sonship, each in his own way. We ought not, therefore, to split into two sons the one Lord Jesus Christ. Such a way of presenting a correct account of the faith will be quite unhelpful, even though some do speak of a union of persons. For Scripture does not say that the Word united the person of a man to Himself, but that He became flesh. The Word's becoming flesh means nothing else than that He partook of flesh and blood like us; He made our body His own, and came forth a man from woman without casting aside His deity or His generation from God the Father, but rather in His assumption of flesh remaining what He was.

This is the account of the true faith everywhere professed. So shall we find that the holy Fathers believed. So have they dared to call the holy Virgin "Mother of God," not as though the nature of the Word or His Godhead received the origin of their being from the holy Virgin, but because there was born from her His holy body rationally ensouled, with which the Word was hypostatically united and is said to have been begotten in the flesh. These things I write out of love in Christ, exhorting you as a brother and calling upon you before Christ and the elect angels, to hold and teach these things with us, in order to preserve the peace of the churches and that the priests of God may remain in an unbroken bond of concord and love.

— NPNF2 14:197-198

TRINITY, INCARNATION, EUCHARIST: UNITY
In a profound interpretation of Jesus' final prayer for unity, St. Cyril, in his Commentary on the Gospel According to St. John, *shows how the Eucharist unites believers to one another, to Christ, and to the Trinity.*

"That they may all be one. As you, Father, are in me and I am in you, may they also be in us" (Jn 17:21).

We must carefully consider what explanation to give here. We have rightly held that the oneness of believers, in agreement of heart and soul, should resemble the divine oneness and essential identity of the Holy Trinity and the intimate relation of each divine Person with the others. But here we wish to point out a sort of natural unity by which we are joined with each other, and all of us to God. We approach a kind of physical unity with each other, even though we are distinguished by having different bodies, and each one of us returns, so to speak, to his own personal environment and individuality. For Peter cannot be Paul, or be spoken of as Paul. Nor can Paul be Peter, even though both are in fact one, because of their union in Christ.

We take for granted, then, the physical unity that exists between the Father and the Son and the Holy Spirit (for we believe and glorify

One Godhead in the Holy Trinity). Now, let us further ask in what manner we are proved to be one with each other and with God, both in a bodily and a spiritual sense.

The only-begotten Son proceeds from the very substance of God the Father, possessing all of His Begetter in His own nature. He became flesh, according to the Scripture, blending Himself, as it were, with our nature by an inexpressible combination and union with this earthly body. Thus He who is God by nature became, and is truly, a Man from heaven. He was not merely "inspired," as some people imagine, who do not rightly understand the depth of the mystery. He is, rather, simultaneously God and Man. He unites in Himself things that are naturally opposed to one another and unable to be fused together. And thus He enables man to share and partake in God's nature.

For the fellowship and abiding presence of the Spirit has reached even to us. It originated through Christ and in Christ. Yet He has become like us — that is, a man — receiving anointing and sanctification, even though He is God by nature. He proceeded from the Father Himself, sanctifying with His own Spirit the temple of His body as well as all creation — which owes Him its very being. The mystery, then, that is in Christ has become a beginning and a way that we may partake of the Holy Spirit and union with God. For in Him we are all sanctified, in the way I have just described.

We also join together ourselves. We are blended into unity with God and with each other. Still, we keep our individual differences. We each have a distinct individuality of soul and body. In order that we may join together this way, the Only Begotten has contrived a means that His own due Wisdom and the Counsel of the Father have sought out. Through the mystery of the Eucharist, one body — His own body — blesses those who believe in Him. He makes us the same body with Himself and with each other. For who could divide the natural union of those who are knit together through His holy body, which is one in union with Christ? If we all share the one bread, we are all made one body (see 1 Cor 10:17); for Christ cannot be severed.

So the Church becomes Christ's body, and we are also individually His members, according to the wisdom of Paul. All of us are united to Christ through His holy body, because we have received, in our own bodies, Him who is one and indivisible. Now we owe the service of our members to Him rather than to ourselves. While Christ is called the Head, the Church is called the rest of the body, joined together of Christian members. Paul proves this to us by his words: "… so that we may no longer be children, tossed to and fro and carried about with every wind of doctrine, by the cunning of men, by their craftiness in deceitful wiles. Rather, speaking the truth in love, we are to grow up in every way into him who is the head, into Christ, from whom the whole body, joined and knit together by every joint with which it is supplied, when each part is working properly, makes bodily growth and upbuilds itself in love" (Eph 4:14-16).

So that those who partake of Christ's holy flesh gain this actual physical unity with Christ, Paul once more bears witness to the mystery of godliness, "which was not made known to the sons of men in other generations as it has now been revealed to his holy apostles and prophets by the Spirit; that is, how the Gentiles are fellow heirs, members of the same body, and partakers of the promise in Christ Jesus" (Eph 3:5-6). If we are all of the same body in Christ — not only with one another, but also with Him who is in us through His flesh — are we not all one, both with one another and with Christ?

Christ is the bond of union, simultaneously God and Man. Remembering the unity that is by the Spirit, we may follow in the same track of inquiry. We may say once more that we all receive one and the same Spirit, the Holy Spirit, and are in some sense blended together with one another and with God. We are many, but Christ, who is the Spirit of the Father, and His own Spirit dwell in each one of us. Still the Spirit is one and indivisible, binding together the divided spirits of the individualities of one and all of us into His own natural unity. He causes us all to be shown forth in Him, through Himself, and as one. The power of His holy flesh makes those in whom it abides to be of the same body. So, too, the one indivisible Spirit of God, who lives in all, binds all together into spiritual unity.

— *LF 48:548-551*

ST. JEROME

Among the Fathers, St. Jerome (342–420) stands out as a sort of eccentric uncle. A man of singular literary and intellectual gifts, he had equally unusual personality quirks. He was irascible to a comic extreme. The poet Phyllis McGinley provides perhaps the best thumbnail profile of the man: "God's angry man, His crotchety scholar, / was Saint Jerome, / the great name-caller, / who cared not a dime / for the laws of libel / and in his spare time / translated the Bible."

Growing up in the province of Dalmatia (in what is today Croatia), Jerome showed great literary skill early in life. At age twelve, he went off to Rome for study at the school of a famous grammarian. Jerome delighted in his studies of the classics, especially in Cicero's ability to shape an argument and turn a clever phrase. He also seems to have indulged in some immoral activity during his student years.

But, probably before he was twenty, he returned to the Christian faith in which he had been raised, and he accepted Baptism from the pope. (Delaying Baptism until adulthood was the fashion at the time.)

Still, Jerome hoped to put his professional skills to use in civil service. But, while traveling with two friends, he met hermits and spoke with them about their life. Eastern-style monasticism was sweeping the West just then, as a result of the popularity of St. Athanasius's biography of St. Anthony of Egypt. Inspired by the hermits' dedication, Jerome abandoned all thought of a secular career and set out, with his friends, to find a place in the monastic life.

At first, they returned to Dalmatia, where they lived in community for a while. But perhaps Jerome's temper had begun to blossom. The companions split because of quarrels. With one of the ascetics, Rufinus, Jerome lit out for the more barren deserts of the East. While traveling, Jerome began to learn the biblical languages, Hebrew and Greek, and undertook study under some of the world's greatest Scripture scholars. A chance encounter with St. Gregory of Nazianzus renewed Jerome's appreciation for Origen's allegorical readings of Scripture.

Also while he was abroad, Jerome had a dream that shook him. He dreamt that he was brought before heaven's throne, where he was accused of being a Ciceronian rather than a Christian. Jerome would cite this as a turning point in his life.

In the early 380s, now laden with great knowledge of the Scriptures, he returned to Rome. There, Jerome became a trusted aide to Pope Damasus, who commissioned him to revise the Latin (or "Vulgate") edition of the four Gospels. While in Rome, he also continued his Hebrew studies under a rabbi.

As a spiritual director, Jerome won renown, encouraging the growing number of aristocratic women who were drawn to consecrate themselves to God as virgins or widows. Some of these set up "house monasteries." Others lived, more or less, as hermits. Jerome tutored them in Scripture and theology. They, in turn, became benefactors for many of his pet projects.

But while Jerome inspired the lives of so many consecrated women, he tended to alienate Rome's priests. There was probably a bit of envy involved. Jerome displayed tremendous intellectual gifts, had easy access to the pope, and enjoyed the company and fortunes of many noblewomen. But surely Jerome aggravated the situation. He tended to make intemperate comments about the degenerate state of the clergy and bishops, suggesting that they might learn from the holy women he directed. Moreover, Rome was just beginning to see a backlash of hostility against the fashions of Eastern monasticism. Some priests whispered rumors about Roman women dying from excessive fasting.

All of these factors made Jerome somewhat unwelcome, but he seems to have been oblivious. When Pope Damasus died, Jerome expressed confidence that he himself would be elected to succeed to the chair of St. Peter.

It did not happen. And Jerome left Rome, going off to sulk and study in the East. His benefactresses followed, and the pilgrims from Rome set up a monastic community in Bethlehem, where Jerome set to work on the biblical translations and commentaries for which he would become duly famous. Meanwhile, he continued to war with ever-new enemies, quarrel with his friends, and repudiate his former masters, such as Origen. (One of these disputes brought on Jerome's brief excommunication.)

Jerome could be most venomous in his attacks upon former companions whom he had alienated. He tells one seafaring friend that the "stench of bilgewater" had addled his brain. As for Rufinus, the dearest companion of his youth, Jerome spends the conclusion of a broadside cruelly satirizing the man's physical features.

In his last years, Jerome bemoaned his failing health, but continued to produce prodigiously. He wrote an encyclopedia of Christian biography, reaching back to biblical times. He fought all comers, including the emerging heresy of Pelagianism, whose adherents burned Jerome's monasteries in 416.

He died about 420. Phyllis McGinley summed up that he "served his Master, / though with complaint. / He wasn't a plaster / sort of saint."

He is, however, one of the Great Fathers, and a Doctor of the Church.

ON MARY'S VIRGINITY
Helvidius was a Roman layman, a champion of ascetical laxity who argued that Mary bore other children after Jesus. In this famous broadside, Jerome demolished Helvidius's arguments — and Helvidius.

Not long ago, I was asked by some of the brethren to reply to a pamphlet written by a Helvidius. I have delayed doing so — not because it is a difficult matter to maintain the truth and refute an ignorant boor who has hardly known the first glimmer of learning — but because I was afraid my reply might make him appear worth defeating.... But all these good reasons for silence no longer influence me, because of the scandal caused to the brethren.... Therefore, the axe of the Gospel must be now laid to the root of the barren tree, and both it and its fruitless foliage cast into the fire, so that Helvidius, who has never learned to speak, may at length learn to hold his tongue....

His first statement was: "Matthew says, 'Now the birth of Jesus Christ took place in this way. When his mother Mary had been betrothed to Joseph, before they came together she was found to be with child of the Holy Spirit; and her husband Joseph, being a just man and unwilling to put her to shame, resolved to send her away quietly.

But as he considered this, behold, an angel of the Lord appeared to him in a dream, saying, "Joseph, son of David, do not fear to take Mary your wife, for that which is conceived in her is of the Holy Spirit"'" (Mt 1:18-20). Notice, says Helvidius, that the word used is betrothed, not *entrusted* as you say, and of course the only reason why she was betrothed was that she might one day be married. And the Evangelist would not have said *before* they came together if they were not to come together, for no one would use the phrase "before he ate" to describe a man who was not going to eat. Then, again, the angel calls her *wife* and speaks of her as *united* to Joseph. We are next invited to listen to the declaration of Scripture: "When Joseph woke from sleep, he did as the angel of the Lord commanded him; he took his wife, but knew her not until she had borne a son; and he called his name Jesus" (Mt 1:24-25).

Before and Until

Let us take the points one by one…. He admits that she was betrothed, and in the next breath will have her to be a man's wife, whom he has admitted to be his betrothed. Again, he calls her wife, and then says the only reason why she was betrothed was that she might one day be married. And, for fear we might not think that enough, "the word used," he says, "is *betrothed* and not *entrusted*, that is to say, not yet a wife, not yet united by the bond of wedlock." But when he continues, "the Evangelist would never have applied the words, '*before* they came together' to persons who were not to come together," … I don't know whether to laugh or cry…. If I choose to say, "the Apostle Paul, before he went to Spain, was put in fetters at Rome" — or (as I certainly might) "Helvidius, before he repented, was cut off by death" — must Paul on being released at once go to Spain, or must Helvidius repent after death …? Must we not, instead, understand that the preposition *before*, although it frequently denotes order in time, yet sometimes refers only to order in thought? So that our plans need not be realized, if sufficient cause intervened to prevent it.

When, then, the Evangelist says "before they came together," he indicates the time immediately preceding marriage, and shows that matters were so far advanced that she who had been betrothed was on the point of becoming a wife. As if he said, "before they kissed and embraced, before the consummation of marriage, she was found to be with child." And she was found to be so by none other than Joseph, who watched the swelling womb of his betrothed with anxious glances, and, at this time, almost the privilege, of a husband.

Yet it does not follow, as the previous examples showed, that he had intercourse with Mary after her delivery, when his desires had been quenched by the fact that she had already conceived.... The passage for discussion now is, "When Joseph woke from sleep, he did as the angel of the Lord commanded him; he took his wife, but knew her not until she had borne a son; and he called his name Jesus." Here, first of all, it is quite needless for our opponent to show so elaborately that the word *know* has reference to coition, rather than to intellectual apprehension: as though anyone denied it, or any sane person could ever imagine the folly that Helvidius takes pains to refute. Then he would teach us that the adverb *until* implies a fixed and definite time, and when that is fulfilled, he says the event takes place that previously did not take place, as in the case before us, "and knew her not until she had brought forth a son." It is clear, says he, that she was known after she brought forth, and that that knowledge was only delayed by her engendering a son. To defend his position, he piles up text upon text, waves his sword like a blindfolded gladiator, rattles his noisy tongue, and ends by wounding no one but himself....

With regard to the word *until*, he is utterly refuted by the authority of Scripture, which often uses a fixed time (he himself told us so) to denote time without limitation, as when God by the mouth of the prophet says to certain persons, "Even to your old age I am He" (Is 46:4). Will He cease to be God when they have grown old? And the Savior in the Gospel tells the Apostles, "Lo, I am with you always, to the close of the age" (Mt 28:20). Will the Lord then, after the end of the world, forsake His disciples?... David also in the fourth Song of Ascents speaks thus, "Behold, as the eyes of servants look to the hand of their master, as the eyes of a maid to the hand of her mistress, so our eyes look to the LORD our God, till he have mercy upon us" (Ps 123:2). Will the prophet, then, look unto the Lord *until* he obtain mercy — and then, when mercy is obtained, will he turn his eyes down to the ground?... The Evangelist pointed out a circumstance which might have given rise to some scandal, namely, that Mary was not known by her husband until she was delivered, and he did so that we might be the more certain that she from whom Joseph refrained while there was room to doubt the import of the vision was not known after her delivery....

Brothers of the Lord

I must now proceed, if my reply is to follow the order of his argument, to the third point. He will have it that Mary bore other sons, and he quotes the passage, "And Joseph also went up from Galilee, from the city of Nazareth, to Judea, to the city of David, which is called Bethlehem, because he was of the house and lineage of David, to be enrolled with Mary his betrothed, who was with child. And while they were there, the time came for her to be delivered. And she gave birth to her first-born son" (Lk 2:4-7). From this he tries to show that the term *first-born* is inapplicable except to a person who has brothers, just as he is called *only-begotten* who is the only son of his parents.

Our position is this: Every only-begotten son is a first-born son, but not every first-born is an only begotten. By first-born we understand not only one who is succeeded by others, but one who has had no predecessor.... The word of God defines first-born as everything that opens the womb. Otherwise, if the title belongs only to those who have younger brothers, the priests cannot claim the firstlings until their successors have been begotten, lest, perchance, in case there were no subsequent delivery it should prove to be the first-born and the only-begotten.... Scripture thus speaks of the Savior, "And when the time came for their purification according to the law of Moses, they brought him up to Jerusalem to present him to the Lord (as it is written in the law of the Lord, 'Every male that opens the womb shall be called holy to the Lord') and to offer a sacrifice according to what is said in the law of the Lord, 'a pair of turtledoves, or two young pigeons'" (Lk 2:22-24). If this law relates only to the first-born, and there can be no first-born unless there are successors, no one ought to be bound by the law of the first-born who cannot tell whether there will be successors!...

The last proposition of Helvidius was this, and it is what he wished to show when he treated of the first-born, that *brethren* of the Lord are mentioned in the Gospels. For example, "Behold, his mother and his brethren stood outside, asking to speak to him" (Mt 12:46). And elsewhere ... "He ... came to his own country; and his disciples followed him. And on the sabbath he began to teach in the synagogue; and many who heard him were astonished, saying, 'Where did this man get all this? What is the wisdom given to him? What mighty works are wrought by his hands! Is not this the carpenter, the son of Mary and brother of James and Joses and Judas and Simon, and are not his sisters here with us?'" (Mk 6:1-3).... Observe, he says, James and Joses are sons of Mary, and the same persons who were called brethren by the Jews....

In Holy Scripture there are four kinds of brethren — by nature, race, kindred, love.... Moreover they are called brethren by kindred who are of one family — that is, *patria*, which corresponds to the Latin *paternitas* — because from a single root a numerous progeny proceeds. In Genesis we read, "Then Abram said to Lot, 'Let there be no strife between you and me, and between your herdsmen and my herdsmen; for we are [brethren]'" (Gen 13:8).... Yet, certainly Lot was not Abraham's brother, but the son of Abraham's brother Aram.... Jacob, the son of Isaac and Rebecca, when in fear of his brother's treachery he had gone to Mesopotamia, drew nigh and rolled away the stone from the mouth of the well, and watered the flocks of Laban, his mother's brother. "Then Jacob kissed Rachel, and wept aloud. And Jacob told Rachel that he was her father's [brother], and that he was Rebekah's son" (Gen 29:11-12). Here is an example of the rule already referred to, by which a nephew is called a brother.... Innumerable instances of the same kind are to be found in the sacred books....

It is clear that Our Lord's brethren bore the name in the same way that Joseph was called His father: "Your father and I have been looking for you anxiously" (Lk 2:48).... Was Joseph His true father? Dull as you are, you will not venture to say that. Was he His reputed father? If so, let the same rule be applied to them when they are called brethren, that you apply to Joseph when he is called father....

Now that I have cleared the rocks and shoals I must spread sail and make all speed to reach his epilogue. Feeling himself to be a smatterer, he there produces Tertullian as a witness.... Of Tertullian I say no more than that he did not belong to the Church.... Might I not array against you the whole series of ancient writers? Ignatius, Polycarp, Irenaeus, Justin Martyr, and many other apostolic and eloquent men, who against Ebion, Theodotus of Byzantium, and Valentinus, held these same views, and wrote volumes replete with wisdom. If you had ever read what they wrote, you would be a wiser man....

— *NPNF2 6:335-337, 339-344*

On Lust

In this letter, Jerome counsels Eustochium, a Roman woman consecrated to virginity, as he recalls his own temptations in the desert.

When I was living in the desert, in the vast solitude that gives hermits a savage dwelling place, parched by a burning sun, how often I imagined myself among the pleasures of Rome! I used to sit alone because I was filled with bitterness. Sackcloth disfigured my unshapely limbs, and my skin, from long neglect, had become as black as an Ethiopian's. Tears and groans were every day my portion; and if drowsiness chanced to overcome my struggles against it, my bare bones, which hardly held together, clashed against the ground. Of my food and drink I say nothing, for even in sickness, the solitaries have nothing but cold water — and to eat one's food cooked is looked upon as self-indulgence.

Now, although in my fear of hell I had consigned myself to this prison, where I had no companions but scorpions and wild beasts, I often found myself amid bevies of girls. My face was pale and my frame chilled with fasting; yet my mind was burning with desire, and the fires of lust kept bubbling up before me when my flesh was as good as dead.

Helpless, I cast myself at the feet of Jesus. I watered them with my tears. I wiped them with my hair. And then I subdued my rebellious body with weeks of abstinence. I do not blush to avow my abject misery. Rather I lament that I am not now what once I was. I remember how I often cried aloud all night till the break of day and did not stop beating my breast till tranquility returned at the chiding of the Lord. I used to dread my very cell as though it knew my thoughts; and stern and angry with myself, I used to make my way alone into the desert. Wherever

I saw hollow valleys, craggy mountains, steep cliffs, there I made my oratory, there the house of correction for my unhappy flesh.

There, also — the Lord Himself is my witness — when I had shed copious tears and had strained my eyes towards heaven, I sometimes felt myself among angelic hosts, and for joy and gladness sang: "Because of the savor of your good ointments we will run after you" (cf. Song 1:3-4).

Now, if such are the temptations of men who, since their bodies are emaciated with fasting, have only evil thoughts to fear, how must it fare with a girl whose surroundings are those of luxury and ease? Surely, to use the Apostle's words, "She ... is dead even while she lives" (1 Tim 5:6). Therefore, if experience gives me a right to advise, or clothes my words with credit, I would begin by urging you and warning you as Christ's spouse to avoid wine as you would avoid poison. For wine is the first weapon used by demons against the young. Greed does not shake, nor pride puff up, nor ambition infatuate so much as this. Other vices we easily escape, but this enemy is shut up within us, and wherever we go we carry him with us. Wine and youth between them kindle the fire of sensual pleasure. Why do we throw oil on the flame — why do we add fresh fuel to a miserable body which is already ablaze?

— NPNF2 6:24-25

ON OLD AGE

St. Jerome complained to his disciples Paula and Eustochium about the advancing infirmities of old age.

I leave it to others to decide how much I have gained by my unflagging study of Hebrew. What I have lost in my own language, I myself can tell. In addition to this, on account of the weakness of my eyes and bodily infirmity generally, I do not write with my own hand; and I cannot make up for my slowness of utterance by greater pains and diligence, as Virgil is said to have done, when he treated his books as a bear treats her cubs, and licked them into shape. Instead I must summon a secretary and say whatever comes first to mind. Or, if I wish to think a little and hope to produce something better, my helper silently reproaches me, clenches his fist, wrinkles his brow, and plainly declares by his whole bearing that he has come for nothing.

— NPNF2 6:497-498

ST. CHROMATIUS OF AQUILEIA

Chromatius was surely blessed, because he was a rather daring peacemaker. A friend from youth of Jerome and Rufinus, he strove to bring their bitter feud to a harmonious end. Though he did not succeed, he managed to keep the friendship of both men. In fact, both dedicated major works to his honor.

Chromatius was born into a large family. His father died when he was very young, and his mother raised the children in a very devout home. Indeed, the family household gradually evolved into a religious community, with Chromatius, his mother, a brother, and several sisters sharing a common life of prayer. The young Jerome and Rufinus, in the flower of their friendship, lived with the family. Ever afterward, Jerome referred to Chromatius's mother as "my mother."

Chromatius was ordained to the priesthood to serve Valerian, Aquileia's fiercely anti-Arian bishop, who was a close ally of St. Ambrose of Milan. In 381, Valerian and Ambrose together presided over the Council of Aquileia, which effectively put an end to Arianism in the Roman West. Though Chromatius was not yet a bishop, he played an active role in the proceedings of the Council. When Bishop Valerian died in 388, Chromatius was named to succeed him and ordained by St. Ambrose.

Aquileia was a prosperous city, with strategic military importance. Its bishop was inevitably a player on the international scene. Chromatius kept in touch with his old friends Jerome and Rufinus, even though they were quarreling. St. John Chrysostom, too, appealed to Chromatius for assistance in his trials. Chromatius sent the emperor a letter supporting Chrysostom (though to no avail).

In his last years, his Church endured much hardship as the Goths began their invasion of Italy. He died in 407 or 408.

Several dozen of Chromatius's homilies have survived, as well as his commentary on Matthew's Gospel. In his preaching we encounter a faith deeply sacramental and Marian: "The Church was united … in the Upper Room with Mary the Mother of Jesus and with his brethren. The Church therefore cannot be referred to as such unless it includes Mary the Mother of our Lord, together with His brethren." [72]

BAPTISM, THE GREAT MYSTERY
Christ was sinless and needed no cleansing. But by His baptism in the Jordan He sanctified all the waters of the world for the sake of our salvation. This is a new translation of Chromatius's Sermon 34.1-3.

On this day, as we just heard in the divine reading, the Lord and Savior was baptized by John in the Jordan, and so it is not merely a Solemnity, but a very great one. For when Our Lord deigned to be baptized, the Holy Spirit descended on Him like a dove, and the voice of the Father was heard to say: "This is my beloved Son, with whom I am well pleased" (Mt 3:17). Oh, what a great mystery is this heavenly baptism! The Father is heard from heaven; the Son appears on earth; the Holy Spirit is manifested in the form of a dove. You cannot, in fact, speak of true baptism, nor the true remission of sins, without the truth of Trinity. No one can grant the remission of sins apart from belief in the perfect Trinity.

The only true baptism belongs to the Church, and it is given only once. In it we are immersed once and come away renewed and pure — pure because we are free from the filth of sins, because we rise again to new life, after having left behind the decrepitude of sin. This bath of baptism makes man whiter than snow, not in the skin of his body, but in the splendor of his spirit and the purity of his soul.

The heavens opened at the Baptism of the Lord, to show that the washing of regeneration opens the kingdom of heaven to believers, according to the decree of the Lord: "unless one is born of water and the Spirit, he cannot enter the kingdom of God" (Jn 3:5). Those who enter are those who do not neglect to keep the grace of their baptism. By contrast, those who do not enter are those who are not reborn.

Our Lord came to give a new baptism. For the salvation of mankind and for the remission of all sins, He condescended to receive the first baptism, not to leave behind sins — for He had committed no sin! — but to sanctify the waters of baptism that they may wash away the sins of all believers reborn in baptism. He was baptized in the waters so that we may be washed clean of all our sin by baptism.

ST. AUGUSTINE OF HIPPO

With St. Augustine (354–430), the patristic achievement reached its peak. He is, beyond doubt, the most influential theologian in the history of the Western Church. From the Lateran Councils to the *Catechism of the Catholic Church*, he is the most-cited individual, outside the Bible, in the Church's dogmatic pronouncements.

So much for his influence on the City of God. His thought has been just as epoch-making in the earthly city. On any short list of those who shaped Western civilization, Augustine's name must appear.

He was the great synthesizer of the Classical and Patristic Eras. In his mind and his preaching, he brought together the philosophy of Plato and the doctrine of Nicaea, the biblical allegories of Alexandria and the historical research of Antioch, the sublimity of Eastern theology with the pastoral practicality of the West.

For his probing introspection in his *Confessions*, he is sometimes called the "father of psychology." The same book sometimes earns him credit for "inventing" the genre of autobiography. His work, in general, marks a milestone in the development of Western philosophy. His book *The City of God* — with Plato's *Republic* and Aristotle's *Politics* — would become one of the foundational works in social thought. Augustine's treatise *On the Trinity* is the great systematic summary of the Church's legacy from Nicaea and Constantinople.

It is hard not to slip into hyperbole when discussing Augustine's contributions to the Church and to the world.

He was born in Thagaste, North Africa, the son of a pagan Roman official, Patricius, and a Christian mother, Monica. He was raised in the Christian faith. At sixteen, he went to the city of Carthage to study law, and then literature and philosophy. Gradually, he gave up the practice of his Christian faith. At age seventeen, he took a mistress, who bore him a son, Adeodatus, in 372. Augustine would live with the woman for the next seventeen years.

A man of deep desires, he had a voracious mind, ambitious to know all that there was to know. He had a great capacity for friendship, and many friends. And, if we are to believe his own recollections, his sensual appetites, too, were rather on the strong side. But in all these ambitions, desires, loves, and longings, Augustine would one day see glimmers of the human heart's deepest need, which is God.

Augustine's interest in philosophy deepened. Having lost his faith in God, he took to reflecting on the material world. He was troubled by the problem of evil. The doctrines of the Manicheans attracted him, because they purported to explain material phenomena and the existence of evil by denigration of both the creator God and His creation. Augustine was intrigued, though not quite convinced. Nonetheless, he began to identify himself with the Manichean heresy.

Meanwhile, he continued to advance in his profession as a teacher of rhetoric. He taught at Thagaste, Carthage, and then Rome, where he opened his own school for one frustrating year. From Rome, he accepted a professorship in Milan. Yet, as his career progressed, so did his sense of unease. He had satisfied his worldly desires, one after another — for friendship, for love, for sex, for success, for fame, for skill, for knowledge — and still there was a gnawing hunger in his heart. Throughout his wanderings, his mother had continually kept him in prayer and often urged him to return to Christian faith. And he loved his mother, so he tried. But, reading the Old Testament unreflectively, he found its teachings contradictory and its laws absurd, so he abandoned the pursuit.

In Milan, he encountered the bishop, St. Ambrose, who had a similar ranging intellect, the same love for truth, the same high degree of professional competence, and perhaps an even greater capacity for friendship. But Bishop Ambrose had something more: he had peace, which attracted Augustine. The elder man was patient, and he gave the rhetorician his precious time in long conversation.

Augustine returned to the faith of his childhood in 387, and he began to live in a somewhat contemplative community with his mother, brother, and some friends. "Our hearts are restless, O Lord, until they rest in You," he would one day write. His heart had found rest, though he would again know sadness. His mother died later in 387; his son died in 389.

Augustine returned to North Africa, where the Christians of Hippo pressed him to receive Holy Orders. In 395, he was ordained a bishop. Augustine's literary production was voluminous in the following years, even as he kept a demanding pastoral schedule — preaching, teaching candidates for Baptism, answering correspondence from throughout the world, and daily receiving the petitions and complaints of local believers in "court." He was a key figure in the Church of Africa and the Church universal. He played an active role, for example, in the regional councils that definitively set the New Testament canon, at the beginning of the fifth century.

He was phenomenally effective as a pastor. Historians give him credit for dealing death blows to three major heresies: Manicheanism, Donatism, and Pelagianism. He also welcomed home the Tertullianists and Montanists who had gone into schism centuries before. Augustine most often attracted heretics with charity and truth. He had, after all, once lived in heresy himself. As Ambrose and Monica had been patient with him, he would be patient and perseverant with others.

Augustine was a world-class rhetorician, and like that other African Tertullian, he had a way of coining phrases. Even today, certain "Augustinisms" are part of the vocabulary of any moderately educated Christian.

- "Love, and do what you will."
- "Give me chastity and continence — but not yet." (His prayer while still resisting God.)
- "Too late have I loved You, O Beauty so ancient and so new."
- "We make a ladder of our vices, if we trample them underfoot."

Augustine died in 430 as barbarians were laying siege to his city. Rome had already fallen. As one age was ending, he entered a new one. St. Augustine is a Great Father and one of the principal Doctors of the Church.

ON HIS MOTHER, MONICA
The ancient world's most famous eulogy, from Augustine's Confessions.

She was brought up modestly and soberly, and made subject by You to her parents, rather than by her parents to You. When she had arrived at a marriageable age, she was given to a husband, whom she served as her lord. And she busied herself to win him over to You, preaching You by her actions. By this You made her beautiful, and reverently lovable, admired by her husband. For she so bore the wronging of her bed as never to have any dissension with her husband on account of it. For she waited for Your mercy upon him, that by believing in You he might become chaste.

Besides this, as he was earnest in friendship, so he was violent in anger. But she had learned that an angry husband should not be resisted, neither in deed, nor even in word. But so soon as he was grown calm and tranquil, and she saw a fitting moment, she would give him a reason for her conduct, should he have been excited without cause.

In short, while many matrons, who had more gentle husbands, carried the marks of beatings on their dishonored faces and would privately blame the lives of their husbands, she would blame their tongues, admonishing them, but with jest, that from the hour they heard the marriage vows read to them, they should think of them as instruments whereby they were made servants; so, keeping in mind their condition, they ought not oppose their lords. They knew what a furious husband she endured, and so they marveled that it had never been reported, nor appeared by any indication, that Patricius had beaten his wife, or that there had been any domestic strife between them, even for a day. When they asked her confidentially why this was so, she taught them her rule, which I have mentioned above. Those who observed it experienced the wisdom of it, and rejoiced; those who did not were kept in subjection, and suffered.

Overcoming Gossip

By submission, persevering with patience and meekness, she also won over her mother-in-law, who was at first prejudiced against her by the gossip of ill-disposed servants. She told her son about the tongues of the meddling servants, and how it had disturbed the domestic peace between herself and her daughter-in-law, and she begged him to punish them for it. He complied with his mother's wish, restoring discipline to his family and ensuring future harmony, by correcting with lashes those she had exposed. She promised a similar reward to any who, in order to please her, should say anything evil to her about her daughter-in-law. Now, none dared to do so, and they lived together with a wonderful sweetness of mutual goodwill.

This great gift You gave — my God, my mercy — to Your good handmaid, from whose womb You created me: that, whenever she could, she showed herself a peacemaker between any differing and discordant souls. She would hear, on both sides, the most bitter things — the sort that arises from growing and unsettled discord, when the crudities of enmity are exhaled in bitter speeches to a present friend against an absent enemy. And then she would disclose nothing about the one to the other, nothing but what might avail to their reconciliation. This would have seemed a small good thing to me, if I did not know (to my sorrow) countless persons, who, through some horrible and far-spreading infection of sin, not only disclose to enemies mutually enraged the things said in passion against each other, but even add some things that were never spoken at all. Whereas, to a generous man, it ought to seem a small thing not to incite or increase the enmities of men by ill-speaking, unless he tries, by kind words, to extinguish them. That is how she was — You, her most intimate Instructor, teaching her in the school of her heart.

Inspiring Conversions

Finally, toward the end of his earthly life, she won over her husband to You. Yet she did not complain to him, as one of the faithful, about the things she had endured before he had found faith.

She was also the servant of Your servants. Whoever knew her would praise and honor and love You in her. By the testimony of her holy conversation, they perceived You in her heart. For she had been the wife of one man, had repaid her parents, had guided her house piously, was well spoken of for good works, had brought up children, laboring in birth for them each time she saw them swerving from You. Lastly, O Lord (since it is by Your permission we speak), she loved all of us, the baptized, who lived together before she rested in You, as if she had been mother of us all, and she served us as if she had been child of all.

As the day approached on which she was to depart this life (a day You knew, though we did not), it happened — that is, You, by Your secret ways, arranged it — that she and I stood alone, leaning in a certain window, from which we looked upon the garden of the house we occupied at Ostia. There, away from the crowd, we rested for the voyage, after the fatigues of our long journey. We were conversing alone very pleasantly, and, "forgetting what lies behind and straining forward to what lies ahead" (Phil 3:13), we were, in the presence of the truth You are, discussing the nature of the eternal life of the saints, which eye has not seen, nor ear heard, neither has entered into the heart of man. We opened wide the mouth of our heart, after those supernal streams of Your fountain, "the fountain of life," which is "with you" (Ps 36:9), that being watered by it according to our capacity, we might in some measure consider so high a mystery.

A Glimpse of Glory

Our conversation arrived at this point: that the highest bodily pleasure, in the brightest earthly light, seemed unworthy of comparison to the sweetness of that life. Lifting ourselves with a more ardent affection towards the Selfsame, we gradually passed through all bodily things, and even the heaven itself, whence sun, moon, and stars shine upon the earth. We soared higher still by inward musing, and conversation, admiring Your works; and we came to our own minds, and went beyond them, that we might go as high as that region of unfailing plenty, where You feed Israel forever with the food of truth, and where life is that Wisdom by whom all these things are made, all that have been and are to come; and she is not made, but is as she has been, and so shall ever be; because to "have been" and "to be in the future" are not in her, but only "to be," since she is eternal; for to "have been" and "to be in the future" are not eternal.

While we were speaking, and straining after her, we slightly touched her with the whole effort of our heart; and we sighed, and there left bound "the first fruits of the Spirit" (Rom 8:23). We returned to the noise of our own mouth, where the word spoken has both beginning and end. But what is like Your Word, Our Lord, who remains in Himself without becoming old, and who "[makes] all things new" (Rev 21:5)?

Lord, You know that, on that day, when we were talking this way, the world with all its delights grew contemptible to us, even while we spoke. Then my mother said, "Son, for myself, I no longer take pleasure in anything in this life. What I want now, and why I am here, I do not know, now that my hopes in this world are satisfied. There was indeed one thing for which I wished to wait in this life, and that was that I might see you a Catholic Christian before I died. My God has exceeded this abundantly, so that I see you despising all earthly happiness, for you have been made His servant. What am I doing here?"

— *NPNF1 136-138*

On Morals

A closely reasoned argument for the good life, this tract is usually titled Of the Morals of the Catholic Church. *St. Augustine demonstrates that humans desire happiness and that the only true and lasting happiness is found in God.*

How then, according to reason, should man live? Surely we all desire to live happily, everyone agrees to that statement almost before it is made. But the term "happy" cannot, in my opinion, belong either to him who lacks what he loves, whatever it may be; or to him who has what he loves, if it is hurtful; or to him who does not love what he has, although it is good in perfection. For one who seeks what he cannot have suffers torture; and one who has what is not desirable is cheated; and one who does not seek what is worth seeking is diseased.

Now, in all these cases the mind cannot help but be unhappy, and happiness and unhappiness cannot reside at the same time in one man. So in none of these cases can the man be happy.

I find, then, a fourth case, where the happy life exists — when man's chief good is both loved and owned. For what do we call enjoyment but having at hand the objects of love? And no one can be happy who does not enjoy what is man's chief good; nor is anyone unhappy who enjoys this. We must, then, have at hand our chief good, if we want to live happily.

We must now inquire what is man's chief good, which of course cannot be anything inferior to man himself. For whoever follows after what is inferior to himself becomes himself inferior. But every man is bound to follow what is best. So man's chief good is not inferior to man. Is it, then, something similar to man himself? It must be so, if there is nothing above man that he is capable of enjoying. But if we find something that is both superior to man and can be possessed by the man who loves it, who can doubt that in seeking for happiness man should try to reach what is more excellent than the being who makes the effort? For if happiness consists in the enjoyment of the greatest good — the chief good — how can a man be properly called happy who has not yet attained to his chief good? Or how can that be the chief good if something better awaits us beyond? The chief good, then, must be something that cannot be lost against the will. For no one can feel confident about a good that he knows can be taken from him, although he wishes to keep and cherish it. But if a man feels no confidence about the good that he enjoys, how can he be happy while afraid of losing it?

What Is Man?

Let us, then, see what is better than man. This must be hard to find, unless we first ask and examine what man is. I am not now called upon to give a definition of man. Since almost all agree, or at least those to whom I am speaking, that we are made up of soul and body, the question here seems to me to be: What is man? Is he both of these? Or is he the body only, or the soul only?

For the things are two, soul and body, and neither without the other could be called man. For the body would not be man without the soul; nor again would the soul be man if there were not a body animated by it. Yet it is possible that one of these may be held to be man, and may be called so. What, then, do we call man? Is he soul and body, as in a double harness, or like a centaur? Or do we mean the body only, as being in the service of the soul that rules it, as the word lamp denotes not the light and the case together, but only the case, though it is because of the light that it receives its name? Or do we mean only the mind, and that on account of the body that it rules — as horseman means not the man and the horse, but the man only, and only as employed in ruling the horse?

This dispute is not easy to settle; or, if the proof is plain, the statement requires time. This is an expenditure of time and strength that we need not incur. For whether the name man belongs to both, or only to the soul, the chief good of man is not the chief good of the body; but whatever is the chief good of both soul and body, or of the soul alone, is man's chief good.

Now, if we ask what is the chief good of the body, reason obliges us to admit that it is whatever enables the body to be in its best state. But of all the things that invigorate the body, there is nothing better or greater than the soul. The chief good of the body, then, is not bodily pleasure, not absence of pain, not strength, not beauty, not swiftness, or whatever else is usually reckoned among the goods of the body, but simply the soul. For all the things mentioned, the soul supplies to the body by its presence, and, what is above them all: life. Hence I conclude that the soul is not the chief good of man, whether we give the name of man to soul and body together, or to the soul alone. For according to reason, the chief good of the body is that which is better than the body, and from which the body receives vigor and life.

So whether the soul itself is man, or soul and body both, we must discover whether there is anything which goes before the soul itself, which the soul follows to the most perfect good of which it is capable.

If such a thing can be found, all uncertainty must be at an end, and we must pronounce this to be really and truly the chief good of man.

An Analogy

If, again, the body is man, it must be admitted that the soul is the chief good of man. But clearly, when we treat of morals — when we inquire what manner of life must be held in order to obtain happiness — it is not the body to which the precepts are addressed, it is not bodily discipline that we discuss. In short, the observance of good customs belongs to that part of us that inquires and learns, which are the prerogatives of the soul.

So, when we speak of attaining to virtue, the question does not regard the body. But if it follows, as it does, that the body that is ruled over by a soul possessing virtue is ruled both better and more honorably, and is in its greatest perfection because of the perfection of the soul that rightfully governs it, that which gives perfection to the soul will be man's chief good, though we call the body man. For if my coachman, in obedience to me, feeds and drives the horses he cares for in the most satisfactory manner — if he enjoys more of my bounty in proportion to his good conduct — can anyone deny that the good condition of the horses, as well as that of the coachman, is due to me? So the question seems not to be whether soul and body is man, or the soul only, or the body only, but what gives perfection to the soul. For when this is obtained, a man can only be either perfect, or at least much better than in the absence of this one thing.

No one will question that virtue gives perfection to the soul. But it is a very proper subject of inquiry whether this virtue can exist by itself or only in the soul. Here again arises a profound discussion, needing lengthy treatment; but perhaps my summary will serve the purpose. God will, I trust, assist me, so that, notwithstanding our feebleness, we may give instruction on these great matters briefly as well as intelligibly. In either case, whether virtue can exist by itself without the soul, or can exist only in the soul, undoubtedly in the pursuit of virtue the soul follows after something, and this must be either the soul itself, or virtue, or something else. But if the soul follows after itself in the pursuit of virtue, it follows after a foolish thing; for before obtaining virtue it is foolish.

Now the height of a follower's desire is to reach that which he pursues. So the soul must either not wish to reach what it pursues, which is utterly absurd and unreasonable, or, in pursuing itself while foolish, it reaches the folly that it flees from. But if it pursues virtue in the desire to reach it, how can it follow what does not exist? Or how can it desire to reach what it already possesses? Either, therefore, virtue exists beyond the soul, or if we are not allowed to give the name of virtue except to the habit and disposition of the wise soul, which can exist only in the soul, we must allow that the soul follows after something else in order that virtue may be produced in itself. For neither by following after nothing, nor by following after folly, can the soul, according to my reasoning, attain to wisdom.

This something else, then, which the soul pursues in order to possess virtue and wisdom, is either a wise man or God. But we have said already that it must be something that we cannot lose against our will. No one needs to ask whether a wise man — supposing we are content to follow after him — can be taken from us in spite of our unwillingness or persistence. God, then, remains. In pursuing Him we live well, and in reaching Him we live both well and happily.

— NPNF1 4:42-44

ON THE TRINITY

Augustine's teaching on the Blessed Trinity, most completely developed in his book On the Trinity, *is a powerful synthesis of the previous centuries' doctrinal development. In passing, he advises Christian apologists to patience and perseverance as they deal with those "who find difficulty in this faith." The following is excerpted from the preface to* On the Trinity.

All those Catholic interpreters of the divine Scriptures, both Old and New, whom I have been able to read, who have written before me concerning the Trinity, who is God, have purposed to teach, according to the Scriptures, this doctrine: that the Father, and the Son, and the Holy Spirit intimate a divine unity of one and the same substance in an indivisible equality; and therefore that They are not three Gods, but one God: although the Father has begotten the Son, and so He who is the Father is not the Son; and the Son is begotten by the Father, and so He who is the Son is not the Father; and the Holy Spirit is neither the Father nor the Son, but only the Spirit of the Father and of the Son, Himself also co-equal with the Father and the Son, and pertaining to the unity of the Trinity.

Yet not that this Trinity was born of the Virgin Mary, and crucified under Pontius Pilate, and, buried, rose again the third day, and ascended into heaven — but only the Son. Nor, again, that this Trinity descended in the form of a dove upon Jesus when He was baptized; nor that, on the day of Pentecost, after the ascension of the Lord, when "a sound came from heaven like the rush of a mighty wind" (Acts 2:2), the same Trinity rested on each of them as "tongues as of fire" (Acts 2:3), but only the Holy Spirit. Nor yet that this Trinity said from heaven, "This is my Son" (Lk 9:35), whether when He was baptized by John, or when the three disciples were with Him on the mount, or when the voice sounded, saying, "I have glorified it, and I will glorify it again" (Jn 12:28); but that it was a word of the Father only, spoken to the Son; although the Father, and the Son, and the Holy Spirit, as They are indivisible, so work indivisibly.

This is also my faith, since it is the Catholic faith.

Some persons, however, find difficulty in this faith. They hear that the Father is God, and the Son God, and the Holy Spirit God, and yet that this Trinity is not three Gods, but one God. And they ask how they are to understand this: especially when it is said that the Trinity works indivisibly in everything that God works, and yet that a certain voice of the Father spoke, which is not the voice of the Son; and that none except the Son was born in the flesh, and suffered, and rose again, and ascended into heaven; and that none except the Holy Spirit came in the form of a dove.

They wish to understand how the Trinity uttered that voice which was only of the Father; and how the same Trinity created that flesh in which only the Son was born of the Virgin; and how the very same Trinity itself wrought that form of a dove, in which only the Holy Spirit appeared. Otherwise, the Trinity does not work indivisibly, but the Father does some things, the Son other things, and the Holy Spirit still others: or else, if They do some things together, some severally, then the Trinity is not indivisible.

It is a difficulty, too, to them, in what manner the Holy Spirit is in the Trinity, whom neither the Father, nor the Son, nor both, have begotten, although He is the Spirit both of the Father and of the Son.

Since, then, men weary us asking such questions, let us unfold to them, as we are able, whatever wisdom God's gift has given our weakness on this subject; neither "let us go on our way with consuming envy." Should we say that we are not accustomed to think about such things, it would not be true; yet if we acknowledge that such subjects commonly dwell in our thoughts, carried away as we are by the love of investigating the truth, then they require us, by the law of charity, to make known what we have been able to find out....

Accordingly I have undertaken the task, by the bidding and help of the Lord my God, not so much of discoursing with authority respecting things I know already, as of learning those things by piously discoursing of them.

— NPNF1 3:20-21

LETTER TO JANUARIUS
St. Augustine offered wise counsel to Januarius, a man troubled by the lack of uniformity in the liturgy as it was celebrated in various places.

In the first place, hold fast to this as the fundamental principle in the present discussion: that our Lord Jesus Christ has appointed to us a "light yoke" and an "easy burden" (cf. Mt 11:30), as He declares in the Gospel: in accordance with which He has bound His people under the new dispensation together in fellowship by sacraments, which are in number very few, in observance most easy, and in significance most excellent, as Baptism solemnized in the name of the Trinity, the Communion of His Body and Blood, and such other things as are prescribed in the canonical Scriptures....

As to those other things which we hold on the authority, not of Scripture, but of Tradition, and which are observed throughout the whole world, it may be understood that they are held as approved and instituted either by the Apostles themselves, or by plenary councils, whose authority in the Church is most useful — for example, the annual commemoration, by special solemnities, of the Lord's passion, resurrection, and ascension, and of the descent of the Holy Spirit from heaven, and whatever else is similarly observed by the whole Church wherever it has been established.

There are other things, however, which differ in different places and countries. For example, some fast on Saturday; others do not. Some partake daily of the Body and Blood of Christ; others receive it on stated days. In some places, no day passes without the sacrifice being offered; in others, it is only on Saturday and the Lord's day, or it may be only on the Lord's day. In regard to these and all other variable observances which may be met anywhere, one is at liberty to comply with them or not as he chooses. There is no better rule for the wise and serious Christian in this matter, than to conform to the practice he finds prevailing in the Church where he happens to be. For such a custom, if it is clearly not contrary to sound faith or morals, should be seen as something indifferent, and ought to be observed for the sake of fellowship with those among whom we live.

You may have heard me tell before what I will nevertheless now mention. When my mother followed me to Milan, she found the Church there not fasting on Saturday. She began to be troubled, and to hesitate as to what she should do. I, though not then taking a personal interest in such things, applied on her behalf to Ambrose, of most blessed memory, for his advice. He answered that he could not teach me anything but what he himself practiced, because if he knew any better rule, he would observe it himself. When I supposed that he intended, on the ground of his authority alone, and without supporting it by any argument, to recommend us to give up fasting on Saturday, he followed me, and said: "When I visit Rome, I fast on Saturday; when I am here, I do not fast. On the same principle, do you observe the custom prevailing in whatever church you come to, if you desire neither to give offense by your conduct, nor to find cause of offense in another's." When I reported this to my mother, she accepted it gladly; and for myself, after frequently reconsidering his decision, I have always esteemed it as if I had received it by an oracle from heaven.

— *NPNF1 1:300-301*

PRUDENTIUS

A Spaniard by birth, Prudentius practiced law and reached the pinnacle of his profession, an appointment at the imperial court. Like many an ambitious professional, ancient and modern, he arrived at earthly success only to find it an empty victory. At fifty, he looked back and regretted what he then saw as a wasted life.

He made a pilgrimage to Rome and took in the sights. There he was deeply moved by the stories of the martyrs. He resolved to spend the rest of his years in prayer and fasting, glorifying God through poetry.

He wrote "Against Symmachus," a long poem refuting idolatrous religion, directed at the senator who strove to have the pagan altar of Victory restored in Rome. His *Cathemerinon*, a book of hymns, is the work most familiar to readers today, because some of the songs were translated for congregational use in the nineteenth century. Through much of history, however, Prudentius was best known for his most ambitious work, the epic *Psychomachia*. In this he follows the familiar classical models, Homer and Virgil, in telling tales of war; but now the story is allegorical, and the true battles are spiritual. His *Peristephanon*, too, has fed the Christian imagination with its stories of the martyrs, especially the Romans St. Lawrence and St. Agnes.

The great scholar of early Christianity Robert Louis Wilken is moved, almost to poetry, as he describes the particular achievement of Prudentius, whom he calls "the first Christian poet": "In Prudentius's verse the love of Christ and love of the Muses embrace, as beauty of language and dignity of form become a vehicle befitting the story of God's sojourn in this world.... Prudentius stands at the beginning of a tradition of Latin literature that stretches without interruption from the fourth century to Dante and beyond."[73]

For all his worldly accomplishments, we know hardly anything more about the man. We do not know when or how he died.

THE STORY OF HIS LIFE

Prudentius begins his book Hymns for the Christian Day *by telling the story of his life. This translation is from R. Martin Pope's* The Hymns of Prudentius *(London: J.M. Dent, 1905).*

Full fifty years my span of life hath run,
Unless I err, and seven revolving years
Have further sped while I the sun enjoy.
Yet now the end draws nigh, and by God's will
Old age's bound is reached: how have I spent
And with what fruit so wide a tract of days?

I wept in boyhood 'neath the sounding rod:
Youth's toga donned, the rhetorician's arts
I plied and with deceitful pleadings sinned:
Anon a wanton life and dalliance gross
(Alas! the recollection stings to shame!)
Fouled and polluted manhood's opening bloom:
And then the forum's strife my restless wits
Enthralled, and the keen lust of victory
Drove me to many a bitterness and fall.
Twice held I in fair cities of renown
The reins of office, and administered
To good men justice and to guilty doom.
At length the Emperor's will beneficent
Exalted me to military power
And to the rank that borders on the throne.
The years are speeding onward, and gray hairs
Of old have mantled o'er my brows
And Salia's consulship from memory dies.
What frost-bound winters since that natal year
Have fled, what vernal suns reclothed
The meads with roses — this white crown declares.
Yet what avail the prizes or the blows
Of fortune, when the body's spark is quenched
And death annuls whatever state I held?
This sentence I must hear: "Whate'er thou art,
Thy mind hath lost the world it loved: not God's
The things thou soughtest, Whose thou now shalt be."
Yet now, ere hence I pass, my sinning soul
Shall doff its folly and shall praise my Lord
If not by deeds, at least with humble lips.
Let each day link itself with grateful hymns
And every night re-echo songs of God:
Yea, be it mine to fight all heresies,
Unfold the meanings of the Catholic faith,
Trample on Gentile rites, thy gods, O Rome,
Dethrone, the Martyrs laud, th' Apostles sing.

O while such themes my pen and tongue employ,
May death strike off these fetters of the flesh
And bear me whither my last breath shall rise!

A CHRISTMAS CAROL
Some of Prudentius's poems have been adapted for inclusion in modern
hymnals. The Christmas carol "Of the Father's Love Begotten" comes from
his "Hymn for All Hours." This popular rendering from the nineteenth
century is by J.M. Neale and H.W. Baker.

Of the Father's love begotten, ere the worlds began to be,
He is Alpha and Omega, He the source, the ending He,
Of the things that are, that have been,
And that future years shall see,
Evermore and evermore!
At His Word the worlds were framèd; He commanded;
    it was done:
Heaven and earth and depths of ocean in their threefold
    order one;
All that grows beneath the shining
Of the moon and burning sun,
Evermore and evermore!

He is found in human fashion, death and sorrow here to know,
That the race of Adam's children doomed by law to endless woe,
May not henceforth die and perish
In the dreadful gulf below,
Evermore and evermore!
O that birth forever blessèd, when the virgin, full of grace,
By the Holy Ghost conceiving, bore the Savior of our race;
And the Babe, the world's Redeemer,
First revealed His sacred face,
Evermore and evermore!

This is He whom seers in old time chanted of with one accord;
Whom the voices of the prophets promised in their faithful word;

Now He shines, the long expected,
Let creation praise its Lord,
Evermore and evermore!

O ye heights of heaven adore Him; angel hosts, His praises sing;
Powers, dominions, bow before Him, and extol our God
    and King!
Let no tongue on earth be silent,
Every voice in concert sing,
Evermore and evermore!

Righteous judge of souls departed, righteous King of
    those who live,
On the Father's throne exalted none in might with thee may strive;
Who at last in vengeance coming
Sinners from Thy face shalt drive,
Evermore and evermore!

Thee let old men, Thee let young men, Thee let boys in
    chorus sing;
Matrons, virgins, little maidens, with glad voices answering:
Let their guileless songs re-echo,
And the heart its music bring,
Evermore and evermore!

Christ, to Thee with God the Father, and, O Holy Ghost, to Thee,
Hymn and chant with high thanksgiving, and unwearied
    praises be:
Honor, glory, and dominion,
And eternal victory,
Evermore and evermore!

ST. PAULINUS OF NOLA

Paulinus was born around 354 into a prominent Christian family in Bordeaux. His tutor, when he was young, was the great poet Ausonius, a pagan, with whom he kept a lifelong correspondence and friendship.

Paulinus lived in Rome for a time, working in government and receiving several promotions, before being appointed governor of the province of Campania. He served there for a few years, until the assassination of the Emperor Gratian. Paulinus then returned to Bordeaux where he married a Spanish Christian named Therasia. After her example, and the influence of others, he began to take his faith seriously. The couple soon conceived a child, a son, but he died at eight days from his birth. Around the same time, Paulinus was accused of murdering his brother. Weary of the world, he and Therasia moved to Spain, wishing to dedicate the rest of their lives to cloistered prayer, living as celibates within marriage.

They were well loved by the local Church, and the inhabitants of Barcelona prevailed upon Paulinus to be ordained a priest. Shortly afterward, he and Therasia sold all they had and retired to Nola in Campania.

Paulinus had long kept a special devotion to St. Felix, a martyr buried at Nola. So he used the remains of his fortune to build an avenue leading to Felix's tomb; he renovated the church, and beside it he built a hospital.

Around 409 Paulinus was named Bishop of Nola, and he served for twenty years, every year composing a poem in honor of St. Felix for the martyr's feast day. He was a prolific author of letters and poetry. He had a warm personality and made many friends. Many of his letters to famous friends have been preserved — including letters to St. Augustine. Augustine, for his part, paid tribute to Paulinus by telling his story repeatedly. In his City of God (1.10) he wrote that Paulinus "willingly abandoned vast wealth and became quite poor, though abundantly rich in holiness." Jerome numbered our poet among his "Illustrious Men," noting that he "was distinguished not only for erudition and holiness of life, but also for his ability to cast out demons."

Thirty-three of his poems have survived. He was a keen observer of detail and a master of description; so his works give us many rare glimpses of ordinary Christian life in his time — of the construction of sanctuaries, the celebration of feast days, and the layout of particular churches, not least St. Peter's in Rome.

Paulinus was known for his fervent devotion to the saints, which even Augustine thought was excessive. But even during his lifetime Paulinus was himself looked upon as saint. Since his death in 431, the Church has honored him as one.

THE COMPANY OF GOD'S SERVANTS

Among Paulinus's many celebrity friends was Sulpicius Severus, to whom he wrote the following account, passionate and poetic, in a letter. The translation is adapted from the book Vigilantius and His Times, *by W. S. Gilly (London: Seeley, Burnside, and Seeley, 1845).*

I love to receive the visits of those who serve God as we do, and whose religious character is visible in their pallid faces, but I have no satisfaction in the company of those who are proud of their embroidered apparel. Give me the society of those who wear hair-shirts; not of those who are arrayed in cloaks and tunics, and girt with sword-belts, but of men clad in sackcloth, and whose loins are girdled with a rope; not of those insolent people who pride themselves on their well-dressed hair, but of those, who for the sake of holy deformity, wear their hair short and badly cut, whose foreheads are shaven, and who possess no ornament except the purity of their lives: who live in honorable disregard and neglect of the niceties of life: who hold personal beauty in contempt, and care only for the internal beauty of their souls: who purposely disfigure themselves, and let their faces be haggard, that their hearts may be clean.

How can they, to whom our mode of life is the odor of death, blame us, if their lives be equally unsupportable to us. They have a horror of my fasting, and I cannot endure their eating. Certain acquaintances of ours avoid the faint-smelling breath of a monk, when he speaks; and I detest the foul vapors of a Thrason overcharged with wine. If the dryness of our mouths is displeasing to them, the fumes of wine that pour out of theirs is not less disgusting to us. If they are shocked by our abstemiousness, we are not less so by their intemperance. It is not from men who are drunk in the morning that we wish to receive visits, but from those who fast till the evening; not from those who on the morrow feel the effects of the preceding evening's debauch, but from men who have not touched wine during the whole day; not from those whose heads reel under the fumes of wine, but of those on whom pious vigils have inflicted holy wounds, and caused a sober intoxication, and who stagger not from satiety, but from want.

POEM ON THE ANNUNCIATION
Enamored of the saints and the Church's feasts, Paulinus gave due notice to the Virgin Mary. This translation appeared in The Blessed Virgin Mary in Early Christian Latin Poetry, *by Rev. Andrew B. Heider, S.M. (Washington: Catholic University of America, 1918).*

> Thereafter, holy Gabriel, the same
> Who messenger had been to Zachary,
> Far greater things to tell, to Mary comes
> Who, trothed to husband, but to God more dear —
> The world's salvation was she to bring forth —
> A virgin chaste, had undefiled preserved
> Her modesty: when stood before her eyes
> The wondrous form in heavenly radiance clothed,
> With modest look to earth she gazed, while glowed
> Her reddened cheeks with blush suffused.
>
> He spoke: "O thou most happy maid of all
> The virgins that have ever been before,
> Are now and shall hereafter be, in all
> The sun-encircled earth; O loved of God,
> Who Mother shalt be called of Him, of whom
> He Father is! Yea, happy one, receive
> The gift divine, untouched of man, exempt
> From nature's law, fecund with word of God.
> To him shalt body give who made the sky

The earth, the sea, the stars; who ever was
Is now and in all time shall ever be:
Lord of the world, Creator of the light,
Himself the light of heaven; He through thee
In mortal members clothed shall be, appear
In visible form and hold converse with men.
Lift up your spirit, undisturbed 'mid praise
So great; for power and faith will He bestow
Who willed — for all things yield to His good pleasure —
To be thy son, though Son of God He be."

This said, he left her sight, and fled the earth
And effortless regained the ethereal realms.
The command of God fulfills itself, the maid
Believes forthwith; her joyous ready faith
Augments the worth of her anterior life:
The secret elements in silence fashion
The form Divine, while grows the sacred burden;
In cherished shrine the Lord of Heaven rests.

ST. VINCENT OF LÉRINS

In the mid-fifth century, Vincent looked back at Christian history
and saw it marred by so many heresies. He sought a universal rule by
which Christians could measure any proposed doctrine. And he found
it in Tradition: the words of Scripture confirmed by the witness of the
Fathers and the teaching office of the Church.

Perhaps it was only natural for Vincent to concern himself with
rules of genealogy and order. He was himself a man of noble birth who
had set out to be a soldier. But at some point, he abandoned his military
career — and with it the world — and entered the monastery on the
Isle of Lérins off the southern coast of Gaul (near modern-day Cannes).

There he was ordained a priest; and he set to writing under the
pen-name Peregrinus ("Pilgrim").

He wrote his *Commonitory*, his most famous (and only surviving) work, around 434. It is there that he crystallized his principle for discerning true from false doctrine. We should hold fast, he wrote, to "the faith that has been believed everywhere, always, and by all." That rule would become known as the Vincentian Canon. In the same passage, Vincent also set the Catholic standards for recognizing a Father of the Church.

The Vincentian Canon is useful, though not fail-safe. Vincent himself applied it in opposition to the doctrine of St. Augustine in the Pelagian controversies, before the Church ruled conclusively in the matter. The Church eventually decided in Augustine's favor. But the Church has also honored Vincent as a saint.

Vincent died sometime between 435 and 450.

How to Study the Fathers

In the first chapter of his Commonitory, *Vincent established clear guidelines for studying Tradition and the Church Fathers.*

In the Catholic Church, all care must be taken to hold to the faith that has been believed everywhere, always, and by all. For that is truly and in the strictest sense "Catholic," which (as the name itself declares) takes in everything universally. This rule we observe if we follow universality, antiquity, and consent. We follow universality if we confess one faith to be true, the faith that the whole Church throughout the world confesses. We follow antiquity if we in no way deviate from the interpretations that our holy ancestors and fathers have proclaimed as inviolable. We follow in consent, in the same way, if in antiquity itself we adhere to the definitions and decisions of all (or at least almost all) the priests and doctors.

But what will a Catholic Christian do if a small portion of the Church should cut itself off from the communion of the universal faith? What, surely, but prefer the soundness of the whole body to the unsoundness of a pestilent and corrupt member? What if some new contagion should seek to infect not merely an insignificant portion of the Church, but the whole? Then it will be his care to cleave to antiquity, which at this day cannot possibly be seduced by any fraud of novelty.

But what if there be found error in antiquity itself, in two or three men, or even a city or a province? Then it will be his care by all means, to prefer the decrees (if there are such decrees) of an ancient general council to the rashness and ignorance of a few.

But what if some error should spring up on which no such decree is found to bear? Then he must collate and consult and interrogate the opinions of the ancients — specifically those who, though living in diverse times and places, yet continuing in the communion and faith of the one Catholic Church, stand as acknowledged and approved authorities. And whatever he shall discover to have been held, written, taught — not just by one or two of these, but by all, equally, with one consent, openly, frequently, persistently — that is what he must himself believe without any doubt or hesitation.

— NPNF2 11:132-133

ST. LEO THE GREAT

There comes a time in doctrinal controversies when someone has to say "Enough!" This is especially true when disputes touch on essential matters of faith and morals and threaten to divide the Church. The heresy of Arius was just such an occasion. Not only did it linger for centuries, despite the clear condemnation of the Church, but it spawned new heresies as theologians reacted to Arianism by "overcorrecting." Nestorianism so deeply distinguished between the divine and human natures of Jesus as to suggest that they represented distinct persons. Monophysitism responded by claiming that Christ had only one nature, which was unique and combined the human and divine.

Bishops had spoken clearly against these errors, but the heresies persisted as heretical emperors convened puppet councils to reach predetermined heretical conclusions. Thus, ordinary Christians faced the daunting task of weighing one council's authority against another's, on matters that even theologians found obscure. The Church needed a final word, which only a pope could give. And that pope was Leo I (reigned 440–461).

Roman-born, Leo served in the Church's diplomatic corps before ascending to the papacy. He was a prolific teacher and preacher, issuing many letters and homilies on doctrinal matters.

The rebel who forced the crisis of Leo's pontificate was Eutyches, an archimandrite (or archabbot) in Constantinople, who argued that the two natures of Jesus Christ were so closely connected that they became one — Christ's human nature was absorbed by the divine. Disciplined by Patriarch Flavian of Constantinople, Eutyches appealed to Pope Leo. Meanwhile, in the spring of 449, the emperor Theodosius II, who supported Eutyches, convened a puppet council at Ephesus. The council, which Leo called a "Robber Synod," was a disaster. The dissident bishops refused to hear the pope's letter to the council, and Patriarch Flavian was beaten to death.

Leo pressed for a council that would be legitimate and truly universal in scope. But this was not possible until the accession of a new emperor who was open to the idea. The council convened in Chalcedon in the fall of 451. At Chalcedon, papal representatives read Leo's letter to the earlier council at Ephesus. The letter clearly stated the traditional doctrine of the incarnation of Jesus Christ — that Jesus Christ is one person with two distinct natures, divine and human: "One and the same Christ, Son, Lord, Only-begotten, known in two natures, without confusion, without change, without division, without separation." The council echoed Pope Leo's teaching, and Leo confirmed the council with the words "Peter has spoken through Leo…. Anathema to him who teaches otherwise."

The decision of Chalcedon set forth the Church's doctrine on Christ, but it also confirmed the authority of the papacy in finally deciding such matters. Chalcedon strengthened Pope Leo's position within the Roman Empire in the West. At a time when Rome's secular power was plummeting, the people looked to Leo for leadership. He had many occasions to draw upon the diplomatic skills he had gained in the years before his papacy. As Attila and the Huns swept toward Rome in 452, Leo went out to meet them. In one of history's most dramatic encounters, the great pope met face-to-face with the notorious barbarian — and persuaded him to turn away from Rome. In 455, he tried the same maneuver with the advancing Vandals, but this time with only moderate success. The Vandals sacked Rome, but stopped short of burning the city.

Leo spent much of the rest of his papacy performing works of mercy for his defeated flock in Rome, and helping to shore up the remnants of civil order in the surrounding lands.

We know almost nothing of Leo's private life or personality. All we have are his writings and the records of the deeds that earned him his title: "the Great." He is a Doctor of the Church.

On Jesus Christ

St. Leo summarized the Church's Christological doctrine in his Letter to Flavian, *sometimes called "The Tome." This letter was suppressed at the Robber Synod of Ephesus, but would later be influential at Chalcedon.*

The whole body of the faithful confess that they believe in God the Father Almighty, and in Jesus Christ, His only Son, our Lord, who was born of the Holy Spirit and the Virgin Mary. By these three statements the devices of almost all heretics are overthrown. For not only is God believed to be both Almighty and the Father, but the Son is shown to be co-eternal with Him, differing in nothing from the Father because He is God from God, Almighty from Almighty, and being born from the Eternal One, is co-eternal with Him; not later in point of time, not lower in power, not unlike in glory, not divided in essence: but at the same time, the only-begotten of the eternal Father was born eternal of the Holy Spirit and the Virgin Mary....

Without detriment, therefore, to the properties of either nature and substance which then came together in one person, majesty took on humility; strength, weakness; eternity, mortality. And to pay off the debt belonging to our condition, inviolable nature was united with passible nature, so that, as suited the needs of our case, one and the same Mediator between God and men, the Man Christ Jesus, could both die with the one and not die with the other. Thus in the whole and perfect nature of true man was true God born, complete in what was His own, complete in what was ours.

— NPNF2 12:39-40

On Rome

In this homily for the Feast of Sts. Peter and Paul, St. Leo shows Providence at work in the ancient history of Rome.

The whole world, dearly beloved, does indeed take part in all holy anniversaries, and loyalty to the one faith demands that whatever is recorded as done for all men's salvation should be everywhere celebrated with common rejoicings. But, besides that reverence which today's festival has gained from all the world, it is to be honored with special and peculiar exultation in our city, that there may be a predominance of gladness on the day of their martyrdom in the place where the chief of the Apostles met their glorious end. For these are the men through whom the light of Christ's Gospel shone on you, O Rome, and through whom you, who were the teacher of error, were made the disciple of truth. These are your holy Fathers and true shepherds, who gave you claims to be numbered among the heavenly kingdoms, and built you under much better and happier auspices than those men by whose zeal the first foundations of your walls were laid: and of whom the one that gave you your name [Romulus] defiled you with the blood of his brother [Remus]. These are the men who promoted you to such glory, making you a holy nation, a chosen people, a priestly and royal state, and the head of the world through the blessed Peter's Holy See. Thus you gained a wider sway by the worship of God than by earthly government. For though you grew by many victories, and extended your rule on land and sea, yet what your toils in war subdued is less than what the peace of Christ has conquered.

For the good, just, and Almighty God, who has never kept His mercy from mankind, and has ever instructed all men alike in the knowledge of Himself by the most abundant benefits, has by a more secret counsel and a deeper love shown pity upon the wanderers' voluntary blindness and tendencies to evil, by sending His co-equal and co-eternal Word. By becoming flesh, the Word so united the Divine Nature with the human that, by lowering His Nature to the uttermost, He has raised our nature to the highest.

Why Rome Ruled

But that the result of this unspeakable grace might be spread abroad throughout the world, God's providence made ready the Roman Empire, whose growth has reached such limits that the whole multitude of nations are brought into close connection. For the divinely planned work particularly required that many kingdoms should be leagued together under one empire, so that the preaching of the world might quickly reach to all people, when they were held beneath the rule of one state. And yet that state, in ignorance of the Author of its aggrandizement (though it ruled almost all nations), was enthralled by the errors of them all, and seemed to itself to have fostered religion greatly because it rejected no falsehood. And hence its emancipation through Christ was the more wondrous, because it had been so securely bound by Satan.

For when the Twelve Apostles, after receiving through the Holy Spirit the power of speaking with all tongues, had distributed the world into parts among themselves, and undertaken to instruct it in the Gospel, the most blessed Peter, chief of the apostolic band, was appointed to the citadel of the Roman Empire, that the light of truth, which was being displayed for the salvation of all the nations, might spread itself more effectively throughout the body of the world from the head itself. What nation had no representatives then living in this city; or what peoples did not know what Rome had learned? Here it was that the tenets of philosophy must be crushed, here that the follies of earthly wisdom must be dispelled, here that the cult of demons must be refuted, here that the blasphemy of all idolatries must be rooted out, here where the most persistent superstition had gathered together all the various errors which had anywhere been devised.

The See of Peter

To this city, then, most blessed Apostle Peter, you did not fear to come. And when the Apostle Paul, the partner of your glory, was still busy with regulating other churches, you entered this forest of roaring beasts, this deep, stormy ocean with greater boldness than when you walked upon the sea. And you who had been frightened by the high priest's maid in the house of Caiaphas now had no fear of Rome, the mistress of the world. Was there any less power in Claudius, any less cruelty in Nero, than in the judgment of Pilate or the Jews' savage rage? So then it was the force of love that conquered the reasons for fear: and you did not think those to be feared whom you had undertaken to love. But this feeling of fearless affection you had even then surely conceived when the profession of your love for the Lord was confirmed by the mystery of the thrice-repeated question. And nothing else was demanded of your earnest purpose than that you should bestow the food as you yourself have been enriched, on feeding His sheep whom you loved....

The Resting Place of Paul

[To Rome] came also your blessed brother-Apostle Paul, "the vessel of election," and the special teacher of the Gentiles. He was associated with you at a time when all innocence, all modesty, all freedom was in jeopardy under Nero's rule. Nero's fury, inflamed by excess of all vices, hurled him headlong into such a fiery furnace of madness that he was the first to assail the Christian name with a general persecution, as if God's grace could be quenched by the death of saints, whose greatest gain it was to win eternal happiness by contempt of this fleeting life. "Precious," therefore, "in the eyes of the Lord is the death of his saints." Nor can any degree of cruelty destroy the religion that is founded on the mystery of Christ's cross. Persecution does not diminish but increase the Church, and the Lord's field is clothed with an ever-richer crop, while the grains, which fall singly, spring up and are multiplied a hundredfold. Hence how large a progeny have sprung from these two heaven-sown seeds is shown by the thousands of blessed martyrs, who, rivaling the Apostles' triumphs, have traversed the city far and wide in purple-clad and ruddy-gleaming throngs, and crowned it, as it were, with a single diadem of countless gems.

And over this band, dearly beloved, whom God has set forth for our example in patience and for our confirmation in the faith, there must be rejoicing everywhere in the commemoration of all the saints, but of these two Fathers' excellence we must rightly make our boast in louder joy, for God's grace has raised them to so high a place among the members of the Church that He has set them like the twin light of the eyes in the body, whose Head is Christ. About their merits and virtues, which pass all power of speech, we must not make distinctions, because they were equal in their election, alike in their toils, undivided in their death. But as we have proved for ourselves, and our forefathers maintained, we believe, and are sure that, amid all the toils of this life, we must always be assisted in obtaining God's mercy by the prayers of special interceders, that we may be raised by the Apostles' merits in proportion as we are weighed down by our own sins. Through our Lord Jesus Christ.

— NPNF2 12:194-196

ST. PETER CHRYSOLOGUS

From 402 until the fall of the Western Roman Empire in 476, Ravenna was the imperial capital. Rome had been breached; Milan proved vulnerable to incursions from the north. But Ravenna was protected by swamps and marshes — a natural defensive moat — and this made it very attractive to the increasingly anxious emperors.

But Peter was not a native of Ravenna. He had grown up in Imola, a town in north-central Italy and was ordained a deacon of that town. According to an ancient tradition, Pope Sixtus III had a vision of St. Peter and St. Appolinaris, the first bishop of Ravenna, and the two saints showed him a young man who should be Ravenna's next bishop. The next day, the Holy Father recognized the young man among a delegation from Imola. It was Peter, and he was sent off to Ravenna.

Peter preached his first homilies in Ravenna with the imperial family in his congregation. It is from his preaching that he received the nickname Chrysologus, which means "Golden-Worded." Almost two hundred of his homilies survive. They are brief, and they explode with word-play, paradox, and poetic flights. One of his homilies preserves his prayer before preaching: "May our God deign to give me the grace of speaking and you the desire of hearing."

In the years Peter was bishop, around 433 to 450, the city enjoyed cultural hegemony in Europe, and he deserves at least some of the credit. He was a great patron of the arts, and he found a ready benefactor in Galla Placidia, the empress regent who was daughter of Theodosius the Great and mother of Valentinian III. The churches and artworks produced in Ravenna during the fifth century are some of the finest from the first millennium. A contemporary mosaic image of Peter survives in Ravenna's Church of St. John the Evangelist: he is depicted saying Mass on a ship, with Galla Placidia attending.

Peter's homilies are deeply biblical, and he returns often to Eucharistic and Marian themes — sometimes all at once: Jesus Christ "is the Bread sown in the Virgin, leavened in the flesh, molded in His Passion, baked in the furnace of the tomb, placed in the churches, and set upon the altars, which daily supplies heavenly food to the faithful."

Peter proceeded confidently and safely through the controversies of his time. Once, the monk Eutyches, who had launched the Monophysite heresy, sought Peter's support. Peter responded gently but firmly with a letter that would be read aloud at the Council of Chalcedon: "We exhort you, honorable brother, that you obediently listen to what has been written by the blessed pope of the city of Rome, since blessed Peter, who lives and presides in his own see, offers the truth of faith to those who seek. For we, in our zeal for peace and faith, cannot decide questions of faith apart from consent of the bishop of Rome."

Peter returned to his hometown of Imola shortly before his death in 450. He is honored as a Doctor of the Church.

Our Daily, Eucharistic Bread
Preaching on the Lord's Prayer, Peter brings his homily around to the Eucharist. This passage from Sermon 71 is adapted from E.B. Pusey's translation in the book The Doctrine of the Real Presence *(London: Rivington, 1855).*

"Give us this day our daily bread." After the fatherhood of God, after hallowing of the divine name, after the kingdom of heaven, we are bidden to ask for daily bread. Christ does not forget; Christ does not contradict His own commands; He Himself said, "Do not be anxious, saying, 'What shall we eat?' or 'What shall we drink?'" (Mt 6:31).

But He is Himself the bread that comes down from heaven (see Jn 6:58) — which, through the millstone of the law and grace, was formed into flour. Which was kneaded by the Passion of the cross. Which was leavened in the sacrament of great goodness. Which bore from the tomb the light dough, to lighten our sorrows. Which in order to bake in the heat of its divinity, itself burnt away the oven of hell. Which is daily brought to the table of the Church for heavenly food. Which is broken for the forgiveness of sins. Which feeds and nourishes those who eat it, to life everlasting.

This bread we daily ask to be given to us, until we enjoy it wholly in that everlasting day.

Praying the "Hail Mary"

This section from Peter's Sermon 140, on the Annunciation, is adapted from the translation in Dom Prosper Gueranger's The Liturgical Year *(Advent, volume 1) (London: Burnes & Oates, 1910).*

God sends the Virgin an angelic messenger, who, while he brings graces, gives her the entrusted pledge and receives hers in return. Then Gabriel returns with Mary's dowry. But, before ascending to heaven, to announce there the consent promised by the Virgin, he delivers to her the gifts due to her virtues. Swiftly does this ambassador fly to the bride, that he may assert God's claim to her as his own.

Gabriel does not take [Mary] from Joseph; he restores her to Christ, to whom she was espoused when she was first formed in the womb. Christ, therefore, merely took His own when He made Mary His bride. It is not a separation He produces, but a union with Himself of His own creature, by becoming incarnate in her womb.

But let us listen to the angel's words. He said to her: "Hail, full of grace! The Lord is with you." These words are not a mere salutation. They *convey* the heavenly gift. Hail — that is, "Take, O Mary, the grace I bring you."

Fear not. This is not the work of nature.

Full of grace! That is, you are not in grace as others are; you are to be filled with it.

The Lord is with you. What does this mean but that He is coming to you not merely as a visitor, but to enter within you by the new mystery of becoming your child?

Blessed are you among women. How fittingly does he add these words. They imply that those who had been mothers, with the curse of Eve upon them, now have the blessed Mary as their joy and honor and type. And while Eve was by nature the mother of children of death, Mary is by grace the mother of children of life.

————————ST. JACOB OF SERUGH————————

Jacob was born in 451 in a village by the Euphrates River, in lands that are now in Turkey. The people in his region had suffered much because their lands skirted the borders between the Roman and Persian Empires. Ownership passed back and forth, and skirmishes were frequent. Local loyalties were sometimes divided, and people were often treated with suspicion by both sides. The non-Christian Persians distrusted Christians as Roman agents. The political divisions exacerbated the theological divisions (and vice versa). In the wake of the Council of Chalcedon, some Syriac Christians accepted the orthodox decrees and some did not. Most people were not theologians, however, and it was difficult enough for theologians to sort it out.

Jacob (or James) of Serugh was a bishop who evidently tried to stay above the fray. His extant writings show no interest in the burning theological controversies of his day. He was ordained a bishop late in life, and he seems to have taken delight in teaching his congregations about the wonders of the sacraments and the glories of the saints. He wrote letters of encouragement to a people who endured hardship, misunderstanding, and persecution, drawing stories of courage and perseverance from the acts of the martyrs. Down the ages, his homilies in verse have been revered almost universally — by Nestorian, Monophysite, and Catholic Syrians.

Jacob died on November 29, 521. In subsequent centuries he has sometimes been described as "monophysite" and avoided by Catholics. A letter attributed to him is somewhat critical of the Council of Chalcedon, but its authorship is in dispute. More recently there has been a revival of interest in his work. Indeed, Pope John Paul II cited

Jacob several times, invoking him as "Saint" and calling him a "Father of the Church."

ON TIME FOR THE LORD

In this portion of a homily on the Holy Mysteries, Jacob tells his people why they should strive never to arrive late to the liturgy or leave early. This translation was made by the Benedictine Hugh Connolly, and it was published in The Downside Review *in 1908.*

The Bridegroom is coming down to see the bride betrothed to Him. Stay, O soul, in the midst of the bridal chamber, that He may see you here. Do not leave the chamber of the Bridegroom, the King. For He is coming down to see you, bearing riches from the house of His Father. The priest, whom you have sent, has called Him. Wait for Him. For if He comes and does not see you, He will be angry.

Together with the priest, the whole people beseeches the Father to send His Son, that He may come down and dwell upon the oblation. And the Holy Spirit, His Power, lights down upon the bread and wine, and sanctifies it, and makes it the Body and the Blood. And everyone who is in the house bestirs himself, in order to cry, "Our Father." ... But he who leaves ... what will he do when they petition him in the house and he is not there to cry, "Our Father." He has cut himself off. No one else has cut him off. What then has he found in the marketplaces whither he is roaming?

Despise business, and despise profits that cannot be held fast, at the hour of the Mysteries you should abide in the house of God. Your enemy is watching, and is athirst for your blood, and so far as he is able he will cut you off from profitable things. When these Mysteries full of life are administered, he fabricates fears of all sorts of losses, and with all sorts of devices he, by his subtlety, drives you out, that you may be removed from that congregation which is crying "Holy."

Satan is distressed by these voices of holiness; and, if he could, he would drive the whole world out. There would not remain one man in the holy place to cry, "Our Father." ... In that hour when the bride cries out, "Forgive me my trespasses" he knows that the Bridegroom, the King, is full of mercy, and that He hears her (the bride), and that the One who died for her also forgives her....

But maybe you say: "I will go about business until the consecration begins, and when they open the doors I will go in and receive." O you who are wise, drive away and cast off these notions.... For the Bridegroom has come down and given you His Body and sealed you with His Blood....

When the Body of the Son of God is set upon His table, earnestly bring Him all your petitions. Reveal your plagues, O sick soul, and show your diseases, and pour out tears before the table of the Godhead. In that hour when the priest sacrifices the Son before His Father, gird yourself, enter, O soul, and ask for pardon with a loud voice. Say to the Father, "Behold your Son, a sacrifice to reconcile You. Pardon me in Him who died for me and was buried. Behold your oblation: accept from my hands Him who is from You."

With these affections stand, O sinner, at the time of the Mysteries; and beg mercy and receive forgiveness, and then go forth. At the hour of the sacrifice, when it is being offered for you, do not leave him who is offering and depart.

Homiliy on Habib the Martyr
In this verse homily Jacob compares Habib and his mother to the Maccabean martyrs of the Old Testament (see 2 Mac 7).

Habib the martyr, clad in flame, has called to me out of the fire, That for him likewise I should fashion an image of beauty among the glorious. Comrade of conquerors, lo! He beckons to me out of the burning, That, as for the glory of his Lord, I should sing concerning him. In the midst of live coals stands the heroic man, and lo! He calls to me, That I should fashion his image: but the blazing fire permits me not. His love is fervid, glowing is his faith;

His fire also burns, and who is adequate to recount his love?...
Zealous he was, because he was concerned for the doctrine
Divine, that he might establish the adherents of the faith.
At the time when the winds of the pagans blew, a lamp was he,

And flamed forth while they blew upon him, and went not out.
All on fire was he, and filled with the love of his Lord, and was
  concerned
For this — that he might speak of Him without hindrance.
The thorns of error sprang up in the land from paganism;
And, as much as in him lay, he rooted them out by his diligence.
He taught, admonished, and confirmed in the faith,
The friends of Christ, who were harassed by persecutors.
Against sword and against fire did he wrestle,
With love hot as the flame, and was not afraid....

Then did his mother, because it was the marriage-feast for her son,
Deck herself in garments nobler than her wont.
Since sordid raiment suited not the banquet-hall,
In magnificent attire all white she clad herself right tastefully.
Hither to the battle came down love to fight
In the mother's soul— the love of nature, and the love of God.
She looked upon her son as he went forth to be put into the flame;
And, forasmuch as there was in her the love of the Lord, she
  suffered not.
The yearnings of her mother's womb cried out on behalf of its
  fruit;
But faith silenced them, so that their tumult ceased.
Nature shrieked over the limb which was severed from her;
But the love of the Lord intoxicated the soul, that she should not
  perceive it.
Nature loved, but the love of the Lord did conquer in the strife
Within the soul of the mother, that she should not grieve for her
  beloved.
And instead of suffering, her heart was filled with all emotions
  of joy;
And, instead of mourning, she went forth in splendid apparel....
And there rose up the sweet perfume of the martyr, and it grew
  sweet thereby.
And the sacrifices ceased, and there was peace in the assemblies;

And the sword was blunted, that it should no more lay waste the
    friends of Christ.
With Sharbil it began, with Habib it ended, in our land;
And from that time even until now not one has it slain, since he
    was burned.
Constantine, chief of conquerors, took the empire,
And the cross has trampled on the diadem of the emperor, and is
    set upon his head.
Broken is the lofty horn of idolatry,
And from the burning of the martyr even until now not one has
    it pierced.
His smoke arose, and it became incense to the Godhead;
And by it was the air purged which was tainted by paganism,
And by his burning was the whole land cleansed:
Blessed be He that gave him a crown, and glory, and a good name!

Here ends the Homily on Habib the martyr, composed by
Mar Jacob.

                                             — ANF 8:708-714

ST. ROMANUS THE SINGER

He is also known as "Romanus the Melodist."

Born in Syria, he served as a deacon in Beirut, but he achieved his
fame in Constantinople, where he was ordained a priest. There is some
dispute about the period in which he lived, but it was likely in the late
fifth and early sixth centuries.

His works are the earliest examples we have of *kontakia*, a form
of metrical Greek sermons, which were sung by a preacher during the
liturgy. A choir would accompany him, singing a refrain. More than a
thousand *kontakia* are attributed to Romanus, though his authorship
of many is contested by scholars. Those considered his masterpieces, his
hymns for Christmas and Easter, are almost certainly genuine.

According to tradition, Romanus received his remarkable gift as a
grace through the Blessed Virgin. She appeared to him in a dream and

gave him a scroll, bidding him to eat it (compare Ezekiel 3:1-3). On waking up, he rushed to the church, took to the pulpit, and sang his Christmas *kontakion*, which follows below.

He wrote in an elevated Greek, and his subject matter is varied — Old Testament, New Testament, lives of the saints, and festivals of the Church. He had a deep familiarity with Jewish customs and figures of speech. Many sources say his background was Jewish, and he may himself have been a convert.

SUNG SERMON AT CHRISTMAS

This translation of Romanus's Christmas Kontakion is by R.F. Littledale, from his Offices from the Service-Books of the Holy Eastern Church *(London: Williams and Norgate, 1863).*

The Virgin bears today
Him who is above all essence,
And the earth
Gives to the Inaccessible the cave.
Angels and shepherds chant his praise;
The magi journey with the star,
For our sake He has been born,
A little child, yet God before the worlds.

Bethlehem has opened Eden,
come, let us behold.
Hidden sweetness we have found,
come and let us take
The gifts of paradise within the cave.
There the unwatered Root appeared
Blossoming in pardon.
There was found the undug well,
Which David longed to drink of old.
And there the Maid,
Bearing her infant, quenched at once the thirst
Of Adam and of David.
So, then, let us hasten on,

Where He was born
A little child, yet God before the worlds.

ST. BENEDICT OF NURSIA

Measured by his own rule, St. Benedict (c. 480–c. 547) was a success, though it is unlikely that he would admit it. For he set humility as an essential virtue of a monk, and Benedict was so humble that he left hardly a trace of himself, except the work he did for God — his work and his prayer.

Indeed, we know little of Benedict from sources contemporary with his life. From later biographies, we know he came from northern Italy, and likely from a wealthy family. He studied in Rome, which was then at an advanced stage of moral and cultural decadence. In short order, Benedict grew disgusted with life. With a trusted servant, he headed for the hills.

His flight was not so extraordinary. Amid the societal disorder following the empire's dissolution, the contemplative life appeared oddly attractive to more men and women. It was more stable and secure, certainly, than life "in the world." So, many took to the wilderness, some living in community, some in isolation. For a growing number, this "flight" was merely an escape from responsibilities and hardship. Some communities were little more than leisure clubs, replete with servants to handle all manual work.

But that was certainly not the case with Benedict. In the Sabine Mountains, near the ruins of a Roman imperial palace, he found a monk named Romanus, who showed Benedict to a cave. There, inside that cave of Subiaco, the young hermit would spend the next three years.

Still, it was not a completely solitary experience. As was the case with St. Basil in the East, word spread that there was a holy man and wise spiritual guide in the mountains not far from Rome, and soon Benedict had visitors — and disciples. In short order, he received an invitation to be abbot over a nearby community, an invitation he declined. But the monks persisted, and Benedict relented.

Yet the monks soon regretted inviting him. His discipline proved too much for a community that had grown used to laxity. The monks tried to poison Benedict. He excused himself from their company and returned to his cave in Subiaco. This time, as men drew near for counsel, Benedict invited them to join him in community. Soon, he had set up a monastery along the lines established in the East, with twelve groups of twelve men.

Trouble entered this corner of paradise when a local priest grew envious of Benedict's success and tried to sabotage the community. First, he tried slandering Benedict, then poisoning him, and finally he introduced prostitutes into the midst of the monks. Benedict, again, thought it best that he leave, since it was envy of the abbot that had aroused the wicked priest against the community at Subiaco.

From there, he traveled southward to a town called Cassino, which had declined miserably with the empire. Its fortunes were spent, its lands barren, and its people had reverted to paganism. Benedict preached the Gospel and won back a handful, and then more, and these he persuaded to raze the local pagan shrines and build chapels.

It was at Monte Cassino that Benedict would build the monastery that would build up Western monasticism. Benedict established a community marked by order, obedience, study, silence, and service. His *Rule* laid out clear guidelines for interaction among monks in a monastery, and between monks and the world. Benedict offered little that was original; instead, he culled the best from the several Eastern rules and synthesized them in a most effective way.

One distinctively Benedictine touch is his emphasis on the dignity of manual labor. He emphasized "prayer and work." Work provided much-needed discipline to a monk's life. Work, Benedict said, was the first step toward goodness.

But he also stressed the need for formal, communal prayer, specifying the times of day when the monks should gather to chant the Psalms and pray the liturgy. This ritual prayer he called *opus dei*, "God's work." Thus, these two, *ora et labora*, "prayer and work," are two sides of the same coin.

Benedict's sister, St. Scholastica, receives credit for establishing communities of women living by Benedict's *Rule*.

Less than three centuries after Benedict's death, the Church would propose his *Rule* as the basic model for monastic life.

To Work and to Pray

This passage from the Rule *shows St. Benedict's distinctive attitude toward work. It is adapted from the translation of* The Holy Rule of St. Benedict, *by Rev. Boniface Verheyen, O.S.B. (1949).*

Idleness is the enemy of the soul. At set times, then, the brethren should be occupied with manual work, and again, at set times, with spiritual reading. We believe therefore that the hours for each should be fixed as follows: that is, from Easter to the first of October, they should go out early in the morning from Prime and work at what has to be done until about the fourth hour, and from the fourth hour spend their time in reading until about the sixth hour. When they rise from eating, after the sixth hour, they should rest on their beds in complete silence, or if one happens to wish to read let him do so without disturbing anyone else. Let None be said in good time, about the middle of the eighth hour; and let them work again at whatever needs to be done until Vespers. And let them not be disturbed if poverty or the necessities of the place compel them to toil at harvesting the crops with their own hands, as did our fathers and the Apostles.... Above all, have one or two seniors appointed to go around the monastery during the hours for reading to see that no restless brother is by chance idle or chattering and not intent on his reading and so of no profit to himself and a distraction to others.... However, if there is anyone so dull or lazy that he either will not or cannot study or read, let him have some task assigned him which he can perform, so that he may not be idle....

ST. VENANTIUS FORTUNATUS

A poet of the sixth century, Venantius Fortunatus was born near Venice and schooled in Ravenna. He studied both Christian and pagan poets, in Latin and Greek. In his youth he wandered through Europe, living the life of a bard while visiting the great shrines along the way. At the court of Sigebert I at Metz, he found success when he was retained to compose a poem for the king's marriage. Afterward he was much in demand among the nobility. Continuing his peregrinations, he visited Paris and finally settled in Poitiers.

He contracted an eye disease and feared he was going blind. At the shrine of St. Martin, in Tours, he anointed his eyes with oil from the lamps burning at the saint's tomb, and he was healed.

At Poitiers, he established a friendship with the Frankish princess St. Radegund, who was then living as a nun. He served as her secretary, and she inspired many of his poems. After her death, he wrote her biography.

Venantius was ordained to the priesthood and, shortly before his death, made bishop of Poitiers. He died in the first years of the 600s.

In the course of his life Venantius wrote eleven books of poetry. His work was profoundly influential as it marked the movement from classical Latin poetry's meter, which counted syllables, to medieval Latin's, which counted stresses or accents. His hymns are still popular today.

Good Friday Hymn

Venantius's Pange Lingua Gloriosi *is often sung on Good Friday. It is sometimes called the* Crux Fidelis *("Faithful Cross"). St. Thomas Aquinas borrowed the opening line for his own famous Eucharistic hymn. This translation is by J.M. Neale, from his book* Mediaeval Hymns and Sequences *(London: Joseph Masters, 1851)*

> Sing, my tongue, the glorious battle!
> With completed victory rife!
> And above the Cross's trophy
> Tell the triumph of the strife:
> How the world's Redeemer conquer'd
> By the offering of His life.
>
> God, his Maker, sorely grieving,
> That the first-made Adam fell,
> When he ate the fruit of sorrow,
> Whose reward was death and hell,

Noted then this Wood, the ruin,
Of the ancient wood to quell.

For this work of our salvation.
Needs must have its order so,
And the manifold deceiver's
Art by art would overthrow,
And from thence would bring the healing,
Whence the insult of the foe.

Wherefore when the appointed fullness
Of the holy time was come,
He was sent who maketh all things
From th' eternal Father's home,
And proceeded, God Incarnate,
Offspring of the Virgin's womb.

Weeps the Infant in the manger
That in Bethlehem's stable stands:
And His Limbs the Virgin Mother
Doth compose in swaddling bands,
Meetly thus in linen folding
Of her God the feet and hands.

Thirty years among us dwelling,
His appointed time fulfilled,
Born for this, He meets His Passion,
For that this He freely willed:
On the Cross the Lamb is lifted,
Where His life-blood shall be spilled.

He endured the nails, the spitting,
Vinegar, and spear, and reed;
From that holy Body broken
Blood and water forth proceed:
Earth, and stars, and sky, and ocean,
By that flood from stain are freed.

Bend thy boughs, O Tree of glory!
Thy relaxing sinews bend;
For awhile the ancient rigor,
That thy birth bestowed, suspend:
And the King of heavenly beauty
On thy bosom gently tend!

Thou alone wast counted worthy
This world's ransom to uphold;
For a shipwrecked race preparing
Harbor, like the Ark of old;
With the sacred Blood anointed
From the smitten Lamb that rolled.

To the Trinity be glory
Everlasting, as is meet:
Equal to the Father, equal
To the Son, and Paraclete:
Trinal Unity, whose praises
All created things repeat. Amen.

HYMN TO THE CROSS

Venantius wrote his Vexilla Regis to welcome a relic of the true cross upon its arrival at Poitiers. This translation, too, is from J.M. Neale's Mediaeval Hymns and Sequences.

The royal banners forward go,
The cross shines forth in mystic glow;
Where He in flesh, our flesh who made,
Our sentence bore, our ransom paid.

Where deep for us the spear was dyed,
Life's torrent rushing from His side,
To wash us in that precious flood,
Where mingled water flowed, and blood.

Fulfilled is all that David told
In true prophetic song of old,
Amidst the nations, God, saith he,
Hath reigned and triumphed from the tree.

O tree of beauty, tree of light!
O tree with royal purple dight!
Elect on whose triumphal breast
Those holy limbs should find their rest.

Blest tree, whose chosen branches bore
The wealth that did the world restore,
The price of humankind to pay,
And spoil the spoiler of his prey.

Upon its arms, like balance true,
He weighed the price for sinners due,
The price which none but He could pay,
And spoiled the spoiler of his prey.

O cross, our one reliance, hail!
Still may thy power with us avail
To give new virtue to the saint,
And pardon to the penitent.

To Thee, eternal Three in One,
Let homage meet by all be done:
As by the cross Thou dost restore,
So rule and guide us evermore.

ST. GREGORY THE GREAT

Almost as soon as Christians had "made it" in the ancient world, "it" began to collapse all around them. Even as Constantine and his successors were Christianizing the empire, the empire was increasingly beset by rebellions within and attacks from barbarians at the frontiers.

Early in the fifth century, the barbarians swept from the frontiers to Rome's city gates. Visigoths sacked Rome in 410. In 455, Vandals seized the city. The last emperor of the West died in 476. And Rome, once synonymous with world rule, descended into anarchy, as did much of western Europe. With the fall of Rome came a gradual collapse of civil order. The law had no force. The military dissolved. Travel, communications, and trade could no longer proceed peaceably as under Roman rule.

No one wanted to see this happen. Anarchy was surely repugnant to the old Roman families, who cherished the memory of imperial order. Neither, however, did chaos serve the barbarian invaders. They, too, wanted to inhabit a prosperous land.

But once the imperial government had vanished, what could take its place?

In a word: Gregory.

With the breakdown of the Roman army and court system, the Church alone survived as a unified, multinational force for order. The Church possessed laws, an educated hierarchy respected for fairness, and an impulse toward charitable works — what today we might call social justice.

Presiding over this intact social system on the local level was the bishop. Presiding over it all, universally, was Gregory.

Gregory (540–604) was born into one of those old Roman families, and he seems to have had an instinctive sense of the rule of law and the authority of rulers. He was prefect, or mayor, of Rome when the Lombards were readying their invasion in 571. Wearied of this world's pomps, Gregory answered the call to religious life, converting his home into a monastery.

But perhaps empire building was in his blood. Before too long, he had founded six more monasteries. He was ordained and, in the late

570s, Pope Pelagius II summoned him to serve in the papal diplomatic corps.

In 590, a plague ravaged Rome and claimed the pope. Gregory was elected his successor.

In rule, Gregory showed himself to be truly Roman. He strengthened the central authority of the papacy; and he defended the bishops, as his legates, against threats from civil leaders in the various lands. He initiated sweeping reforms and renewal of the clergy and the liturgy, both of which had fallen into a scandalous state of slovenliness. Gregorian chant was named for him, its initial promoter.

Yes, Gregory's genius was peculiarly Roman. Yet, he was not nostalgic about old Rome. He saw the future of the world and of the Church in the conversion of the vast populations of so-called barbarians beyond the former boundaries of the empire. Gregory looked with hope to the mission fields to the north and west, where he sent an increasing number of his monks. (He showed a great partiality to Benedictines.)

In confronting the heathen, Gregory suggested "adaptation," rather than destruction, of pagan temples. The pontiff wrote to his English mission in 601: "The idol temples of that race should by no means be destroyed, but only the idols in them. Take holy water and sprinkle it in these shrines, build altars and place relics in them." Gregory told the missionaries to encourage the locals to continue slaughtering their animals, as if for sacrifice, but now for celebration and praise of God instead. "Thus while some outward rejoicings are preserved, they will be able more easily to share in inward rejoicings."[74]

With "rejoicings," then, he led Europe from enveloping darkness to a first glimmer of dawn.

Yet, saving the known world was a demanding job, even for an old Roman, and it is said that St. Gregory worked himself first to a skeleton, and then to death in 604. He is both a Great Father and a Doctor of the Church.

On Bashing the Clergy

The great pope, in this letter to a bishop, shows his passion for order and for pastoral care.

If I were to destroy what my predecessors established, I should be justly convicted of being a destroyer rather than a builder. So testifies the voice of the Truth, who says, "Every kingdom divided against itself is laid waste" (Lk 11:17); and every science and law divided against itself shall be destroyed. We all, together, need to follow the guidelines of our holy Fathers, doing nothing adversarial. But, unanimous in every pious aim, we must, with the Lord's help, obey the holy and apostolic constitutions....

Now, you asked us about the harassment of bishops. We know that the life of prelates ought to be marred by no disturbances. It is unseemly for those who are called "thrones of God" to be disturbed by any action of kings or their subjects. If David, the most righteous king, did not presume to lay his hand on Saul — who was apparently already rejected by God — how much more should everyone be careful not to lay the hand of insults, abuse, indiscretion, or dishonor on the Lord's anointed, or on the preachers of the holy Church, since harassing or insulting them inevitably touches Christ, whom they represent in the Church!

All the faithful should be very careful never — neither secretly nor publicly, by insults or abuse — to attack their bishop. For he is the Lord's anointed. Consider the case of Miriam, who was punished with the uncleanness of leprosy because she spoke against Moses the servant of God for taking an Ethiopian wife (Num 12).

Subordinates, whether priests or lay people, should take care not to blame rashly the lives of their bishops or superiors, even if they see them do anything blamable. Otherwise, from their position of correcting evil they may be sunk into greater depths through the impulse of elation. Those who investigate the faults of their superiors must also be admonished so that they do not grow too bold and rebellious,... nor refuse to carry the yoke of reverence.

The things done by bishops and superiors are not to be smitten with the sword of the mouth, even when they seem to be blameworthy. It has been laid down by our predecessors, and by many other holy bishops, that sheep should not be eager to blame their shepherds, or presume to charge them or accuse them. For when we sin against our superiors, we go against the decree of Him who gave them to us. Moses, when he learned that the people complained against him and Aaron, said, "What are we? Your murmurings are not against us but against the LORD" (Ex 16:8). This is why subordinates of either order should be admonished, when they observe the deeds of their superiors, to return to their own heart, and presume not to upbraid them. The disciple is not above his master, nor the servant above his lord (Mt 10:24).

— NPNF2 13:110

ON THE RIGHTS OF THE JEWS
At the urging of a faithful Jew, St. Gregory admonished a bishop who had twice expelled a congregation from its synagogues.

A Jew named Joseph, the bearer of these gifts, has informed us that you, my brother, have expelled the Jews of Terracina, who had been accustomed to gathering in a certain place for celebrating their feast days. He said that they had, with your knowledge and consent, moved their festivities to another place. Now they complain that they have been expelled from this second place. If this is the case, we wish that you, our brother, would abstain from giving cause for this kind of complaint. They should be allowed, as was their custom, to gather in the meeting-place they had obtained with your knowledge.

Those who dissent from the Christian religion should be gathered into the unity of faith by gentleness, kindness, admonition, and persuasion. Otherwise, those who might have been attracted by the sweetness of preaching and the dread of future judgment might be repelled by threats and terrors. It is better for them to gather to hear the kindly word of God from you rather than to become fearful of your overstrained austerity.

— NPNF2 12:85

DIONYSIUS THE (PSEUDO-) AREOPAGITE

There was certainly a St. Dionysius (or Denis) the Areopagite. He is mentioned in the Acts of the Apostles (17:34) as one of the very few people St. Paul converted on his otherwise disappointing mission trip to Athens. Eusebius tells us that that Dionysius later became the first bishop of Athens.[75]

But that first-century man is almost certainly not the author of the body of works that bear his name. Of the real author of those texts, we know nothing for sure.

Yet it is hard to ignore the "Dionysian Corpus" in a book about the Fathers, because it was very influential on the theologians of later centuries. St. Maximus the Confessor considered his own work to be a mere footnote to the work of the Areopagite.

The corpus includes four treatises — *The Divine Names, The Mystical Theology, The Celestial Hierarchy,* and *The Ecclesiastical Hierarchy* — and ten letters.

The author follows through on the fiction, dropping the names of an all-star cast of New Testament characters: John the Evangelist, Paul, Timothy, Titus, Justus, and Carpus — all of whom, he claims, are close, personal friends.

The language, however, and the brilliant philosophy are engaged with the issues, and use the vocabulary, of a much later period in Church history. They are shot through with the language of fifth-century philosophers of the school of Plato; and they everywhere imply a preoccupation with the Christological controversies surrounding the Council of Chalcedon. They were likely written in the late fifth or early sixth century.

The earliest known reference to the works of Dionysius appears in a critical report from the year 532. Even this earliest reference questions the authenticity and orthodoxy of the corpus.

Still, all fictional devices aside, the Dionysian Corpus is as profound a work of theology as has ever been written, and it exercised a profound influence upon theologians and mystics in every generation since its publication. The author studies the metaphysical depths of Catholic doctrine on the angels, the liturgy, the priesthood, heaven, and the Blessed Trinity. Future theologians as diverse as St. Thomas Aquinas and St. John of the Cross have acknowledged their utter dependence on the doctrine of Dionysius.

The works themselves refer to other books supposedly by the same author, but history records not a single quotation or even a reference to these books. It is likely that these titles, too, are part of the fiction.

Dionysius is the great ancient expositor of *negative*, or *apophatic*, theology, which backs into a knowledge of God by emphasizing what He is not and acknowledging that He utterly transcends all created being. Dionysius also developed a beautiful theology of hierarchy as a great chain of spiritual beings, the higher serving the lower, from God Himself through the angels to the least person on the earth.

The Dionysian Corpus is one of the great masterpieces of Christian literature, the fruit of deep contemplation, and yet the true author will never receive the slightest credit!

PRAYER BEFORE THEOLOGY
The author speaks of the need to invoke God before considering His nature or attributes. All passages here are adapted from The Works of Dionysius the Areopagite, *translated by John Parker (Oxford: James Parker, 1897). The following selection appears in volume 1, pages 127-128.*

Let us examine the all-perfect name, Goodness, which manifests all the progressions of Almighty God.

But first let us invoke the Trinity, the source of all good which is above all good.... For, we must first be raised up to It, as the source of good, by our prayers; and by approaching nearer to It. We must be introduced to the all-good gifts that are established around It. For It is indeed present to all, but all are not present to It.

When we have invoked It, by all pure prayers and unpolluted mind, and by our inclination towards Divine Union, we also are present to It. It is not in a place, so It cannot be absent from a particular place. Nor can It pass from one to another. But even the statement that "It is in all existing beings" falls short of Its infinity, which is above everything, embracing everything.

So, with our prayers, let us elevate ourselves to the higher ascent of the Divine and good rays. It is as if a luminous chain were suspended from the celestial heights, reaching down to us. By clutching upwards, first with one hand, and then with the other, we seem indeed to draw it down, but in reality we do not. It remains both above and below. But we ourselves are carried upward to the higher splendors of the luminous rays.

Or it is as if we are on a ship. Cables moor us to a rock. We take them and pull them, but we do not draw the rock to us. We draw, rather, ourselves and the ship to the rock. Or consider it from the other side: If anyone standing on the ship pushes away the rock by the shore, he will do nothing to the stationary and unmoved rock. Rather, he separates himself from it; and as much as he pushes it away, so much is he hurled from it.

That is why, before everything, and especially before our considerations of God, we must begin with prayer. It is not as if we ourselves were drawing the power, which is everywhere and nowhere present; but rather that, by our godly recollections and invocations, we conduct ourselves to it, and making ourselves one with it.

HIERARCHY: THE LADDER OF LIGHT
In this classic passage from the Celestial Hierarchy *(Parker translation, volume 2, pages 113 and following), Dionysius shows how hierarchy is a great chain of service, beginning with God, who humbles Himself to serve all.*

What is hierarchy and what is it for?

In my opinion, hierarchy is a sacred order, a kind of knowledge and an activity that approximates the likeness of God, as much as that is possible. It is lifted up to the imitation of God according to the illuminations granted to it. Now the beauty of God — so simple and good, the source of perfection — is altogether free from any dissimilarity. It gives its own proper light to each according to capacity, and perfects in divine initiation, and harmoniously it gives its own form to those being perfected.

The purpose of hierarchy is to enable beings, as much as possible, to be like God and have union with Him. The hierarchy has God as its Leader in all knowledge and activity. A hierarchy looks unflinchingly at His most divine beauty.

A hierarchy, as much as possible, perfects its own followers to be divine images, luminous and flawless reflections, receiving the primal light in its supremely divine ray. When the followers are devoutly filled, the hierarchy ensures that they spread this radiance unsparingly to those lower beings, according to God's will.

It would be unlawful for the mystic rites of sacred things, or for those who participate in them, to practice anything beyond the sacred regulations of their own proper function. They must never act otherwise, if they want to reach its deifying splendor and look to it religiously — and if they are formed to the splendor proportionate to each mind.

When someone speaks of hierarchy, he means a certain altogether holy order, an image of the supremely divine freshness, dispensing the mysteries of its own enlightenment in hierarchical ranks and levels of knowledge, each assimilated to its own proper Head as far as permitted.

For all who have been called into the hierarchy find their perfection in being borne, in their own proper degree, to the imitation of God — and, what is most divine of all, they become "God's fellow workers" (1 Cor 3:9), as the Scriptures say, manifesting in themselves, as much as possible, the work of God.

For it is the law of the hierarchy that some are purified while others purify. Some are enlightened while others enlighten. Some are perfected while others perfect. The imitation of God will suit each one in this fashion. The divine happiness, to use human terms, is something unstained by dissimilarity, and it is full of invisible light. It is perfect and lacks no perfection. It is cleansing, enlightening, and perfecting. More than that, it is a holy purification and illumination and perfection, above purification, above light, preeminently perfect. It is the self-perfect source and cause of every hierarchy, and elevated preeminently above every holy thing.

It appears to me that those who are being purified should be entirely perfected, without stain, and be freed from all dissimilar confusion. Those who are being illuminated should be filled with the divine Light, raised up in the habit and faculty of contemplation in all purity of mind. Those who are being initiated should be separated from the imperfect, and become recipients of that perfecting knowledge of the sacred things they contemplate.

What is more, those who purify should give, from their own overflowing purity, their own proper holiness. Those who illuminate have more luminous intelligence, and it is their task to receive and to bestow light. And they are joyful and filled with holy gladness that these gifts should overflow, in proportion to their own overflowing light, toward those who are worthy to be enlightened. Those who perfect others are skilled in bestowing perfection, and they should indeed perfect those in their charge, through their sacred teaching, in the knowledge and contemplation of holy things.

Thus each rank of the hierarchical order is led, in its own degree, to be coworkers with God. By grace and God-given power, it does things that are naturally and supernaturally proper to God, things accomplished by Him transcendently, and manifested in the hierarchy, for the attainable imitation of the God-loving minds.

ST. MAXIMUS THE CONFESSOR

Maximus the Confessor (580–662) was well born, bred, and schooled, all among the nobility of the chief city of the world, Constantinople. Early in life, he drew notice for the subtlety of his mind and his great literary skill. He was quite young when he was tagged to be first secretary to the emperor Heraclius.

He excelled in the imperial service, but then discerned a vocation to be a monk. So he quit the world of government for a monastic retreat. He seems to have spent time in several monasteries in Asia Minor and North Africa. At one of them, Maximus met the man who would, more than any other, influence the direction of his life and thought. It was St. Sophronius, the future patriarch of Jerusalem, who raised Maximus's awareness of the dangers in certain new ways of thinking.

The Monothelite (or "one will") school of thought arose as many churchmen were seeking a way to reconcile the Monophysite heretics of Egypt and Syria. The Monophysites believed that Christ had but a single nature, the divine, which completely absorbed His humanity.

The Church condemned this belief because it voided the Incarnation; Christ could not be both "true God and true man" if His human nature were compromised in this way.

Some theologians thought they had found a solution in the Monothelite doctrine. They proposed that Christ had two natures, but only one will, His divine will. This proposal caused much excitement among authorities in both Church and state. Many people had grown weary of the seemingly endless — and increasingly violent — controversies about fine points of doctrine. The emperor himself was eager to restore unity to his realm, the better to resist the rising threats of invasion from the east. Almost everyone, it seems, was anxious for an easy answer.

But Maximus was not, and for good reason. The rush for easy answers, compromises, and quick fixes was at least one reason why earlier theologians had cascaded from one heresy to another. The Monothelite doctrine raised new and serious problems. How, for example, could Christians understand Jesus' agony in the garden (Mt 26:36-46) except as the struggle of human will to conform to God's will? If He had only one will, what was the struggle? The agony was reduced to a sham.

Maximus opposed the doctrine of the Monothelites in public debates, which he won handily, and at the African synods. Maximus raised the stakes by traveling to Rome to consult with the pope and participate in the Lateran Council of 649. There, too, he prevailed. Still, the emperor, Constans II, sided with the Monothelites, and so did the patriarch of Constantinople. In 653, the emperor ordered the arrest of both Maximus and the pope. Since both refused to accept the new formula, they were exiled.

Recalled to Constantinople in 661, they still refused. The judge decided to silence Maximus once and for all. He ordered the torturers to cut out his tongue and cut off his right hand, so that he would never again be able to speak or write against the Monothelite doctrine.

Maximus died from the effects of these tortures in 662. But he was vindicated when the Church ruled at the Council of Constantinople in 680 that Christ had two wills, divine and human.

Maximus's theological style and method were rather remarkable. He moved easily from pure theology to practical spirituality, and he — better than any other theologian of the Patristic Era — managed to fuse the best qualities of both Eastern and Western thought.

There has been a recent groundswell of interest in St. Maximus, with beautiful translations appearing in the ACW, CWS, ECF, and PP series.

WHEN SOMEONE GOSSIPS ABOUT YOU
Maximus compiled collections of concise statements about the spiritual life, for monks to use in their meditation. He collected them together in batches of one hundred, called "centuries." These are numbers 83, 84, 88, and 89 in his fourth Century on Love. The translation is a composite, adapted from several.

Someone has gossiped about you. Do not hate him, but rather the gossip and the demon who encouraged the gossip. If you hate the one who gossips, you hate a person and break the commandment, and what he did by his word you do by your action. But if you keep the commandment, show proof of your love, and if possible, give him help so that he can be delivered from such evil.

Christ does not want you to hate anyone, or be grieved or angry or grudging at all, for any temporal reason whatsoever. This is clearly proclaimed in the four Gospels.

There is no difficulty more oppressive to the soul than slander, whether one is slandered for his faith or for his way of life. No one can ignore it except the one who, like Susanna, looks to God; for He alone can rescue those in need. He rescued her, to reassure everyone, as He did in her case, and to comfort the soul with hope.

To the extent that you pray from your heart for the one who spread gossip about you, God will reveal the truth to those who heard the gossip.

THE ULTIMATE AUTHORITY ON EARTH
St. Maximus wrote the following in a letter to the governor of Syria and Palestine, who had written to ask whether the deposed patriarch of Constantinople, Pyrrhus, was a heretic. St. Maximus defers judgment to

the pope and the Church of Rome. The translation is adapted from The Catholic Encyclopedia *(1912 edition).*

[The authorities in Constantinople] have not conformed to the sense of the Apostolic See. And what is laughable — or rather lamentable, because it proves their ignorance — is that they have not hesitated to lie against the Apostolic See itself.... Moreover, they have claimed the great [deceased Pope] Honorius to be on their side.... What did the divine Honorius do, and after him the aged Severinus, and John who followed him? Yet further, what supplication has the blessed pope, who now sits, not made? Have not the whole East and West brought their tears, laments, and pleas, both before God in prayer and before men in their letters? If the Roman See recognizes [the former patriarch of Constantinople] Pyrrhus to be not only a reprobate but a heretic, it is certainly plain that everyone who rejects those who have rejected Pyrrhus, rejects the See of Rome itself — that is, he rejects the Catholic Church. I need hardly add that he excommunicates himself as well, if indeed he is in communion with the Roman See and the Church of God....

It is not right that one who has been condemned and cast out by the Apostolic See of the city of Rome for his wrong opinions should be named with any kind of honor, until he is received by her, having returned to her — no, to Our Lord — by a pious confession and orthodox faith. Only by this can he receive holiness and the title of holy....

Let him hasten first of all to satisfy the Roman See, for if it is satisfied everyone will agree to call him pious and orthodox. For it is futile for anyone to try to persuade or entrap someone like me without trying instead to satisfy and implore the blessed pope of the most holy Church of the Romans. For that is the Apostolic See, which has received, from the incarnate Son of God Himself, universal and supreme dominion, authority, and the power of binding and loosing over all the holy churches of God. This is confirmed by all holy synods, according to the holy canons and definitions, which are in the whole world. For with it the Word, who is above the celestial powers, binds and looses in heaven as well.

If [Pyrrhus] thinks he must satisfy others, but fails to implore the most blessed Roman pope, he is acting like a man who, when accused of murder or some other crime, wastes his time proving his innocence to private individuals, who have no power to acquit him, rather than to the judge appointed by law.

ST. ISIDORE OF SEVILLE

Isidore lived at a time when the memory (or fantasy) of a homogeneous Roman culture was rapidly fading. The conquering "barbarians," the Visigoths, had now been resident in Spain for generations. They were no longer foreigners. Rather, a new culture was forming, a "melting pot" of Roman and northern elements. Isidore's writings gathered the best from both cultures and laid a solid foundation on which medieval Europe could be built. For the situation was not peculiar to Spain. It was the same all over the continent.

Isidore was born around 560 to a devoutly Catholic family, whose members labored for the conversion of the Visigoths from the Arian heresy. Two of his brothers came to be prominent bishops in Spain; his sister Florentina was a religious superior who governed a large number of monasteries. All his siblings are recognized as saints.

Isidore received his schooling at the cathedral in Seville. It was then an experimental form of education, but it was demanding and would eventually catch on as the standard for the continent. Isidore managed to learn a number of languages as well as history, classical literature, music, arithmetic, geometry, rhetoric, and the natural sciences. He studied the customs and history of the Visigoths as well as the Romans.

Around 600 he succeeded his brother Leander as archbishop of Seville. He would serve in that office for close to thirty-five years. Recognizing the need for an assimilation of cultures, he applied the Church's resources to education. He himself wrote great textbooks that provide an invaluable record of the process of transition and cultural redefinition. Though Isidore wrote in Latin, he used well over a thousand "new" Spanish words.

He was a prolific author, producing important works in history, science, theology, and biblical studies. His greatest book is undoubtedly his *Etymologies*, an encyclopedic dictionary in which he hunts down the origins of words, not for mere curiosity's sake, but in order to lead readers to the true essence of the things that are represented by the words. Sometimes his definitions are more allegorical than historical. He wants his readers to understand God's intention in creating this or that thing with certain peculiar attributes. The *Etymologies* was a work in progress throughout Isidore's life, still unfinished at the time of his death.

With that book, Isidore invented a new genre, one that would be developed through the centuries. Modern encyclopedias can trace their own origin to his seventh-century work. The *Etymologies* has even been called the progenitor of the World Wide Web, and there has been a movement in recent years to recognize Isidore as the patron saint of the Internet.

A man of holy ambition, Isidore succeeded in producing a library of learning that could serve as a light to the Dark Ages. The last of the Western Fathers, he laid strong foundations for the great medieval civilization. He is honored as a Doctor of the Church.

A CENSUS OF THE ANGELS

In his Etymologies, *Isidore presents all creation hierarchically, in what would come to be known as a great "chain of being," with God at the top, followed by the angels, who are followed in turn by the human race, and so on down to slugs and stones. In this passage, he culls ideas on the angels from sources as diverse as Augustine and Dionysius and gives basic definitions of each angelic order. This translation comes from Ernest Brehaut's An Encyclopedist of the Dark Ages: Isidore of Seville (New York: Columbia, 1912).*

The word *angel* is the name of a function, not of a nature; for they are always spirits, but are called angels when they are sent. And the creativity of painters makes wings for them in order to denote their swift passage in every direction, just as also in the fables of the poets the winds are said to have wings on account of their velocity.... The sacred writings testify that there are nine orders of angels: namely, angels, archangels, thrones, dominions, virtues, principalities, powers, cherubim, and seraphim. And we shall explain by derivation why the names of these functions were so applied.

Angels are so called because they are sent down from heaven to carry messages to men....

Archangels in the Greek tongue means *summi nuntii* (highest messengers) in the Latin. For those who carry small or trifling messages are called *angels;* and they who announce the most important things are called *archangels....* Archangels are so called because they hold the leadership among angels.... For they are leaders and chiefs under whose control services are assigned to each and every angel.

Certain functions of angels by which signs and wonders are done in the world are called *virtues,* on account of which the virtues are named.

Those are *powers* to whom hostile virtues are subject, and they are called by the name of *powers* because evil spirits are constrained by their power not to harm the world as much as they desire.

Principalities are those who are in command of the hosts of the angels. And they have received the name of *principality* because they send the subordinate angels here and there to do the divine service....

Dominions are those who are in charge even of the virtues and principalities, and they are called *dominions* because they rule the rest of the hosts of the angels.

Thrones are the hosts of angels who in Latin are called *sedes* (seats); and they are called *thrones* because the creator presides over them, and through them accomplishes his decisions.

Cherubim ... are the higher hosts of angels who, being placed nearer, are fuller of the divine wisdom than the rest....

The *seraphim* in like manner are a multitude of angels, and the word is translated from the Hebrew into the Latin as *ardentes* or *incendentes,* and they are called *ardentes* because between them and God no other angels stand, and therefore the nearer they stand in His presence the more they are lighted by the brightness of divine light. And they veil the face and feet of God sitting on His throne, and therefore the rest of the throng of angels are not able to see fully the essence of God, since the seraphim cover Him.

To each and every one, as has been said before, his proper duties are appointed, and it is agreed that they obtained these according to merit at the beginning of the world.

That angels have charge over both places and men, an angel testifies through the prophet, saying: " The prince of the kingdom of Persia withstood me" (Dn 10:13). Whence it is evident that there is no place that angels have not charge of. They have charge also over the beginnings of all works.

Such is the order or classification of the angels who after the fall of the wicked stood in celestial strength. For after the apostate angels fell, these were established in the continuance of eternal blessedness.

As to the two seraphim that are read of in Isaiah, they show in a figure the meaning of the Old and the New Testament. But as to their covering the face and feet of God, it is because we cannot know the past before the universe, nor the future after the universe, but according to their testimony we contemplate only the intervening time.

ST. JOHN OF DAMASCUS

Of all the controversies in the early Church, perhaps the most violent was that of the eighth-century iconoclasts. They won their name, which means "icon-smasher," for their destructive raids on churches throughout the Christian East.

The iconoclasts, led by a succession of Byzantine emperors, believed that praying before images was idolatry, a violation of the First Commandment. Tradition was against them — as Sts. Athanasius, Basil, Gregory of Nyssa, and many others had defended the practice — but they had the court theologians on their side. In 726, the emperor Leo III committed the unthinkable act of outlawing religious images in the Eastern empire. The bishops of the East reacted swiftly, by excommunicating the emperor and all iconoclasts.

But it took an accountant, a Syrian bureaucrat, to settle the matter in a more definitive way. His name was John, and he was the chief treasury official of the Muslim caliph of Damascus. Yet he was a devout Christian, and he was unashamed to bow before sacred icons.

John of Damascus took it upon himself to write a refutation of the iconoclasts' position. His first tract appeared about 728, with two more by 730. Sometime during that interval, he left behind his high position and journeyed to the Monastery of St. Sabbas, ten miles south of Jerusalem.

In his refutations, John appealed to Scripture, Tradition, and common sense. He acknowledged that the Old Covenant forbade prayer before images. But, he added, the Incarnation changed everything. "In former times, God, being without form or body, could in no way be represented. But today, since God has appeared in the flesh and lived among men, I can represent what is visible in God. I do not worship matter, but I worship the Creator of matter who became matter for my sake ... and who, through matter, accomplished my salvation."

Next, he listed the times when God either commanded or approved the making of images: Moses' raising of the bronze serpent in the desert; the figures of cherubim woven round the Ark of the Covenant; and the angels of gold in Solomon's Temple. Yet all these, though commanded by God, would be forbidden by the iconoclasts.

John went on to make a now-classic distinction that may be his greatest contribution to theology. He explained the difference between *latria*, which is adoration or worship due only to God, and *proskinesis*, which is honor or veneration given to creatures. A Christian offers *latria* in prayer to God and in the liturgy; he offers *proskinesis* to his parents, to civil authorities, to the flag, to the saints and angels, and to the images and relics of Christ.

"Discern between the different kinds of worship. Abraham bowed down to the sons of Hamor, men who had neither faith nor knowledge of God.... Jacob bowed to the ground before Esau, his brother, and also before the tip of his son Joseph's staff. He bowed down, but he did not adore. Joshua ... and Daniel bowed in veneration before an angel of God, but they did not adore him. For adoration is one thing, and that which is offered in order to honor something of great excellence is another."

John also pointed out that Leo's purge was a sort of class warfare. While the men of the imperial court had the leisure to read and the money to buy books, most people did not. To deprive the congregations of icons was, really, to deprive them of the Gospel stories. "Since, however, not all know letters, nor do all have the leisure to read, the Fathers deemed it fit that these events should be depicted as a sort of memorial and terse reminder. It certainly happens frequently that at times when we do not have the Lord's passion in mind we may see the image of His crucifixion and, being thus reminded of His saving passion, fall down and adore."

John suspected that there was more to iconoclasm than met the eye. He feared that these men had Manichean tendencies, despising God's creation and especially human flesh; they wished to spiritualize — "purify" — the incarnational faith. John argued the orthodox position: that matter is good because God created it, and that Christ sanctified the flesh by taking it on Himself. In iconoclasm, John saw the revival of all the old Christological heresies.

John's arguments prevailed, but not in his lifetime. He died in 749, and the fury of iconoclasm continued. A general council at Nicaea condemned iconoclasm in 787, but in 814 another iconoclast emperor came to the throne, and the trouble started all over again. The trouble didn't finally end until 842, when the empress Theodora restored the icons and ended the power of the iconoclasts forever. Her decree is still celebrated by a great feast in the Eastern Church.

The last of the Fathers, John is sometimes called the first of the medievals, because his comprehensive manual, *On the Orthodox Faith*, anticipates that distinctive genre of the theology of the Middle Ages: the *summa theologica*.

On the Veneration of Saints
From his work On the Orthodox Faith.

To the saints honor must be paid as friends of Christ, as sons and heirs of God. In the words of John the theologian and evangelist, "But to all who received him, who believed in his name, he gave power to become children of God" (Jn 1:12). So that they are no longer servants, but sons: and if sons, also heirs, heirs of God and joint heirs with Christ (see Gal 4:7). And the Lord in the holy Gospels says to His Apostles, "You are my friends if you do what I command you. No longer do I call you servants, for the servant does not know what his master is doing" (Jn 15:14-15).

And further, if the Creator and Lord of all things is called also King of kings and Lord of lords and God of gods, surely also the saints are gods and lords and kings. For of these God is and is called God and Lord and King. "[For] I am the God of Abraham," He said to Moses, "the God of Isaac, and the God of Jacob" (Ex 3:6). And God made Moses a god to Pharaoh. Now I mean gods and kings and lords not in nature, but as rulers and masters of their passions, and as preserving a truthful likeness to the divine image according to which they were made (for the image of a king is also called king), and as being united to God of their own free will and receiving Him as an indweller and becoming by grace through participation with Him what He is Himself by nature. Surely, then, the worshipers and friends and sons of God are to be held in honor. For the honor shown to the most thoughtful of fellow servants is a proof of good feeling towards the common Master.

These are made treasuries and pure habitations of God: For I will dwell in them, said God, and walk in them, and I will be their God. The divine Scripture likewise says that the souls of the just are in God's hand and death cannot lay hold of them. For death is rather the sleep of the saints than their death. For they travailed in this life and shall to the end, and "Precious in the sight of the Lord is the death of his saints" (Ps 116:15). What, then, is more precious than to be in the hand of God? For God is Life and Light, and those who are in God's hand are in life and light.

Further, that God dwelt spiritually even in their bodies, the Apostle tells us, saying, "Do you not know that your body is a temple of the Holy Spirit within you?" (1 Cor 6:19). The Lord is that Spirit, and if anyone destroy the temple of God, him will God destroy. Surely, then, we must ascribe honor to the living temples of God, the living tabernacles of God. These while they lived stood with confidence before God.

The Master Christ made the remains of the saints to be fountains of salvation to us, pouring forth manifold blessings and abounding in oil of sweet fragrance: and let no one disbelieve this. For if water burst in the desert from the steep and solid rock at God's will and from the jawbone of an ass to quench Samson's thirst, is it incredible that fragrant oil should burst forth from the martyrs' remains? By no means, at least to those who know the power of God and the honor which He accords His saints.

In the law, everyone who touches a dead body was considered impure, but these are not dead. For from the time when He who is Himself life and the Author of life was reckoned among the dead, we do not call those dead who have fallen asleep in the hope of the resurrection and in faith in Him. For how could a dead body work miracles? How, therefore, are demons driven off by them, diseases dispelled, sick persons made well, the blind restored to sight, lepers purified, temptations and troubles overcome, and how does every good gift from the Father of lights come down through them to those who pray with sure faith? How much labor would you not undergo to find a patron to introduce you to a mortal king and speak to him on your behalf? Are not those, then, worthy of honor who are the patrons of the whole race, and make intercession to God for us? Yes, truly, we ought to give honor to them by raising temples to God in their name, bringing them fruit offerings, honoring their memories and taking spiritual delight in them, in order that the joy of those who call on us may be ours, that in our attempts at worship we may not on the contrary cause them offense. For those who worship God will take pleasure in those things whereby God is worshiped, while His shield-bearers will be wroth at those things wherewith God is wroth. In psalms and hymns and spiritual songs, in contrition and in pity for the needy, let us believers honor the saints, as God also is most worshiped in this way.

Let us raise monuments to them and visible images, and let us ourselves become, through imitation of their virtues, living monuments and images of them. Let us give honor to her who bore God as being strictly and truly the Mother of God. Let us honor also the prophet John as forerunner and baptist, as Apostle and martyr: For among them that are born of women there has not risen a greater than John the Baptist, as says the Lord, and he became the first to proclaim the kingdom. Let us honor the Apostles as the Lord's brothers, who saw Him face-to-face and ministered to His passion, for whom God the Father did foreknow He also did predestine to be conformed to the image of His Son — first, Apostles; second, prophets; third, pastors and teachers. Let us also honor the martyrs of the Lord chosen out of every class, as soldiers of Christ who have drunk His cup and were then baptized with the baptism of His life-bringing death, to be partakers of His passion and glory: of whom the leader is Stephen, the first deacon of Christ and apostle and first martyr.

Also let us honor our holy Fathers, the God-possessed ascetics, whose struggle was the longer and more toilsome one of the conscience: who wandered about in sheepskins and goatskins, being destitute, afflicted, tormented; they wandered in deserts and in mountains and in dens and caves of the earth, of whom the world was not worthy. Let us honor those who were prophets before grace, the patriarchs and just men who foretold the Lord's coming. Let us carefully review the life of these men, and let us emulate their faith and love and hope and zeal and way of life, and endurance of sufferings and patience even to blood, in order that we may be sharers with them in their crowns of glory.

— NPNF2 9:86-87

On Images
A capsule of his arguments against the iconoclasts, from On the Orthodox Faith.

But since some find fault with us for worshiping and honoring the image of our Savior and that of Our Lady, and those, too, of the rest of the saints and servants of Christ, let them remember that in the beginning God created man after His own image. On what grounds, then, do we show reverence to one another unless it is because we are made after God's image? For as Basil, that much-versed expounder of divine things, says, the honor given to the image passes over to the prototype.

Now a prototype is that which is imaged, from which the derivative is obtained. Why was it that the Mosaic people honored on all hands the tabernacle which bore an image and type of heavenly things, or rather of the whole creation? God indeed said to Moses, "See that you make them after the pattern for them, which is being shown you on the mountain" (Ex 25:40). The cherubim, too, which overshadow the mercy seat, are they not the work of men's hands? What, further, is the celebrated Temple at Jerusalem? Is it not handmade and fashioned by the skill of men?

Moreover the divine Scripture blames those who worship graven images, but also those who sacrifice to demons. The Greeks sacrificed and the Jews also sacrificed: but the Greeks to demons and the Jews to God. And the sacrifice of the Greeks was rejected and condemned, but the sacrifice of the just was very acceptable to God. For Noah sacrificed, and God smelled a sweet savor, receiving the fragrance of the right choice and goodwill towards Him. And so the graven images of the Greeks, since they were images of deities, were rejected and forbidden.

But besides this, who can make an imitation of the invisible, incorporeal, uncircumscribed, formless God? Therefore to give form to the Deity is the height of folly and impiety. And hence it is that in the Old Testament the use of images was not common. But after God in the depths of His bowels of pity became in truth man for our salvation, not as He was seen by Abraham in the semblance of a man, nor as He was seen by the prophets, but in being truly man, and after He lived upon the earth and dwelt among men, worked miracles, suffered, was crucified, rose again, and was taken back to heaven, since all these things actually took place and were seen by men, they were written for the remembrance and instruction of us who were not alive at that time in order that though we saw not, we may still, hearing and believing, obtain the blessing of the Lord. But seeing that not every one has a knowledge of letters nor time for reading, the Fathers gave their sanction to depicting these events on images as being acts of great heroism, in order that they should form a concise memorial of them. Often, doubtless, when we have not the Lord's passion in mind and see the image of Christ's crucifixion, His saving passion is brought back to remembrance, and we fall down and worship not the material but that which is imaged: just as we do not worship the material of which the Gospels are made, nor the material of the cross, but that which these typify.

For wherein does the cross, which typifies the Lord, differ from a cross that does not do so? It is just the same also in the case of the Mother of the Lord. For the honor which we give to her is referred to

Him who was made of her incarnate. And similarly also the brave acts of holy men stir us up to be brave and to emulate and imitate their valor and to glorify God. For as we said, the honor that is given to the best of fellow servants is a proof of goodwill towards our common Lady, and the honor rendered to the image passes over to the prototype.

— *NPNF2 9:88*

THE MOTHERS

"Fathers of the Church" is not just a title, but a metaphor as well. And to many modern minds it raises the question: Were there "Mothers of the Church"?

Since I've answered that question at length in another book, *Mothers of the Church: The Witness of Early Christian Women* (Huntington, IN: Our Sunday Visitor, 2012), we'll spend just a moment on it here.

We possess very few writings by women from the ancient world. Christian women are probably slightly better represented than their pagan counterparts. Even in Christian societies, however, women faced fewer educational opportunities than men. If women were not in a position to teach and write, then they were not performing the duties usually associated with the Fathers of the Church.

This does not, however, mean that women were passive members of the Church. The sociologist Rodney Stark, in his compelling study of the first three Christian centuries, *The Rise of Christianity*, concludes that women made up a disproportionate number of converts, that Christianity improved the lives of women in the world, and that women played active roles in the running of the Church. Women were never ordained to the priesthood, but the ordained priesthood was hardly the only — or even the primary — mode of Christian leadership.

Women made up a great number of the early martyrs, and their stories and their cult of honor were often more popular than those of their male companions. This was true in every part of the Christian world. In Gaul (what is today France), the Christians esteemed St. Blandina as the most courageous of all. In ancient Africa, they honored Sts. Perpetua and Felicity. The Roman Mass, from the Patristic Era till now, has invoked the names of Perpetua and Felicity along with other women of the ancient Church: Agatha, Lucy, Agnes, Cecilia, and Anastasia.

Women were just as active in the monastic movement. The many collections of "Sayings of the Desert Fathers" actually include proverbs by women ascetics, who were addressed as "Amma," or "Mother."

St. John Chrysostom (fifth century) carried on extensive correspondence with an abbess named Olympias, but her letters have not survived. His contemporary St. Jerome corresponded with many holy and scholarly women — Melania, Lea, Asella, Principia, Paula, Eustochium, Demetrias — but, again, we have mostly Jerome's end of the conversation. In the late fourth century, St. Gregory of Nyssa wrote a profoundly moving biography of his sister St. Macrina, who had won renown as a spiritual director; but Macrina herself left us no books.

Their contemporaries honored these women as maternal figures. The Church has always honored them as saints. The liturgies for their feast days address them as "Mother." There is no custom of calling them "Mothers of the Church," but there is no reason why individual Christians might not revere them as such.

ST. PERPETUA

Perpetua, an educated noblewoman, was arrested with her slave Felicity and several others in Carthage, North Africa, in 202 or 203. The emperor Septimius Severus had initiated yet another persecution. Perpetua's crime was her Christian faith; she was a recent convert, who had just completed her preparation for Baptism.

While in prison, Perpetua wrote an account of the days leading up to their martyrdom. The narrative, of course, was finished by another hand. Perpetua was frank in her discussion of the difficulties and temptations faced by the condemned Christians — the gross discomforts of the prisons, the fear of pain and death, and the desire to please their uncomprehending family members, many of whom were pagan. Her narrative also provides an early witness to many Catholic doctrines, such as purgatory and the sacraments.

Perpetua's story was corroborated and preserved by her near-contemporary Tertullian and was revered by St. Augustine.

THE PASSION OF ST. PERPETUA

In this opening passage of The Passion of Perpetua, *the saint's narrative ranges from extraordinary visions to the quite ordinary anxieties of a new mother. In her vision, she experiences a mystical Communion from the hand of an angel or, perhaps, God Himself. Some ancient Christian (perhaps Tertullian) wrote the brief introduction that opens this excerpt.*

The young catechumens — Revocatus and his fellow servant Felicity, Saturninus, and Secundulus — were arrested. Among them also was Vivia Perpetua, a noblewoman, well educated, a married matron. She had a father and mother and two brothers, one of whom, like herself, was a catechumen, and an infant son whom she was breastfeeding. She was about twenty-two years of age. From this point onward she shall herself narrate the whole course of her martyrdom, as she left it described by her own hand and with her own mind....

———————

While we were still with the persecutors, my father, out of affection, persisted in trying to turn me away and cast me down from the faith.

"Father," I said, "do you see this vessel lying here to be a little pitcher, or something else?"

He said, "That is what I see."

And I replied to him, "Can it be called by any other name than what it is?"

And he said, "No."

"Neither can I call myself anything else than what I am, a Christian."

Then my father, provoked at this saying, threw himself upon me, as if he would tear my eyes out. But he only distressed me, and went away overcome by the devil's arguments.

A few days after I had been without my father, I gave thanks to the Lord; and his absence became a source of consolation to me. In that same period of a few days we were baptized, and to me the Spirit prescribed that nothing else but the water of Baptism would be needed for bodily endurance.

The Dungeon a Palace

After a few days more, we were taken into the dungeon, and I was very much afraid, because I had never felt such darkness. What a terrible day! Oh, the fierce heat of the shock of the soldiery, because of the crowds!

I was unusually distressed by anxiety for my infant. So the blessed deacons who ministered to us, Tertius and Pomponius, arranged by means of a bribe for us to find a few hours of refreshment in a more pleasant part of the prison.

Then, going out of the dungeon, all attended to their own wants. I nursed my child, who was now weak with hunger. In my anxiety for it, I addressed my mother and comforted my brother, and commended my son to their care. I was languishing because I had seen them languishing on my account. Such solicitude I suffered for many days, and I arranged for my infant to remain in the dungeon with me; and afterward I grew strong and was relieved from distress and anxiety about my infant; and the dungeon became like a palace to me, so that I preferred being there to being elsewhere.

A Vision

Then my brother said to me, "My dear sister, you are already in a position of dignity so great that you may ask for a vision, that it may be revealed to you whether this will result in suffering or escape."

I knew that I was privileged to converse with the Lord, whose kindnesses I had found to be so great. So I boldly promised him, "Tomorrow I will tell you."

And I asked, and this was what was shown to me. I saw a golden ladder of marvelous height, reaching up to heaven. It was very narrow, so that persons could only ascend it one by one; and on the sides of the ladder was fixed every kind of iron weapon. There were there swords, lances, hooks, daggers; so that if anyone went up carelessly, not looking upward, he would be torn to pieces and his flesh would cleave to the iron weapons. And under the ladder itself crouched a dragon of wonderful size, who lay in wait for those who ascended, and frightened them from the ascent.

Saturus went up first ... and he reached the top of the ladder and turned towards me, saying, "Perpetua, I am waiting for you; but be careful that the dragon does not bite you."

And I said, "In the name of the Lord Jesus Christ, he shall not hurt me."

From under the ladder itself, as if in fear of me, he slowly lifted up his head; and as I stepped upon the first rung, I stepped upon his head. I went up, and I saw an immense garden, and in the midst of the garden a white-haired man sitting in the dress of a shepherd. He was large in stature, milking sheep; and standing around were many thousands in white robes. He raised his head, and looked upon me, and said to me, "You are welcome, daughter." And he called me, and from the cheese as he was milking he gave me a little cake, and I received it with folded hands; and I ate it, and all who stood around said, "Amen." And at the sound of their voices I was awakened, still tasting a sweetness which I cannot describe.

I immediately described this to my brother, and we understood that the result was to be suffering, and we ceased afterward to have any hope in this world.

— ANF 3:699-700

ST. SYNCLETICA

St. Syncletica was born in the fourth century into a wealthy family in Alexandria, Egypt. She took a vow of virginity and refused many suitors. When her parents died, she retired with her blind sister to live as hermits in an unused tomb.

Many people, looking to her as "Amma," or "Mother," sought her out for spiritual counsel. These disciples preserved her sayings for posterity, and they are all we have of her. Syncletica's advice was seasoned with examples drawn from domestic life; she often compared the spiritual disciplines to the familiar tasks of cooking and cleaning.

In her seclusion, Syncletica battled both demons and cancer. She died around the year 400.

THE SAYINGS
The following passages appear in The Sayings of the Desert Fathers: The Alphabetical Collection, *translated by Mother Benedicta Ward (Kalamazoo, MI: Cistercian Publications, 1975).*

Amma Syncletica said, "In the beginning there are a great many battles and a good deal of suffering for those who are advancing towards God and, afterwards, ineffable joy. It is like those who wish to light a fire. At first, they are choked with smoke and cry, until they obtain what they seek. As it is written, 'Our God is a consuming fire' (Heb 12:29); so we also must kindle the divine fire in ourselves through tears and hard work."

She also said, "Do not let yourself be seduced by the delights of the riches of the world, as though they contained something useful on account of vain pleasure. Worldly people esteem the art of cooking, but you, through fasting and thanks to cheap food, go beyond their abundance of food. It is written: 'He who is sated loathes honey' (Prov 27:7). Do not fill yourself with bread and you will not desire wine."

Blessed Syncletica was asked if poverty is a perfect good. She said, "For those who are capable of it, it is a perfect good. Those who can sustain it receive suffering in the body but rest in the soul, for just as one washes coarse clothes by trampling them underfoot and turning them about in all directions, even so the strong soul becomes much more stable thanks to voluntary poverty."

Amma Syncletica said, "There are many who live in the mountains and behave as if they were in the town, and they are wasting their time. It is possible to be a solitary in one's mind while living in a crowd, and it is possible for one who is a solitary to live in the crowd of his own thoughts."

EGERIA THE PILGRIM

We know nothing about Egeria (sometimes rendered Etheria or Hegeria) except what she recorded in her pilgrim diary. A nun from Spain or Gaul (modern-day France), she set out on a pilgrimage to the

Holy Land. Her journey, which lasted at least three years (381–384), took her to Constantinople, Palestine, Syria, Mesopotamia, Arabia, and Egypt.

Along the way, she recorded what she saw, noting many valuable details of scenery, language, architecture, monastic life, popular devotion, local custom, and liturgy. Her language is colloquial and intimate, addressed to her sisters in the community back home.

For its quality of observation, Egeria's diary is unique in the fourth century. Our sense of history and sense of place would be impoverished without it, as many of the lands she visited are no longer Christian lands. And without Egeria's witness, we would never know that, when St. Cyril of Jerusalem preached about the sacraments (the very sermons that are included in this book), his congregation of newly baptized adults erupted into applause — applause that was audible throughout the neighborhood.

Only portions of her account have survived.

Climbing Mount Sinai

This excerpt is adapted from The Pilgrimage of Etheria, *translated by M. L. McClure and C. L. Feltoe (London: SPCK, 1919).*

We reached the mountain late on the sabbath, and arriving at a certain monastery, the monks who dwelt there received us very kindly, showing us every kindness. There is also a church and a priest there. We stayed there that night, and early on the Lord's day, together with the priest and the monks who dwelt there, we began the ascent of the mountains one by one. These mountains are ascended with infinite toil, for you cannot go up gently by a spiral track — snail-shell wise, as we say — but you climb straight up the whole way, as if up a wall, and you must come straight down each mountain until you reach the very foot of the middle one, which is specially called Sinai.

By this way, then, at the bidding of Christ our God, and helped by the prayers of the holy men who accompanied us, we arrived at ten in the morning at the summit of Sinai, the holy mountain of God, where the law was given — at the place where the Glory of the Lord descended on the day when the mountain smoked (see Ex 19:18).

Thus the toil was great, for I had to go up on foot, the ascent being impossible in the saddle, and yet I did not feel the toil, on the side of the ascent — I say "the toil" because I realized that the desire that I had was being fulfilled at God's bidding.

In that place there is now a church, not great in size, for the place itself, the summit of the mountain, is not very great. Nevertheless, the church itself is great in grace.

When, therefore, at God's bidding, we had arrived at the summit, and had reached the door of the church, the priest who was appointed to the church came from his cell and met us — a hale old man, a monk from early life, and an ascetic as they say here: in short, one worthy to be in that place. The other priests also met us, together with all the monks who dwelt on the mountain, those who were not hindered by age or infirmity. No one, however, dwells on the very summit of the central mountain; there is nothing there except the church and the cave where holy Moses was.

When the whole passage from the book of Moses had been read in that place, and when the liturgy had been duly offered, at which we received Communion, and as we were coming out of the church, the priests of the place gave us *eulogiae* — that is, blessed fruits that grow on the mountain. The holy mountain Sinai is rocky throughout, and has not even a shrub on it; yet down below, near the foot of the mountains, around either the central height or those which encircle it, there is a little plot of ground where the holy monks diligently plant little trees and orchards, and set up chapels with cells nearby, so that they may gather fruits that they have evidently cultivated with their own hands from the soil of the mountain itself.

So, after we had received Communion, and the holy men had given us *eulogiae*, and we had come out of the door of the church, I began to ask them to show us the several sites. The holy men immediately agreed to show us the various places. They showed us the cave where holy Moses was when he had gone up again into the mount of God (see Ex 34:4), that he might receive the second tables after he had broken the first ones when the people sinned. They also showed us the other sites we wanted to see, which they themselves well knew.

But I would have you know, ladies, reverend sisters, that from the place where we were standing, round outside the walls of the church — from the summit of the central mountain — those mountains, which we could scarcely climb at first, seemed to be so far below us when compared with the central one on which we were standing, that they appeared to be little hills. Yet they were so very large that I thought that I had never seen higher — except that this central one excelled them by far.

From there we could see Egypt and Palestine, and the Red Sea and the Parthenian Sea, which leads to Alexandria and the boundless territories of the Saracens — all so much below us as to be hardly believable. But the holy men pointed out each one of them to us.

POSTSCRIPT

What we have heard and know,
and what our Fathers have declared to us
we will declare to the generation to come:
the glorious deeds of the LORD and His strength
and the wonders that He wrought.

> — Psalm 78:3-4, Responsorial Psalm for the
> Eighteenth Sunday in Ordinary Time

ABOUT THE AUTHOR

Mike Aquilina is the author of many books, including *St. Monica and the Power of Persistent Prayer*, *The Mass of the Early Christians*, and *Roots of the Faith*. He has cohosted eight series on EWTN. He is married and the father of six children.

APPENDIX

For Further Study

This book offers a first glance at the Church Fathers. This implies that readers should take a second glance, and a third, and many more, each time looking ever more deeply into the thought and prayer of the Fathers, and so into the mind and heart of the Church. Below is a listing of resources, in many media, which offer opportunities for richer study of the Fathers. (For a key to my abbreviations, please see page 12.)

THE FATHERS IN GENERAL

The twentieth century produced a great many seminary and university textbooks on the study of the Church Fathers. They're usually known by the names of their authors, rather than by their titles, which are almost indistinguishable anyway. So you'll sometimes hear fans of the Fathers arguing, for example, the comparative merits of "Quasten" and "Altaner."

Most of the manuals are out of print, but used copies are waiting for you on the shelves of bookshops around the world. Affordable copies turn up regularly online at ABEBooks, Bookfinder, Alibris, and Amazon. The following are my favorites. I note their page counts, because some readers are looking for a summary treatment and others for the cyclopedic.

Altaner, Berthold. *Patrology.* Translated by Hilda C. Graef. New York: Herder and Herder, 1960. 660 pages.

Bardenhewer, Otto. *Patrology: The Lives and Works of the Fathers of the Church.* Translated by Thomas J. Shahan. Freiburg: Herder, 1908. (Reprint: St. Irenaeus Press, 2012). 697 pages.

Beatrice, Pier Franco. *Introduction to the Fathers of the Church*. Vicenzo, Italy: Istituto San Gaetano, 1983. 351 pages. Summaries, texts, and beautiful full-color illustrations.

Benedict XVI, Pope. *The Fathers* (two volumes). Huntington, IN: Our Sunday Visitor, 2008 and 2010. Volume 1: 201 pages. Volume 2: 170 pages. A collection of his Wednesday audience talks on the early Christians.

Cayré, F. *Manual of Patrology* (two volumes). Translated by H. Howitt. Paris: Desclée, 1940. Vol. 1: 742 pages. Vol. 2: 916 pages.

Dirksen, Aloys. *Elementary Patrology: The Writings of the Fathers of the Church*. St. Louis, MO: Herder, 1959. 314 pages.

Drobner, Hubertus R. *The Fathers of the Church: A Comprehensive Introduction*. Translated by Siegfried S. Schatzmann. Peabody, MA: Hendrickson, 2005. 596 pages. A detailed, one-volume Catholic patrology, currently in print and relatively affordable, that includes the most up-to-date scholarship. It focuses on a few select Fathers and spends more time explaining cultural background and intellectual currents.

Femantle, Anne. *A Treasury of Early Christianity*. New York: Mentor, 1960. 511 pages. A selection of readings.

Hamell, Patrick J. *Handbook of Patrology*. New York: Alba House, 1968. 170 pages.

Musurillo, Herbert A. *The Fathers of the Primitive Church*. New York: Mentor, 1966.

Papandrea, James. *Reading the Early Church Fathers: From the Didache to Nicaea*. New York: Paulist, 2012. 352 pages.

Quasten, Johannes. *Patrology* (four volumes). Allen, TX: Christian Classics, 1997. Vol. 1: 450 pages. Vol. 2: 349 pages. Vol. 3: 605 pages. Vol. 4: 667 pages. Still in print after several decades, this survey is like an encyclopedia of patrology, providing by far the most detailed analysis of each Father's life, work, and importance in the history of the Church.

Russell, Claire. *Glimpses of the Church Fathers*. London: Scepter, 1996. 549 pages. A devotional collection, useful for prayer and meditation.

Schmid, Bernard. *Manual of Patrology.* Translated by a Benedictine monk. St. Louis, MO: Herder, 1911. 351 pages.

Tixeront, J. *A Handbook of Patrology.* Translated by S. A. Raemers. St. Louis, MO: Herder, 1920. 380 pages.

Wuerl, Donald W. *Fathers of the Church.* Boston: Daughters of St. Paul, 1982. 144 pages.

COLLECTIONS AND ANTHOLOGIES

The best and most complete series are ACW (Mahwah, NJ: Paulist Press) and FC (Washington: Catholic University of America Press), both of which are Catholic — and both still growing. The most affordable series are the nineteenth-century Protestant ANF and NPNF (reprinted by Hendrickson), whose commentary and footnotes are sometimes very good and sometimes extremely anti-Catholic. Most annoying, though, is the ANF/NPNF editors' habit of deleting passages that favor distinctively Catholic doctrines (usually the papacy). I've found egregious instances of this in the translations of Clement of Rome and Ambrose of Milan.

Jurgens, William A., ed. *The Faith of the Early Fathers* (three volumes). Collegeville, MN: Liturgical Press, 1979. Three volumes of the Fathers' testimony on a host of dogmas, doctrines, and disciplines. This is an excellent resource for those who explain, defend, or teach the faith.

Toal, M. F., ed. *Sunday Sermons of the Great Fathers: A Manual of Preaching, Spiritual Reading, and Meditation* (four volumes). San Francisco: Ignatius Press, 1996. St. Thomas Aquinas gathered these patristic homilies together into the collection he called "The Golden Chain." The readings follow the Church's calendar.

New Advent Supersite, an outstanding Catholic website, includes text of the ANF and NPNF editions (without the anti-Catholic footnotes and introductory matter): www.newadvent.org.

The Tertullian Project is a patristics website that includes texts from the ANF and NPNF series (as published) as well as other scattered works, primary texts and translations, and secondary scholarship. The site's contents are also available on a handy CD-ROM.

The North American Patristics Society's site includes links to many scholarly pages dedicated to the Fathers and their schools of thought: www.patristics.org.

THE APOSTOLIC FATHERS

Search any well-stocked online bookstore using the words "The Apostolic Fathers," and you'll turn up several translations.

My favorite is still a work in progress. Kenneth Howell has so far translated and published *Ignatius of Antioch and Polycarp of Smyrna: A New Translation and Theological Commentary* (Zanesville, OH: Coming Home Resources, 2009). He promises more to come.

The cheapest English edition of the Apostolic Fathers is *Early Christian Writings* in the Penguin Classics series (London: Penguin, 1987), translated by Maxwell Staniforth and revised by Andrew Louth.

If you prefer to have the original language handy, you can choose from many editions. I prefer Michael W. Holmes' *The Apostolic Fathers: Greek Texts and English Translations* (Grand Rapids, MI: Baker, 2007). The old bilingual *The Apostolic Fathers*, edited by J. B. Lightfoot and J. R. Harmer (1891, reprinted by Baker 1984), is currently out of print, but used copies can often be found at affordable prices.

Accessible overviews of the period are *The Apostolic Fathers* by Simon Tugwell, O.P. (Harrisburg, PA: Morehouse, 1989) and *Reading the Apostolic Fathers* by Clayton N. Jefford (Peabody, MA: Hendrickson, 1996).

A beautiful, moving, almost novelistic treatment is Rod Bennett's *Four Witnesses: The Early Church in Her Own Words* (San Francisco: Ignatius Press, 2002).

HISTORICAL OVERVIEWS AND RAMBLES

Bunson, Matthew. *Encyclopedia of Catholic History*. Huntington, IN: Our Sunday Visitor, 2004. Reliable basic data on the Fathers, creeds, councils, heresies.

Newman, John Henry Cardinal. *The Church of the Fathers*. Notre Dame, IN: Notre Dame University Press, 2002. Vivid historical sketches about some of the main characters and events of the Patristic Era.

Ramsey, Boniface. *Beginning to Read the Fathers.* Mahwah, N.J.: Paulist Press, 1985. A good introduction to the Fathers, with in-depth explorations of the Fathers' doctrine on selected topics, such as Jesus Christ, Scripture, and consecrated virginity.

Sommer, Carl J. *We Look for a Kingdom: The Everyday Lives of the Early Christians.* San Francisco, CA: Ignatius, 2007. Provides vivid details about the Fathers' world: social life, entertainment, military life, Roman religion.

Stark, Rodney. *The Rise of Christianity: How the Obscure Jesus Movement Became the Dominant Religious Force in the Western World in a Few Centuries.* San Francisco: HarperCollins, 1997. A sociological study of the Church's growth in the first three centuries — all the more remarkable because it was written by a nonbeliever.

Whitehead, Kenneth. *One, Holy, Catholic, and Apostolic: The Early Church Was the Catholic Church.* San Francisco: Ignatius Press, 2000.

Wilken, Robert L. *The Christians as the Romans Saw Them.* New Haven, CT: Yale University Press, 1984.

———. *The Spirit of Early Christian Thought: Seeking the Face of God.* New Haven, CT: Yale University Press, 2003. An intelligent yet popular and quite moving introduction to the Christian culture of the Fathers.

EASTERN SCHOOLS, TRADITIONS, RITES

Brightman, F. E. *Eastern Liturgies.* Piscataway, NJ: Gorgias (reprint), 2002.

Brock, Sebastian, trans. and ed. *Syriac Fathers on Prayer and the Spiritual Life.* Kalamazoo, MI: Cistercian Publications, 1988.

Gruber, Mark. *Sacrifice in the Desert: A Study of an Egyptian Minority through the Prism of Coptic Monasticism.* Lanham, MD: University Press of America, 2003.

Meinardus, Otto F. A. *Two Thousand Years of Coptic Christianity.* Cairo: American University in Cairo Press, 2002.

Meredith, Anthony. *The Cappadocians.* Crestwood, NY: St. Vladimir's Seminary Press, 2000.

Roberson, Ronald G. *The Eastern Christian Churches: A Brief Survey.* Rome: Oriental Institute Press, 1986.

THE FATHERS ON THE BIBLE

Danielou, Jean, S.J. *The Bible and the Liturgy.* Notre Dame, IN: Notre Dame University, 1956.

de Margerie, Bertrand, S.J. *An Introduction to the History of Exegesis,* three volumes. Petersham, MA: St. Bede's Publications, 1993.

Froehlich, Karlfried. *Biblical Interpretation in the Early Church.* Philadelphia: Fortress Press, 1984. A collection of texts on the reading of Scripture, culled from the Fathers themselves.

Hall, Christopher A. *Reading Scripture with the Church Fathers.* Downers Grove, IL: InterVarsity Press, 1998. A readable and winsome introduction to the Fathers' methods of biblical interpretation, written by a Protestant theologian for an evangelical publisher.

Oden, Thomas, gen. ed. *The Ancient Christian Commentary on Scripture* series. Downers Grove, Ill.: InterVarsity Press, 1998. A multivolume set that collects the Fathers' interpretations of all the Scriptures, verse by verse, book by book.

Shea, Mark P. *Making Senses Out of Scripture: Reading the Bible as the First Christians Did.* San Diego, CA: Basilica Press, 1999.

Simonetti, Manlio. *Biblical Interpretation in the Early Church.* Edinburgh: T. & T. Clark, 1994.

THE FATHERS ON PRAYER

Aquilina, Mike. *The Way of the Fathers: Praying with the Early Christians.* Huntington, IN: Our Sunday Visitor, 1999. A collection of sayings of the Fathers, organized by topic.

Aumann, Jordan. *Christian Spirituality in the Catholic Tradition.* San Francisco: Ignatius Press, 1985. Father Aumann's early chapters offer profound insight into the patristic experience of prayer, liturgy, Scripture, and community.

Bouyer, Louis, et al. *The Spirituality of the New Testament and the Fathers. A History of Christian Spirituality,* vol. 1. New York: Seabury, 1963.

Cayré, F. *Spiritual Writers of the Early Church*. Twentieth Century *Encyclopedia of Catholicism*, vol. 39. New York: Hawthorn, 1958.

Hahn, Scott. *Understanding "Our Father": Biblical Reflections on the Lord's Prayer*. Steubenville, OH: Emmaus Road, 2002. A synthesis of patristic, historical, and spiritual exegesis, with several lengthy commentaries from the Fathers themselves.

Spidlík, Thomas. *Drinking from the Hidden Fountain: A Patristic Breviary*. Kalamazoo, MI: Cistercian Publications, 1994. Selections from the Fathers, chosen and arranged for meditation.

THE FATHERS ON CHURCH, PRIESTHOOD, AND HIERARCHY

Cochini, Christian. *The Apostolic Origins of Priestly Celibacy*. San Francisco: Ignatius, 1990.

Fortescue, Adrian. *The Early Papacy: To the Synod of Chalcedon in 451*. San Francisco: Ignatius, 2008.

Guarducci, Margherita. *The Primacy of the Church of Rome: Documents, Reflections, Proofs*. San Francisco: Ignatius Press, 2003.

Halton, Thomas. *The Church*. MFC, vol. 4. Wilmington, DE: Michael Glazier, 1985. A selection of texts.

Heid, Stefan. *Celibacy in the Early Church: The Beginnings of Obligatory Continence for Clerics in East and West*. San Francisco: Ignatius Press, 2000.

Heston, Edward L., C.S.C. *The Priest of the Fathers*. Milwaukee: Bruce, 1945.

Kaitholil, George. *Church, The Sacrament of Christ: Patristic Vision and Modern Theology*. Staten Island, NY: Alba House, 1998.

Lienhard, Joseph T. *Ministry*. MFC, vol. 8. Wilmington, DE: Michael Glazier, 1984. A selection of texts.

Martimort, Aimé Georges. *Deaconesses: An Historical Study*. San Francisco, CA: Ignatius, 1986.

Shotwell, James T., and Louise Ropes Loomis. *The See of Peter*. New York: Columbia University Press, 1991. A collection of texts and traditions that link the papacy and Roman primacy with succession from St. Peter.

THE FATHERS ON THE SACRAMENTS

Aquilina, Mike. *The Mass of the Early Christians* (second edition). Huntington, IN: Our Sunday Visitor, 2007. Background, commentary, and many texts of the earliest liturgies.

Bouyer, Louis. *Eucharist: Theology and Spirituality of the Eucharistic Prayer*. Notre Dame, IN: Notre Dame University Press, 1968.

Deiss, Lucien. *Springtime of the Liturgy: Liturgical Texts of the First Four Centuries*. Collegeville, MN: Liturgical Press, 1979. A rich stock of ancient liturgies, well translated into dignified modern English. Many unusual prayers and blessings.

Hahn, Scott, and Mike Aquilina. *Living the Mysteries: A Guide for Unfinished Christians*. Huntington, IN: Our Sunday Visitor, 2003. Fifty patristic meditations covering the Church's sacraments.

Mazza, Enrico. *Mystagogy: A Theology of Liturgy in the Patristic Age*. Collegeville, MN: Pueblo, 1989.

————. *The Celebration of the Eucharist: The Origin of the Rite and the Development of Its Interpretation*. Collegeville, MN: Pueblo, 1999.

————. *The Origin of the Eucharistic Prayer*. Collegeville, MN: Pueblo, 1995.

THE FATHERS ON DOCTRINE

Congar, Yves M. J. *A History of Theology*. New York: Doubleday, 1968. Excellent chapters on the rise of theology as a discipline, and the Fathers' challenges and accomplishments in this area.

————. *The Meaning of Tradition*. San Francisco: Ignatius Press, 2004.

Daley, Brian. *On the Dormition of Mary: Early Patristic Homilies*. Crestwood, NY: St. Vladimir's Seminary Press, 1997.

————. *The Hope of the Early Church: A Handbook of Patristic Eschatology*. Peabody, MA: Hendrickson, 2005. An overview of the Fathers' teachings on the end times and the last things.

Gambero, Luigi. *Mary and the Fathers of the Church: The Blessed Virgin Mary in Patristic Thought*. San Francisco: Ignatius Press, 2004.

Gasparro, Giulia Sfameni, et al., eds. *The Human Couple in the Fathers*. Pauline Patristic Series, vol. 1. Boston: St. Pauls, 1999. Brings out the richness of the Fathers' thoughts on love, sex, and marriage. Includes selections from the Fathers with detailed and useful introductions.

Hogan, Richard M. *Dissent from the Creed: Heresies Past and Present.* Huntington, IN: Our Sunday Visitor, 2001. The best popular study of the most wayward ancients.

Kelly, J. N. D. *Early Christian Doctrines.* New York: Continuum, 2000.

Newman, John Henry Cardinal. *An Essay on the Development of Christian Doctrine.* Notre Dame, IN: Notre Dame University Press, 1989. A clear explanation and demonstration of the Fathers' authority in doctrinal matters.

Pelikan, Jaroslav. *The Emergence of the Catholic Tradition (100-600)*, vol. 1 in *The Christian Tradition*. Chicago: University of Chicago Press, 1971.

Ray, Stephen K. *Crossing the Tiber.* San Francisco: Ignatius Press, 1997. The story of how one man, led by study of the Church Fathers, converted from "Bible-only" Christianity to the fullness of Catholic faith. Each of his doctrinal points is thoroughly documented with patristic references.

Reynolds, Brian K. *Gateway to Heaven: Marian Doctrine and Devotion, Image and Typology in the Patristic and Medieval Periods.* Hyde Park, NY: New City Press, 2012.

Scott, David. *The Catholic Passion: Rediscovering the Power and Beauty of the Faith.* Chicago: Loyola Press, 2005. A beautiful retrieval of the Fathers' understanding of Catholic faith. Scott takes the words of the Fathers and applies them to our lives today.

Tixeront, Joseph. *History of Dogmas. Milestones in Catholic Thought*, vol. 1. Westminster, MD: Christian Classics, 1984.

Willis, John R. *The Teachings of the Church Fathers.* San Francisco: Ignatius Press, 2002. Selections from the Fathers, organized by doctrinal theme.

MARTYRDOM IN THE EARLY CHURCH

Musurillo, Herbert, ed. and trans. *The Acts of the Christian Martyrs.* Oxford: Oxford University Press, 1972.

Ricciotti, Giuseppe. *The Age of Martyrs: Christianity from Diocletian to Constantine*. Translated by Anthony Bull. Milwaukee: Bruce, 1959.

Young, Robin Darling. *In Procession before the World: Martyrdom as Public Liturgy in Early Christianity*. Milwaukee: Marquette University Press, 2001.

MONASTICISM IN THE EARLY CHURCH

Burton-Christie, Douglas. *The Word in the Desert: Scripture and the Quest for Holiness in Early Christian Monasticism*. Oxford: Oxford University Press, 1993.

Harmless, William. *Desert Christians: An Introduction to the Literature of Early Monasticism*. Oxford: Oxford University Press, 2004.

Petersen, Joan M., ed. and trans. *Handmaids of the Lord: Holy Women in Late Antiquity and the Early Middle Ages*. Kalamazoo, MI: Cistercian Publications, 1996.

Ward, Benedicta, ed. and trans. *The Sayings of the Desert Fathers: The Alphabetical Collection*. Kalamazoo, MI: Cistercian Publications, 1975.

FICTION

De Wohl, Louis. *Citadel of God: A Novel about Saint Benedict*. San Francisco: Ignatius Press, 1994.

———. *The Restless Flame: A Novel about Saint Augustine*. San Francisco: Ignatius Press, 1997.

Giesler, Michael. *Junia: The Fictional Life and Death of an Early Christian*. Princeton: Scepter, 2002.

———. *Marcus*. Princeton: Scepter, 2004.

———. *Grain of Wheat*. Princeton: Scepter, 2008.

Newman, John Henry. *Callista: A Tale of the Third Century*. Notre Dame, IN: University of Notre Dame Press, 2001.

Waugh, Evelyn. *Helena*. Chicago: Loyola Press, 2005. A great novelist's portrait of Constantine's amazing mother.

OTHER MEDIA

Collections of the Fathers can be found at New Advent (NewAdvent.org) and The Tertullian Project (Tertullian.org/Fathers).

"Early Christianity and the First Christians," an audio course on the Fathers, taught by Fr. Brian Daley, S.J., of Notre Dame University, is available from NowYouKnowMedia.com.

Eighth Day Books. A catalog with a wide selection of works by and about the Fathers. Many of the items in this listing are in Eighth Day's catalog: 1-800-841-2541, www.eighthdaybooks.com.

I update my own blog, FathersOfTheChurch.com, with occasional news and observations on the Fathers.

BY THE AUTHOR OF THIS BOOK

Aquilina, Mike. *The Mass of the Early Christians (second edition).* Huntington, IN: Our Sunday Visitor, 2007.

———. *Companion Guide to Pope Benedict's 'The Fathers.'* Huntington, IN: Our Sunday Visitor, 2008. Good for group study.

———. *The Early Church.* New Haven, CT: Knights of Columbus, 2008.

———. *Roots of the Faith: From the Church Fathers to You.* Cincinnati, OH: Servant, 2010. A thematic study of the Fathers' doctrine and practices.

———. *A Year with the Church Fathers: Patristic Wisdom for Daily Living.* Charlotte, NC: St. Benedict's Press, 2010. A devotional collection.

———. *A Year with the Angels: Daily Meditations with the Messengers of God.* Charlotte, NC: St. Benedict's Press, 2011. A devotional on the angels, all taken from the Church Fathers.

———. *Faith Charts: The Fathers of the Church at a Glance.* Huntington, IN: Our Sunday Visitor, 2011.

———. *Faith of Our Fathers: Why the Early Christians Still Matter and Always Will.* Steubenville, OH: Emmaus Road, 2012. A collection of essays and occasional journalism.

Aquilina, Mike, and Christopher Bailey. *Mothers of the Church: The Witness of Early Christian Women.* Huntington, IN: Our Sunday Visitor, 2012.

Aquilina, Mike, and Christopher Bailey. *Praying the Psalms with the Early Christians.* Ijamsville, MD: Word Among Us, 2009.

Aquilina, Mike, and Scott Hahn. *Living the Mysteries: A Guide for Unfinished Christians.* Huntington, IN: Our Sunday Visitor, 2008. Fifty meditations, by the Fathers, on the sacraments.

Aquilina, Mike, and Lea Marie Ravotti. *Signs and Mysteries: Revealing Ancient Christian Symbols.* Huntington, IN: Our Sunday Visitor, 2008. An illustrated guide to early Christian art.

THE TIMES OF THE FATHERS

◄─────◇─────►

Timeline of Events

Note: Many dates assigned to events 1,500 to 2,000 years ago are in dispute among reputable scholars. What follows are approximations.

30–33	• Jesus ascends to heaven.
	• The Apostles receive the Holy Spirit at Pentecost.
48	• Composition of some parts of the Didache.
49–66	• The letters of St. Paul.
64	• Burning of Rome.
65	• Nero purges "vast numbers" of Christians in Rome.
	• Death of St. Peter in Rome.
67	• Death of St. Paul in Rome.
70	• Jerusalem falls to the Romans.
88–97	• Reign of Pope St. Clement.
90–100	• Death of the last Apostle, St. John.
92–96	• Persecution of Domitian.
107	• St. Ignatius of Antioch's journey to martyrdom.
130	• Papias writes his recollections of the Apostles.
130s	• St. Irenaeus studies under St. Polycarp.
140s	• The heretic Marcion gains a following in Rome.
155	• Death of St. Polycarp.
	• St. Justin writes his Apology to the emperor.
165	• Death of St. Justin in Rome.
Late 100s	• Montanus leads his followers into schism.
180	• Founding of the School of Alexandria.
190–200	• Muratorian Canon lists New Testament books.
	• St. Hippolytus reports an early creed.
200	• St. Clement leads the School of Alexandria.

202	• Death of St. Irenaeus in Lyons.
	• Beginning of systematic persecution under Emperor Septimius Severus.
203	• Origen succeeds St. Clement as rector in Alexandria.
222	• Death of Tertullian.
248	• St. Cyprian is named bishop of Carthage.
250	• Emperor Decius decrees a persecution.
251	• Epidemic sweeps the Roman Empire.
253	• Death of Origen.
257	• Emperor Valerian begins persecution.
293–305	• Ruthless persecution is led by Emperor Diocletian.
310s	• Donatist schism begins.
313	• Constantine's Edict of Milan decrees toleration of Christianity.
318	• Arius begins teaching his heresy.
325	• Council of Nicaea condemns Arianism.
327	• St. Athanasius is named bishop of Alexandria.
330	• Constantine orders St. Athanasius to readmit Arius to priesthood.
	• Founding of Constantinople, administrative center of the eastern empire.
335	• Synod of Tyre excommunicates St. Athanasius.
336	• St. Athanasius is exiled to Germany.
	• Death of Arius.
350	• St. Cyril delivers his catechetical lectures in Jerusalem.
361–363	• Emperor Julian tries to revive paganism.
366	• St. Athanasius is restored to Alexandria.
370	• St. Basil is named bishop of Caesarea in Pontus, reforms monastic life.
374	• St. Ambrose is named bishop of Milan.
380	• Emperor Theodosius I declares Christianity official religion of the empire.
381	• Council of Constantinople confirms decisions of Nicaea.
382	• St. Jerome revises the Latin Gospels.
387	• St. Augustine returns to the Catholic faith.
390	• St. Ambrose denies the sacraments to the emperor.
390–405	• St. Jerome revises the Latin New Testament.

393	• Synod of Hippo Regius discusses the New Testament canon.
395	• Roman Empire divides into East and West.
	• St. Augustine is made bishop.
397, 419	• Synod of Carthage settles the New Testament canon.
398	• St. John Chrysostom is named patriarch of Constantinople.
400	• Montanist and Donatist heretics submit to St. Augustine.
403	• St. John Chrysostom is exiled.
410	• Visigoths sack Rome.
428	• The heretic Nestorius is named patriarch of Constantinople.
429	• Vandals invade Africa.
430	• Death of St. Augustine.
431	• Council of Ephesus condemns Nestorianism.
448	• Eutyches is denounced for holding the Monophysite heresy.
449	• The "Robber Synod" of Ephesus.
451	• Council of Chalcedon condemns Monophysitism.
452	• Pope Leo turns Attila and the Huns away from Rome.
455	• Vandals seize Rome.
476	• Death of Rome's last Western emperor.
529	• St. Benedict founds Monte Cassino.
553	• Second Council of Constantinople.
571	• Lombards invade Rome.
590	• St. Gregory the Great is elected pope.
622–632	• Mohammed founds Islam.
632	• Muslim caliphates begin.
636	• Death of St. Isidore of Seville, the last Western Father.
638	• Jerusalem is captured by Muslims.
680	• Third Council of Constantinople.
726	• Sacred images are outlawed by the Byzantine emperor.
728–730	• St. John of Damascus writes tracts defending icons.
749	• Death of St. John of Damascus, the last Eastern Father.

NOTES

1. St. Basil the Great, *Letter 37*.
2. NPNF2 11:132.
3. NPNF2 11:132.
4. ANF 3:261.
5. NPNF2 1:172.
6. Not everyone agrees that Tertullian, Origen, and Eusebius should be called Fathers. At least two of the standard textbooks, F. Cayré's *Manual of Patrology* (1935) and J. Tixeront's *Handbook of Patrology* (1920), grant them the title by way of exception. But B. Schmid's *Manual of Patrology* (1911) denies them the title, as does Yves Congar's *The Meaning of Tradition*. However, the *Catechism of the Catholic Church* cites Tertullian explicitly as a Father of the Church (n. 1446) and nine times invokes Origen as an authority. Cayré says, "The valuable services that these men have rendered to the Church explain these exceptions."
7. Yves Congar, *A History of Theology* (New York: Doubleday, 1968), 37.
8. ANF 1:5.
9. ANF 1:16.
10. NPNF1 8:268.
11. Origen, *On Exodus*, 13.3. See Mike Aquilina, *The Mass of the Early Christians* (Huntington, IN: Our Sunday Visitor, 2001), 143.
12. NPNF2 10:28.
13. St. Jerome, *Commentary on Isaiah*, 1.2.
14. Pope Leo XIII, encyclical *Providentissimus Deus*, 7.
15. Pontifical Biblical Commission, *Interpretation of the Bible in the Church*, III.B.2.
16. Cf. 2 Cor 3:14-16.
17. Cf. 1 Pet 3:21.
18. Jn 6:32; cf. 1 Cor 10:1-6.
19. ANF 1:34.
20. St. Jerome, *Commentary on Isaiah*, 54.12.
21. ANF 1:34.
22. ANF 7:381.
23. The Greek word for this is usually translated as "sanctuary." See the discussion in Patr. 1:66.
24. ANF1:49.
25. ANF 1:81.
26. ANF 1:89-90.

27. ANF 1:89.

28. St. Justin, *Apol.* 1, 65-67: PG 6, 428-429; the text before the asterisk (*) is from chap. 67.

29. ANF 1:185.

30. Quoted in CCC 1106. NPNF2 9:83.

31. ANF 1:62.

32. ANF 7:380.

33. ANF 1:51-52.

34. ANF 1:64-65.

35. NPNF2 6:93.

36. ACW 1:45.

37. NPNF2 1:147.

38. ANF 1:415-416. See also the extended study of these texts "St. Irenaeus and the Roman Primacy," by Dominic J. Unger, in *Theological Studies* (September 1952), 359-418.

39. ANF 1:254.

40. ANF 3:55.

41. ANF 3:107.

42. ANF 3:695.

43. Tacitus, *Annals*, 15:44.

44. ANF 1:75.

45. ANF 1:42.

46. Ibid.

47. *Catechism of the Catholic Church* (n. 186): St. Cyril of Jerusalem, *Catech. illum.* 5, 12: PG 33, 521-524.

48. Patr. 1:26.

49. John Henry Cardinal Newman, *Discussions and Arguments on Various Subjects* (London: Longmans, Green, 1907), 46.

50. Vatican Council I, *Dogmatic Constitution on the Faith*, 2.9.

51. Newman, 45.

52. Cf. *Catechesi Tradendae*, 12.

53. This translation is taken from newspaper reports at the time of the sermon's discovery. For a different and full translation, see WSA3 11:383.

54. ANF 1:34.

55. ANF 1:196ff.

56. Anyone who wishes to understand the sometimes heated rhetoric that passed between Christians and Jews in late antiquity should read two books by Robert Louis Wilken: *Judaism and the Early Christian Mind: A Study of Cyril of Alexandria's Exegesis and Theology* (New Haven, CT: Yale University, 1971) and *John Chrysostom and the Jews: Rhetoric and Reality in the Late Fourth Century* (Berkeley, CA: University of California, 1983). An excellent study from the Jewish perspective is Rabbi Jacob Neusner's *Aphrahat and Judaism* (Atlanta, GA: Scholars Press, 1999). Rodney Stark's *The Rise of Christianity*

(San Francisco: HarperCollins, 1997) provides the social context. For the unpleasant extremes of Jewish anti-Christian rhetoric, see Peter Schäfer's *Jesus in the Talmud* (Princeton, NJ: Princeton University Press, 2007).

57. For details on Melito's life, see Eusebius in NPNF2 1:203-206.

58. Cf. 1 Cor 10:6, 11; Heb 10:1; 1 Pet 3:21.

59. 1 Cor 15:28.

60. ANF 3:525.

61. ANF 3:246.

62. ANF 3:55.

63. ANF 4:99.

64. ANF 4:100.

65. Preserved in Eusebius, *Church History* 6.45.

66. NPNF2 6:329.

67. Jacob Neusner, *Aphrahat and Judaism: The Christian-Jewish Argument in Fourth-Century Iran* (Atlanta, GA: Scholars Press, 1999), iii.

68. Elizabeth Barrett Browning, *The Greek Christian Poets and the English Poets* (London: Chapman and Hall, 1863).

69. Theodore of Mopsuestia, *Commentary on the Lord's Prayer, Baptism and the Eucharist*, chapter 5.

70. Johannes Quasten, *Patrology*, volume 3 (Allen, TX: Christian Classics, no date), 417.

71. William Jurgens, *The Faith of the Early Fathers*, volume 2 (Collegeville, MN: Liturgical Press, 1979), 78.

72. Chromatius, Sermon 30.1.

73. Robert Louis Wilken, *The Spirit of Early Christian Thought: Seeking the Face of God* (New Haven, CT: Yale, 2001), 213-214.

74. St. Bede the Venerable, *Ecclesiastical History of the English Nation*, 1.30.

75. See NPNF2 1:137.

INDEX